KEEP THE ASPIDISTRA FLYING

Books by George Orwell

DOWN AND OUT IN PARIS AND LONDON   1933

BURMESE DAYS   1934

A CLERGYMAN'S DAUGHTER   1935

KEEP THE ASPIDISTRA FLYING   1936

THE ROAD TO WIGAN PIER   1937

HOMAGE TO CATALONIA   1938

COMING UP FOR AIR   1939

INSIDE THE WHALE AND OTHER ESSAYS   1940

THE LION AND THE UNICORN   1941

ANIMAL FARM   1945

CRITICAL ESSAYS
(*IN THE U.S.*, DICKENS, DALI AND OTHERS)   1946

NINETEEN EIGHTY-FOUR   1949

SHOOTING AN ELEPHANT AND OTHER ESSAYS   1950

SUCH, SUCH WERE THE JOYS   1953

THE ORWELL READER   1956

THE COLLECTED ESSAYS, JOURNALISM AND LETTERS
OF GEORGE ORWELL (4 VOLS.)   1968

A COLLECTION OF ESSAYS   1970

GEORGE ORWELL

KEEP THE ASPIDISTRA FLYING

Amereon
■House■

First published in England in 1936

KEEP THE ASPIDISTRA FLYING

Though I speak with the tongues of men and of angels, and have not money, I am become as a sounding brass, or a tinkling cymbal. And though I have the gift of prophecy, and understand all mysteries, and all knowledge; and though I have all faith, so that I could remove mountains, and have not money, I am nothing. And though I bestow all my goods to feed the poor, and though I give my body to be burned, and have not money, it profiteth me nothing. Money suffereth long, and is kind; money envieth not; money vaunteth not itself, is not puffed up, doth not behave unseemly, seeketh not her own, is not easily provoked, thinketh no evil; rejoiceth not in iniquity, but rejoiceth in the truth; beareth all things, believeth all things, hopeth all things, endureth all things. . . . And now abideth faith, hope, money, these three; but the greatest of these is money.

I Corinthians xiii (adapted)

Chapter One

THE CLOCK struck half past two. In the little office at the back of Mr. McKechnie's bookshop, Gordon—Gordon Comstock, last member of the Comstock family, aged twenty-nine and rather moth-eaten already—lounged across the table, pushing a fourpenny packet of Player's Weights open and shut with his thumb.

The ding-dong of another, remoter clock—from the Prince of Wales, the other side of the street—rippled the stagnant air. Gordon made an effort, sat upright and stowed his packet of cigarettes away in his inside pocket. He was perishing for a smoke. However, there were only four cigarettes left. To-day was Wednesday and he had no money coming to him till Friday. It would be too bloody to be without tobacco to-night as well as all to-morrow.

Bored in advance by to-morrow's tobaccoless hours, he got up and moved towards the door—a small frail figure, with delicate bones and fretful movements. His coat was out at elbow in the right sleeve and its middle button was missing; his ready-made flannel trousers were stained and shapeless. Even from above you could see that his shoes needed re-soling.

The money clinked in his trouser pocket as he got up. He knew the precise sum that was there. Fivepence halfpenny—twopence halfpenny and a Joey. He paused, took out the miserable little threepenny-bit and looked at it. Beastly, useless thing! And bloody fool to have taken it! It had happened yesterday, when he was buying cigarettes. "Don't mind a three-penny-bit, do you, sir?" the little bitch of a shop-girl had

3

chirped. And of course he had let her give it him. "Oh no, not at all!" he had said—fool, bloody fool!

His heart sickened to think that he had only fivepence halfpenny in the world, threepence of which couldn't even be spent. Because how can you buy anything with a threepenny-bit? It isn't a coin, it's the answer to a riddle. You look such a fool when you take it out of your pocket, unless it's in among a whole handful of other coins. "How much?" you say. "Threepence," the shop-girl says. And then you feel all round your pocket and fish out that absurd little thing, all by itself, sticking on the end of your finger like a tiddleywink. The shop-girl sniffs. She spots immediately that it's your last threepence in the world. You see her glance quickly at it—she's wondering whether there's a piece of Christmas pudding still sticking to it. And you stalk out with your nose in the air, and can't ever go to that shop again. No! We won't spend our Joey. Twopence halfpenny left—twopence halfpenny to last till Friday.

This was the lonely after-dinner hour, when few or no customers were to be expected. He was alone with seven thousand books. The small dark room, smelling of dust and decayed paper, that gave on the office, was filled to the brim with books, mostly aged and unsaleable. On the top shelves near the ceiling the quarto volumes of extinct encyclopædias slumbered on their sides in piles like the tiered coffins in common graves. Gordon pushed aside the blue, dust-sodden curtains that served as a doorway to the next room. This, better lighted than the other, contained the lending library. It was one of those "twopenny no-deposit" libraries beloved of book-pinchers. No books in it except novels, of course. And *what* novels! But that too was a matter of course.

Eight hundred strong, the novels lined the room on three sides ceiling-high, row upon row of gaudy oblong backs, as though the walls had been built of many-coloured bricks laid upright. They were arranged alphabetically. Arlen, Burroughs, Deeping, Dell, Frankau, Galsworthy, Gibbs, Priestley, Sapper, Walpole. Gordon eyed them with inert hatred. At this moment he hated all books, and novels most of all. Horrible to think of all that soggy, half-baked trash massed together in one place.

4

Pudding, suet pudding. Eight hundred slabs of pudding, walling him in—a vault of puddingstone. The thought was oppressive. He moved on through the open doorway into the front part of the shop. In doing so, he smoothed his hair. It was an habitual movement. After all, there might be girls outside the glass door. Gordon was not impressive to look at. He was just five feet seven inches high, and because his hair was usually too long he gave the impression that his head was a little too big for his body. He was never quite unconscious of his small stature. When he knew that anyone was looking at him he carried himself very upright, throwing a chest, with a you-be-damned air which occasionally deceived simple people.

However, there was nobody outside. The front room, unlike the rest of the shop, was smart and expensive-looking, and it contained about two thousand books, exclusive of those in the window. On the right there was a glass show-case in which children's books were kept. Gordon averted his eyes from a beastly Rackhamesque dust-jacket; elvish children tripping Wendily through a bluebell glade. He gazed out through the glass door. A foul day, and the wind rising. The sky was leaden, the cobbles of the street were slimy. It was St. Andrew's day, the thirtieth of November. McKechnie's stood on a corner, on a sort of shapeless square where four streets converged. To the left, just within sight from the door, stood a great elm-tree, leafless now, its multitudinous twigs making sepia-coloured lace against the sky. Opposite, next to the Prince of Wales, were tall hoardings covered with ads for patent foods and patent medicines. A gallery of monstrous doll-faces—pink vacuous faces, full of goofy optimism. Q.T. Sauce Truweet Breakfast Crisps ("Kiddies clamour for their Breakfast Crisps"), Kangaroo Burgundy, Vitamalt Chocolate, Bovex. Of them all, the Bovex one oppressed Gordon the most. A spectacled rat-faced clerk, with patent-leather hair, sitting at a café table grinning over a white mug of Bovex. "Corner Table enjoys his meal with Bovex," the legend ran.

Gordon shortened the focus of his eyes. From the dust-dulled pane the reflection of his own face looked back at him. Not a

5

good face. Not thirty yet, but moth-eaten already. Very pale, with bitter, ineradicable lines. What people call a "good" forehead—high, that is—but a small pointed chin, so that the face as a whole was pear-shaped rather than oval. Hair mouse-coloured and unkempt, mouth unamiable, eyes hazel inclining to green. He lengthened the focus of his eyes again. He hated mirrors nowadays. Outside, all was bleak and wintry. A tram, like a raucous swan of steel, glided groaning over the cobbles, and in its wake the wind swept a debris of trampled leaves. The twigs of the elm tree were swirling, straining eastward. The poster that advertised Q.T. Sauce was torn at the edge; a ribbon of paper fluttered fitfully like a tiny pennant. In the side street too, to the right, the naked poplars that lined the pavement bowed sharply as the wind caught them. A nasty raw wind. There was a threatening note in it as it swept over; the first growl of winter's anger. Two lines of a poem struggled for birth in Gordon's mind:

Sharply the something wind—for instance, threatening wind? No, better, menacing wind. The menacing wind blows over—no, sweeps over, say.

The something poplars—yielding poplars? No, better, bending poplars. Assonance between bending and menacing? No matter. The bending poplars, newly bare. Good.

Sharply the menacing wind sweeps over
The bending poplars, newly bare.

Good. "Bare" is a sod to rhyme; however, there's always "air," which every poet since Chaucer has been struggling to find rhymes for. But the impulse died away in Gordon's mind. He turned the money over in his pocket. Twopence halfpenny and a Joey—twopence halfpenny. His mind was sticky with boredom. He couldn't cope with rhymes and adjectives. You can't, with only twopence halfpenny in your pocket.

His eyes refocused themselves upon the posters opposite. He had his private reasons for hating them. Mechanically he re-read their slogans. "Kangaroo Burgundy—the wine for Britons." "Asthma was choking her!" "Q.T. Sauce Keeps Hubby Smiling." "Hike all day on a Slab of Vitamalt!" "Curve

6

Cut—the Smoke for Outdoor Men." "Kiddies clamour for their Breakfast Crisps." "Corner Table enjoys his meal with Bovex." Ha! A customer—potential, at any rate. Gordon stiffened himself. Standing by the door, you could get an oblique view out of the front window without being seen yourself. He looked the potential customer over.

A decentish middle-aged man, black suit, bowler hat, umbrella and dispatch-case—provincial solicitor or Town Clerk—peeking at the window with large pale-coloured eyes. He wore a guilty look. Gordon followed the direction of his eyes. Ah! So that was it! He had nosed out those D. H. Lawrence first editions in the far corner. Pining for a bit of smut, of course. He had heard of Lady Chatterley afar off. A bad face he had, Gordon thought. Pale, heavy, downy, with bad contours. Welsh, by the look of him—Nonconformist, anyway. He had the regular Dissenting pouches round the corners of his mouth. At home, president of the local Purity League or Seaside Vigilance Committee (rubber-soled slippers and electric torch, spotting kissing couples along the beach parade), and now up in town on the razzle. Gordon wished he would come in. Sell him a copy of *Women in Love*. How it would disappoint him!

But no! The Welsh solicitor had funked it. He tucked his umbrella under his arm and moved off with righteously turned backside. But doubtless to-night, when darkness hid his blushes, he'd slink into one of the rubber-shops and buy *High Jinks in a Parisian Convent*, by Sadie Blackeyes.

Gordon turned away from the door and back to the bookshelves. In the shelves to your left as you came out of the library the new and nearly-new books were kept—a patch of bright colour that was meant to catch the eye of anyone glancing through the glass door. Their sleek unspotted backs seemed to yearn at you from the shelves. "Buy me, buy me!" they seemed to be saying. Novels fresh from the press—still unravished brides, pining for the paperknife to deflower them—and review copies, like youthful widows, blooming still though virgin no longer, and here and there, in sets of half a dozen, those pathetic spinster-things, "remainders," still guarding hopefully their long preserv'd virginity. Gordon turned his

7

eyes away from the "remainders." They called up evil memories. The single wretched little book that he himself had published, two years ago, had sold exactly a hundred and fifty-three copies and then been "remaindered"; and even as a "remainder" it hadn't sold. He passed the new books by and paused in front of the shelves which ran at right angles to them and which contained more second-hand books.

Over to the right were shelves of poetry. Those in front of him were prose, a miscellaneous lot. Upwards and downwards they were graded, from clean and expensive at eye-level to cheap and dingy at top and bottom. In all bookshops there goes on a savage Darwinian struggle in which the works of living men gravitate to eye-level and the works of dead men go up or down—down to Gehenna or up to the throne, but always away from any position where they will be noticed. Down in the bottom shelves the "classics," the extinct monsters of the Victorian age, were quietly rotting. Scott, Carlyle, Meredith, Ruskin, Pater, Stevenson—you could hardly read the names upon their broad dowdy backs. In the top shelves, almost out of sight, slept the pudgy biographies of dukes. Below those, saleable still and therefore placed within reach, was "religious" literature—all sects and all creeds, lumped indiscriminately together. *The World Beyond*, by the author of *Spirit Hands Have Touched Me*. Dean Farrar's *Life of Christ. Jesus the First Rotarian*. Father Hilaire Chestnut's book of R.C. propaganda. Religion always sells provided it is soppy enough. Below, exactly at eye-level, was the contemporary stuff. Priestley's latest. Dinky little books of reprinted "middles." Cheer-up "humour" from Herbert and Knox and Milne. Some highbrow stuff as well. A novel or two by Hemingway and Virginia Woolf. Smart pseudo-Strachey predigested biographies. Snooty, refined books on safe painters and safe poets by those moneyed young beasts who glide so gracefully from Eton to Cambridge and from Cambridge to the literary reviews.

Dull-eyed, he gazed at the wall of books. He hated the whole lot of them, old and new, highbrow and lowbrow, snooty and chirpy. The mere sight of them brought home to him his own sterility. For here was he, supposedly a "writer," and he

8

couldn't even "write"! It wasn't merely a question of not getting published; it was that he produced nothing, or next to nothing. And all that tripe cluttering the shelves—well, at any rate it existed; it was an achievement of sorts. Even the Dells and Deepings do at least turn out their yearly acre of print. But it was the snooty "cultured" kind of books that he hated the worst. Books of criticism and belles-lettres. The kind of thing that those moneyed young beasts from Cambridge write almost in their sleep—and that Gordon himself might have written if he had had a little more money. Money and culture! In a country like England you can no more be cultured without money than you can join the Cavalry Club. With the same instinct that makes a child waggle a loose tooth, he took out a snooty-looking volume—*Some Aspects of the Italian Baroque*—opened it, read a paragraph and shoved it back with mingled loathing and envy. That devasting omniscience! That noxious, horn-spectacled refinement! And the money that such refinement means! For after all, what is there behind it, except money? Money for the right kind of education, money for influential friends, money for leisure and peace of mind, money for trips to Italy. Money writes books, money sells them. Give me not righteousness, O Lord, give me money, only money.

He jingled the coins in his pocket. He was nearly thirty and had accomplished nothing; only his miserable book of poems that had fallen flatter than any pancake. And ever since, for two whole years, he had been struggling in the labyrinth of a dreadful book that never got any further, and which, as he knew in his moments of clarity, never would get any further. It was the lack of money, simply the lack of money, that robbed him of the power to "write." He clung to that as to an article of faith. Money, money, all is money! Could you write even a penny novelette without money to put heart in you? Invention, energy, wit, style, charm—they've all got to be paid for in hard cash.

Nevertheless, as he looked along the shelves he felt himself a little comforted. So many of the books were faded and unreadable. After all, we're all in the same boat. Memento mori. For you and for me and for the snooty young men from

9

Cambridge, the same oblivion waits—though doubtless it'll wait rather longer for those snooty young men from Cambridge. He looked at the time-dulled "classics" near his feet. Dead, all dead. Carlyle and Ruskin and Meredith and Stevenson—all are dead, God rot them. He glanced over their faded titles. *Collected Letters of Robert Louis Stevenson.* Ha, ha! That's good. *Collected Letters of Robert Louis Stevenson!* Its top edge was black with dust. Dust thou art, to dust returnest. Gordon kicked Stevenson's buckram backside. Art there, old false-penny? You're cold meat, if ever Scotchman was.

Ping! The shop bell. Gordon turned round. Two customers, for the library.

A dejected, round-shouldered, lower-class woman, looking like a draggled duck nosing among garbage, seeped in, fumbling with a rush basket. In her wake hopped a plump little sparrow of a women, red-cheeked, middle-middle class, carrying under her arm a copy of *The Forsyte Saga*—title outwards, so that passers-by could spot her for a highbrow.

Gordon had taken off his sour expression. He greeted them with the homey, family-doctor geniality reserved for library-subscribers.

"Good afternoon, Mrs. Weaver. Good afternoon, Mrs. Penn. What terrible weather!"

"Shocking!" said Mrs. Penn.

He stood aside to let them pass. Mrs. Weaver upset her rush basket and spilled on to the floor a much-thumbed copy of Ethel M. Dell's *Silver Wedding*. Mrs. Penn's bright bird-eye lighted upon it. Behind Mrs. Weaver's back she smiled up at Gordon, archly, as highbrow to highbrow. Dell! The lowness of it! The books these lower classes read! Understandingly, he smiled back. They passed into the library, highbrow to highbrow smiling.

Mrs. Penn laid *The Forsyte Saga* on the table and turned her sparrow-bosom upon Gordon. She was always very affable to Gordon. She addressed him as Mister Comstock, shopwalker though he was, and held literary conversations with him. There was the free-masonry of highbrows between them.

"I hope you enjoyed *The Forsyte Saga*, Mrs. Penn?"

"What a perfectly *marvellous* achievement that book is, Mr. Comstock! Do you know that that makes the fourth time I've read it? An epic, a real epic!"

Mrs. Weaver nosed among the books, too dim-witted to grasp that they were in alphabetical order.

"I don't know what to 'ave this week, that I don't," she mumbled through untidy lips. "My daughter she keeps on at me to 'ave a try at Deeping. She's great on Deeping, my daughter is. But my son-in-law, now, 'e's more for Burroughs. I don't know, I'm sure."

A spasm passed over Mrs. Penn's face at the mention of Burroughs. She turned her back markedly on Mrs. Weaver.

"What I feel, Mr. Comstock, is that there's something so *big* about Galsworthy. He's so broad, so universal, and yet at the same time so thoroughly English in spirit, so *human*. His books are real *human* documents."

"And Priestley, too," said Gordon. "I think Priestley's such an awfully fine writer, don't you?"

"Oh, he is! So big, so broad, so human! And so essentially English!"

Mrs. Weaver pursed her lips. Behind them were three isolated yellow teeth.

"I think p'raps I can't do better'n 'ave another Dell," she said. "You 'ave got some more Dells, 'aven't you? I *do* enjoy a good read of Dell, I must say. I says to my daughter, I says, 'You can keep your Deepings and your Burroughses. Give me Dell,' I says."

Ding Dong Dell! Dukes and dogwhips! Mrs. Penn's eye signalled highbrow irony. Gordon returned her signal. Keep in with Mrs. Penn! A good, steady customer.

"Oh, certainly, Mrs. Weaver. We've got a whole shelf by Ethel M. Dell. Would you like *The Desire of His Life?* Or perhaps you've read that. Then what about *The Altar of Honour?*"

"I wonder whether you have Hugh Walpole's latest book?" said Mrs. Penn. "I feel in the mood this week for something epic, something *big*. Now Walpole, you know, I consider a really *great* writer, I put him second only to Galsworthy. There's something so *big* about him. And yet he's so human with it."

"And so essentially English," said Gordon.

"Oh, of course! So essentially English!"

"I b'lieve I'll jest 'ave *The Way of an Eagle* over again," said Mrs. Weaver finally. "You don't never seem to get tired of *The Way of an Eagle*, do you, now?"

"It's certainly astonishingly popular," said Gordon, diplomatically, his eye on Mrs. Penn.

"Oh, as*ton*ishingly!" echoed Mrs. Penn, ironically, her eye on Gordon.

He took their twopences and sent them happy away, Mrs. Penn with Walpole's *Rogue Herries* and Mrs. Weaver with *The Way of an Eagle*.

Soon he had wandered back to the other room and towards the shelves of poetry. A melancholy fascination, those shelves had for him. His own wretched book was there—skied, of course, high up among the unsaleable. *Mice,* by Gordon Comstock; a sneaky little foolscap octavo, price three and sixpence but now reduced to a bob. Of the thirteen B.F.s who had reviewed it (and *The Times Lit. Supp.* had declared that it showed "exceptional promise") not one had seen the none too subtle joke of that title. And in the two years he had been at McKechnie's bookshop, not a single customer, not a single one, had ever taken *Mice* out of its shelf.

There were fifteen or twenty shelves of poetry. Gordon regarded them sourly. Dud stuff, for the most part. A little above eye-level, already on their way to heaven and oblivion, were the poets of yesteryear, the stars of his earlier youth. Yeats, Davies, Housman, Thomas, De la Mare, Hardy. Dead stars. Below them, exactly at eye-level, were the squibs of the passing minute. Eliot, Pound, Auden, Campbell, Day Lewis, Spender. Very damp squibs, that lot. Dead stars above, damp squibs below. Shall we ever again get a writer worth reading? But Lawrence was all right, and Joyce even better before he went

12

off his coconut. And if we did get a writer worth reading, should we know him when we saw him, so choked as we are with trash?

Ping! Shop bell. Gordon turned. Another customer.

A youth of twenty, cherry-lipped, with gilded hair, tripped Nancifully in. Moneyed, obviously. He had the golden aura of money. He hadn't been in the shop before. Gordon assumed the gentlemanly-servile mien reserved for new customers. He repeated the usual formula:

"Good afternoon. Can I do anything for you? Are you looking for any particular book?"

"Oh, no, not weally." An R-less Nancy voice. "May I just *bwowse?* I simply couldn't wesist your fwont window. I have such a tewwible weakness for bookshops! So I just floated in—tee-hee!"

Float out again, then, Nancy. Gordon smiled a cultured smile, as booklover to booklover.

"Oh, please do. We like people to look round. Are you interested in poetry, by any chance?"

"Oh, of course! I *adore* poetwy!"

Of course! Mangy little snob. There was a subartistic look about his clothes. Gordon slid a "slim" red volume from the poetry shelves.

"These are just out. They might interest you, perhaps. They're translations—something rather out of the common. Translations from the Bulgarian."

Very subtle, that. Now leave him to himself. That's the proper way with customers. Don't hustle them; let them browse for twenty minutes or so; then they get ashamed and buy something. Gordon moved to the door, discreetly, keeping out of Nancy's way; yet casually, one hand in his pocket, with the insouciant air proper to a gentleman.

Outside, the slimy street looked grey and drear. From somewhere round the corner came the clatter of hooves, a cold hollow sound. Caught by the wind, the dark columns of smoke from the chimneys veered over and rolled flatly down the sloping roofs. Ah!

13

Sharply the menacing wind sweeps over
The bending poplars, newly bare,
And the dark ribbons of the chimneys
Veer downward tumty tumty (something like "murky") *air.*

Good. But the impulse faded. His eye fell again upon the ad-posters across the street.

He almost wanted to laugh at them, they were so feeble, so dead-alive, so unappetising. As though anybody could be tempted by *those!* Like succubi with pimply backsides. But they depressed him all the same. The money-stink, everywhere the money-stink. He stole a glance at the Nancy, who had drifted away from the poetry shelves and taken out a large expensive book on the Russian ballet. He was holding it delicately between his pink non-prehensile paws, as a squirrel holds a nut, studying the photographs. Gordon knew his type. The moneyed "artistic" young man. Not an artist himself, exactly, but a hanger-on of the arts; frequenter of studios, retailer of scandal. A nice-looking boy, though, for all his Nancitude. The skin at the back of his neck was as silky-smooth as the inside of a shell. You can't have a skin like that under five hundred a year. A sort of charm he had, a glamour, like all moneyed people. Money and charm; who shall separate them?

Gordon thought of Ravelston, his charming, rich friend, editor of *Antichrist,* of whom he was extravagantly fond, and whom he did not see so often as once in a fortnight; and of Rosemary, his girl, who loved him—adored him, so she said—and who, all the same, had never slept with him. Money, once again; all is money. All human relationships must be purchased with money. If you have no money, men won't care for you, women won't love you; won't, that is, care for you or love you the last little bit that matters. And how right they are, after all! For, moneyless, you are unlovable. Though I speak with the tongues of men and of angels. But then, if I haven't money, I *don't* speak with the tongues of men and of angels.

He looked again at the ad-posters. He really hated them this time. That Vitamalt one, for instance! "Hike all day on a Slab of Vitamalt!" A youthful couple, boy and girl, in clean-minded hiking kit, their hair picturesquely tousled by the wind, climbing a stile against a Sussex landscape. That girl's face! The awful bright tomboy cheeriness of it! The kind of girl who goes in for Plenty of Clean Fun. Windswept. Tight khaki shorts but that doesn't mean you can pinch her backside. And next to them—Corner Table. "Corner Table enjoys his meal with Bovex." Gordon examined the thing with the intimacy of hatred. The idiotic grinning face, like the face of a self-satisfied rat, the slick black hair, the silly spectacles. Corner Table, heir of the ages; victor of Waterloo, Corner Table, Modern man as his masters want him to be. A docile little porker, sitting in the money-sty, drinking Bovex.

Faces passed, wind-yellowed. A tram boomed across the square, and the clock over the Prince of Wales struck three. A couple of old creatures, a tramp or beggar and his wife, in long greasy overcoats that reached almost to the ground, were shuffling towards the shop. Book-pinchers, by the look of them. Better keep an eye on the boxes outside. The old man halted on the kerb a few yards away while his wife came to the door. She pushed it open and looked up at Gordon, between grey strings of hair, with a sort of hopeful malevolence.

"'Ju buy books?" she demanded hoarsely.

"Sometimes. It depends what books they are."

"I gossome *lovely* books 'ere."

She came in, shutting the door with a clang. The Nancy glanced over his shoulder distastefully and moved a step or two away, into the corner. The old woman had produced a greasy little sack from under her overcoat. She moved confidentially nearer to Gordon. She smelt of very, very old breadcrusts.

"Will you 'ave 'em?" she said, clasping the neck of the sack. "Only 'alf a crown the lot."

"What are they? Let me see them, please."

"*Lovely* books, they are," she breathed, bending over to open the sack and emitting a sudden very powerful whiff of breadcrusts.

" 'Ere!" she said, and thrust an armful of filthy-looking books almost into Gordon's face.

They were an 1884 edition of Charlotte M. Yonge's novels,

and had the appearance of having been slept on for many years. Gordon stepped back, suddenly revolted.

"We can't possibly buy those," he said shortly.

"Can't buy em? *Why* can't yer buy 'em?"

"Because they're no use to us. We can't sell that kind of thing."

"Wotcher make me take 'em out o' me bag for, then?" demanded the old woman ferociously.

Gordon made a detour round her, to avoid the smell, and held the door open, silently. No use arguing. You had people of this type coming into the shop all day long. The old woman made off, mumbling, with malevolence in the hump of her shoulders, and joined her husband. He paused on the kerb to cough, so fruitily that you could hear him through the door. A clot of phlegm, like a little white tongue, came slowly out between his lips and was ejected into the gutter. Then the two old creatures shuffled away beetle-like in the long greasy overcoats that hid everything except their feet.

Gordon watched them go. They were just by-products. The throw-outs of the money-god. All over London, by tens of thousands, draggled old beasts of that description; creeping like unclean beetles to the grave.

He gazed out at the graceless street. At this moment it seemed to him that in a street like this, in a town like this, every life that is lived must be meaningless and intolerable. The sense of disintegration, of decay, that is endemic in our time, was strong upon him. Somehow it was mixed up with the ad-posters opposite. He looked now with more seeing eyes at those grinning yard-wide faces. After all, there was more there than mere silliness, greed and vulgarity. Corner Table grins at you, seemingly optimistic, with a flash of false teeth. But what is behind the grin? Desolation, emptiness, prophecies of doom. For can you not see, if you know how to look, that behind that slick self-satisfaction, that tittering fat-bellied triviality, there is nothing but a frightful emptiness, a secret despair? The great death-wish of the modern world. Suicide pacts. Heads stuck in gas-ovens in lonely maisonettes. French letters and Amen Pills. And the reverberations of future wars. Enemy aeroplanes flying over London; the deep threatening hum of the propellers, the shattering thunder of the bombs. It is all written in Corner Table's face.

More customers coming. Gordon stood back, gentlemanly-servile.

The door-bell clanged. Two upper-middle-class ladies sailed noisily in. One pink and fruity, thirty-fivish, with voluptuous bosom burgeoning from her coat of squirrel-skin, emitting a super-feminine scent of Parma violets; the other middle-aged, tough and curried—India, presumably. Close behind them a dark, grubby, shy young man slipped through the doorway as apologetically as a cat. He was one of the shop's best customers—a flitting, solitary creature who was almost too shy to speak and who by some strange manipulation kept himself always a day away from a shave.

Gordon repeated his formula:

"Good afternoon. Can I do anything for you? Are you looking for any particular book?"

Fruity-face overwhelmed him with a smile, but curry-face decided to treat the question as an impertinence. Ignoring Gordon, she drew fruity-face across to the shelves next the new books where the dog-books and cat-books were kept. The two of them immediately began taking books out of the shelves and talking loudly. Curry-face had the voice of a drill-sergeant. She was no doubt a colonel's wife, or widow. The Nancy, still deep in the big book on the Russian ballet, edged delicately away. His face said that he would leave the shop if his privacy were disturbed again. The shy young man had already found his way to the poetry shelves. The two ladies were fairly frequent visitors to the shop. They always wanted to see books about cats and dogs, but never actually bought anything. There were two whole shelves of dog books and cat books. "Ladies' Corner," old McKechnie called it.

Another customer arrived, for the library. An ugly girl of twenty, hatless, in a white overall, with a sallow, blithering, honest face and powerful spectacles that distorted her eyes. She was assistant at a chemist's shop. Gordon put on his homey library manner. She smiled at him, and with a gait as clumsy as a bear's followed him into the library.

"What kind of book would you like this time, Miss Weeks?"

"Well—" She clutched the front of her overall. Her distorted black-treacle eyes beamed trustfully into his. "Well, what I'd *really* like's a good hot-stuff love-story. You know—something *modern*."

"Something modern? Something by Barbara Bedworthy, for instance? Have you read *Almost a Virgin?*"

"Oh no, not her. She's too Deep. I can't bear Deep books. But I want something—well, *you* know—*modern*. Sex-problems and divorce and all that. *You* know."

"Modern, but not Deep," said Gordon, as lowbrow to lowbrow.

He ranged among the hot-stuff modern love-stories. There were not less than three hundred of them in the library. From the front room came the voices of the two upper-middle-class ladies, the one fruity, the other curried, disputing about dogs. They had taken out one of the dog books and were examining the photographs. Fruity-voice enthused over the photograph of a Peke, the ickle angel pet, wiv his gweat big Soulful eyes and his ickle black nosie—oh, so ducky-duck! But curry-voice— yes, undoubtedly a colonel's widow—said Pekes were soppy. Give her dogs with guts—dogs that would fight, she said; she hated these soppy lapdogs, she said. "You have no Soul, Bedelia, no Soul," said fruity-voice plaintively. The door-bell pinged again. Gordon handed the chemist's girl *Seven Scarlet Nights* and booked it on her ticket. She took a shabby leather purse out of her overall pocket and paid him twopence.

He went back to the front room. The Nancy had put his book back in the wrong shelf and vanished. A lean, straight-nosed, brisk woman, with sensible clothes and gold-rimmed pince-nez—schoolmarm possibly, feminist certainly—came in and demanded Mrs. Wharton-Beverley's history of the suffrage movement. With secret joy Gordon told her that they hadn't got it. She stabbed his male incompetence with gimlet eyes and went out again. The thin young man stood apologetically in the corner, his face buried in D. H. Lawrence's Collected

Poems, like some long-legged bird with its head buried under its wing.

Gordon waited by the door. Outside, a shabby-genteel old man with a strawberry nose and a khaki muffler round his throat was picking over the books in the sixpenny box. The two upper-middle-class ladies suddenly departed, leaving a litter of open books on the table. Fruity-face cast reluctant backward glances at the dog-books, but curry-face drew her away, resolute not to buy anything. Gordon held the door open. The two ladies sailed noisily out, ignoring him.

He watched their fur-coated upper-middle-class backs go down the street. The old strawberry-nosed man was talking to himself as he pawed over the books. A bit wrong in the head, presumably. He would pinch something if he wasn't watched. The wind blew colder, drying the slime of the street. Time to light up presently. Caught by a swirl of air, the torn strip of paper on the Q.T. Sauce advertisement fluttered sharply, like a piece of washing on the line. Ah!

> Sharply the menacing wind sweeps over
> The bending poplars, newly bare,
> And the dark ribbons of the chimneys
> Veer downward; flicked by whips of air,
> Torn posters flutter.

Not bad, not bad at all. But he had no wish to go on—could not go on, indeed. He fingered the money in his pocket, not chinking it, lest the shy young man should hear. Twopence halfpenny. No tobacco all to-morrow. His bones ached.

A light sprang up in the Prince of Wales. They would be swabbing out the bar. The old strawberry-nosed man was reading an Edgar Wallace out of the twopenny box. A tram boomed in the distance. In the room upstairs Mr. McKechnie, who seldom came down to the shop, drowsed by the gas-fire, white-haired and white-bearded, with snuff-box handy, over his calf-bound folio of Middleton's *Travels in the Levant*.

The thin young man suddenly realised that he was alone and looked up guiltily. He was an habitué of bookshops, yet never stayed longer than ten minutes in any one shop. A passionate hunger for books, and the fear of being a nuisance, were constantly at war in him. After ten minutes in any shop he would grow uneasy, feel himself de trop, and take to flight, having bought something out of sheer nervousness. Without speaking he held out the copy of Lawrence's poems and awkwardly extracted three florins from his pocket. In handing them to Gordon he dropped one. Both dived for it simultaneously; their heads bumped against one another. The young man stood back, blushing sallowly.

"I'll wrap it up for you," said Gordon.

But the shy young man shook his head—he stammered so badly that he never spoke when it was avoidable. He clutched his book to him and slipped out with the air of having committed some disgraceful action.

Gordon was alone. He wandered back to the door. The strawberry-nosed man glanced over his shoulder, caught Gordon's eye and moved off, foiled. He had been on the point of slipping Edgar Wallace into his pocket. The clock over the Prince of Wales struck a quarter past three.

Ding Dong! A quarter past three. Light up at half past. Four and three-quarter hours till closing time. Five and a quarter hours till supper. Twopence halfpenny in pocket. No tobacco to-morrow.

Suddenly a ravishing, irresistible desire to smoke came over Gordon. He had made up his mind not to smoke this afternoon. He had only four cigarettes left. They must be saved for tonight, when he intended to "write"; for he could no more "write" without tobacco than without air. Nevertheless, he had got to have a smoke. He took out his packet of Player's Weights and extracted one of the dwarfish cigarettes. It was sheer stupid indulgence; it meant half an hour off to-night's "writing" time. But there was no resisting it. With a sort of shameful joy he sucked the soothing smoke into his lungs.

The reflection of his own face looked back at him from the greyish pane. Gordon Comstock, author of *Mice;* en l'an trentième de son eage, and moth-eaten already. Only twenty-six teeth left. However, Villon at the same age was poxed, on his own showing. Let's be thankful for small mercies.

He watched the ribbon of torn paper whirling, fluttering on the Q.T. Sauce advertisement. Our civilisation is dying. It *must* be dying. But it isn't going to die in its bed. Presently the aeroplanes are coming. Zoom—whizz—crash! The whole western world going up in a roar of high explosives.

He looked at the darkening street, at the greyish reflection of his face in the pane, at the shabby figures shuffling past. Almost involuntarily he repeated:

> *C'est l'Ennui—l'œil chargé d'un pleur involontaire,*
> *Il rêve d'échafauds en fumant son houka!"*

Money, money! Corner Table! The humming of the aeroplanes and the crash of the bombs.

Gordon squinted up at the leaden sky. Those aeroplanes are coming. In imagination he saw them coming now; squadron after squadron, innumerable, darkening the sky like clouds of gnats. With his tongue not quite against his teeth he made a buzzing, blue-bottle-on-the-window-pane sound to represent the humming of the aeroplanes. It was a sound which, at that moment, he ardently desired to hear.

Chapter Two

Gordon walked homeward against the rattling wind, which blew his hair backward and gave him more of a "good" forehead than ever. His manner conveyed to the passers-by—at least, he hoped it did—that if he wore no overcoat it was from pure caprice. His overcoat was up the spout for fifteen shillings, as a matter of fact.

Willowbed Road, N.W., was not definitely slummy, only dingy and depressing. There were real slums hardly five minutes' walk away. Tenement houses where familes slept five in a bed, and, when one of them died, slept every night with the corpse until it was buried; alley-ways where girls of fifteen were deflowered by boys of sixteen against leprous plaster walls. But Willowbed Road itself contrived to keep up a kind of mingy, lower-middle-class decency. There was even a dentist's brass plate on one of the houses. In quite two-thirds of them, amid the lace curtains of the parlour window, there was a green card with "Apartments" on it in silver lettering, above the peeping foliage of an aspidistra.

Mrs. Wisbeach, Gordon's landlady, specialised in "single gentlemen." Bed-sitting-rooms, with gaslight laid on and find your own heating, baths extra (there was a geyser), and meals in the tomb-dark dining-room with the phalanx of clotted sauce-bottles in the middle of the table. Gordon, who came home for his midday dinner, paid twenty-seven and six a week.

The gaslight shone yellow through the frosted transom above the door of Number 31. Gordon took out his key and fished about in the keyhole—in that kind of house the key never quite fits the lock. The darkish little hallway—in reality it was only a passage—smelt of dishwater, cabbage, rag mats and bedroom slops. Gordon glanced at the japanned tray on the hall-stand. No letters, of course. He had told himself not to hope for a letter, and nevertheless had continued to hope. A stale feeling, not quite a pain, settled upon his breast. Rosemary might have written! It was four days now since she had written. Moreover, there were a couple of poems that he had sent out to magazines and had not yet had returned to him. The one thing that made the evening bearable was to find a letter waiting for him when he got home. But he received very few letters—four or five in a week at the very most.

On the left of the hall was the never-used parlour, then came the staircase, and beyond that the passage ran down to the kitchen and to the unapproachable lair inhabited by Mrs. Wisbeach herself. As Gordon came in, the door at the end of the passage opened a foot or so. Mrs. Wisbeach's face emerged, inspected him briefly but suspiciously, and disappeared again. It was quite impossible to get in or out of the house, at any time before eleven at night, without being scrutinised in this manner. Just what Mrs. Wisbeach suspected you of it was hard to say; smuggling women into the house, possibly. She was one of those malignant respectable women who keep lodging-houses. Age about forty-five, stout but active, with a pink, fine-featured, horribly observant face, beautiful grey hair and a permanent grievance.

Gordon halted at the foot of the narrow stairs. Above, a coarse rich voice was singing, "Who's afraid of the Big Bad Wolf?" A very fat man of thirty-eight or nine came round the angle of the stairs, with the light dancing step peculiar to fat men, dressed in a smart grey suit, yellow shoes, a rakish trilby hat and a belted blue overcoat of startling vulgarity. This was Flaxman, the first-floor lodger and travelling representative of the Queen of Sheba Toilet Requisites Co. He saluted Gordon with a lemon-coloured glove as he came down.

"Hullo, chappie!" he said blithely. (Flaxman called everyone "chappie.") "How's life with you?"

"Bloody," said Gordon shortly.

23

Flaxman had reached the bottom of the stairs. He threw a roly-poly arm affectionately round Gordon's shoulders.

"Cheer up, old man, cheer up! You look like a bloody funeral. I'm off down to the Crichton. Come on down and have a quick one."

"I can't. I've got to work."

"Oh, hell! Be matey, can't you? What's the good of mooning about up here? Come on down to the Cri and we'll pinch the barmaid's bum."

Gordon wriggled free of Flaxman's arm. Like all small frail people, he hated being touched. Flaxman merely grinned, with the typical fat man's good humour. He was really horribly fat. He filled his trousers as though he had been melted and then poured into them. But of course, like other fat people, he never admitted to being fat. No fat person ever uses the word "fat" if there is any way of avoiding it. "Stout" is the word they use—or, better still, "robust." A fat man is never so happy as when he is describing himself as "robust." Flaxman, at his first meeting with Gordon, had been on the point of calling himself "robust," but something in Gordon's greenish eye had deterred him. He compromised on "stout" instead.

"I do admit, chappie," he said, "to being—well, just a wee bit on the stout side. Nothing unwholesome, you know." He patted the vague frontier between his belly and his chest. "Good firm flesh. I'm pretty nippy on my feet, as a matter of fact. But—well, I suppose you might call me *stout*."

"Like Cortez," Gordon suggested.

"Cortez? Cortez? Was that the chappie who was always wandering about in the mountains in Mexico?"

"That's the fellow. He was stout, but he had eagle eyes."

"Ah? Now that's funny. Because the wife said something rather like that to me once. 'George,' she said, 'you've got the most wonderful eyes in the world. You've got eyes just like an eagle,' she said. That would be before she married me, you'll understand."

Flaxman was living apart from his wife at the moment. A little while back the Queen of Sheba Toilet Requisites Co.

24

had unexpectedly paid out a bonus of thirty pounds to all its travellers, and at the same time Flaxman and two others had been sent across to Paris to press the new Sexapeal Naturetint lipstick on various French firms. Flaxman had not thought it necessary to mention the thirty pounds to his wife. He had had the time of his life on that Paris trip, of course. Even now, three months afterwards, his mouth watered when he spoke of it. He used to entertain Gordon with luscious descriptions. Ten days in Paris with thirty quid that wifie hadn't heard about! Oh, boy! But unfortunately there had been a leakage somewhere; Flaxman had got home to find retribution awaiting him. His wife had broken his head with a cut-glass whisky decanter, a wedding present which they had had for fourteen years, and then fled to her mother's house, taking the children with her. Hence Flaxman's exile in Willowbed Road. But he wasn't letting it worry him. It would blow over, no doubt; it had happened several times before.

Gordon made another attempt to get past Flaxman and escape up the stairs. The dreadful thing was that in his heart he was pining to go with him. He needed a drink so badly— the mere mention of the Crichton Arms had made him feel thirsty. But it was impossible, of course; he had no money. Flaxman put an arm across the stairs, barring his way. He was genuinely fond of Gordon. He considered him "clever"— "cleverness," to him, being a kind of amiable lunacy. Moreover, he detested being alone, even for so short a time as it would take him to walk to the pub.

"Come on, chappie!" he urged. "You want a Guinness to buck you up, that's what you want. You haven't seen the new girl they've got in the saloon bar yet. Oh, boy! There's a peach for you!"

"So that's why you're all dolled up, is it?" said Gordon, looking coldly at Flaxman's yellow gloves.

"You bet it is, chappie! Coo, what a peach! Ash blonde she is. And she knows a thing or two, that girlie does. I gave her a stick of our Sexapeal Naturetint last night. You ought to have seen her wag her little bottom at me as she went past my table. Does she give me the palpitations? Does she? Oh, boy!"

Flaxman wriggled lasciviously. His tongue appeared between his lips. Then, suddenly pretending that Gordon was the ash-blonde barmaid, he seized him by the waist and gave him a tender squeeze. Gordon shoved him away. For a moment the desire to go down to the Crichton Arms was so ravishing that it almost overcame him. Oh, for a pint of beer! He seemed almost to feel it going down his throat. If only he had had any money! Even sevenpence for a pint. But what was the use? Twopence halfpenny in pocket. You can't let other people buy your drinks for you.

"Oh, leave me alone, for God's sake!" he said irritably, stepping out of Flaxman's reach, and went up the stairs without looking back.

Flaxman settled his hat on his head and made for the front door, mildly offended. Gordon reflected dully that it was always like this nowadays. He was forever snubbing friendly advances. Of course it was money that was at the bottom of it, always money. You can't be friendly, you can't even be civil, when you have no money in your pocket. A spasm of self-pity went through him. His heart yearned for the saloon bar at the Crichton; the lovely smell of beer, the warmth and bright lights, the cheery voices, the clatter of glasses on the beer-wet bar. Money, money! He went on, up the dark evil-smelling stairs. The thought of his cold lonely bedroom at the top of the house was like a doom before him.

On the second floor lived Lorenheim, a dark, meagre, lizard-like creature of uncertain age and race, who made about thirty-five shillings a week by touting vacuum-cleaners. Gordon always went very hurriedly past Lorenheim's door. Lorenheim was one of those people who have not a single friend in the world and who are devoured by a lust for company. His loneliness was so deadly that if you so much as slowed your pace outside his door he was liable to pounce out upon you and half drag, half wheedle you in to listen to interminable paranoiac tales of girls he had seduced and employers he had scored off. And his room was more cold and squalid than even a lodging-house bedroom has any right to be. There were always half-eaten bits of bread and margarine lying about everywhere. The only other lodger in the house was an engineer of some kind, employed on nightwork. Gordon only saw him occasionally—a massive man with a grim, discoloured face, who wore a bowler hat indoors and out.

In the familiar darkness of his room, Gordon felt for the gas-jet and lighted it. The room was medium-sized, not big enough to be curtained into two, but too big to be sufficiently warmed by one defective oil-lamp. It had the sort of furniture you expect in a top floor back. White-quilted single bed; brown lino floor-covering; wash-hand-stand with jug and basin of that cheap white ware which you can never see without thinking of chamberpots. On the window-sill there was a sickly aspidistra in a green-glazed pot.

Up against this, under the window, there was a kitchen table with an inkstained green cloth. This was Gordon's "writing" table. It was only after a bitter struggle that he had induced Mrs. Wisbeach to give him a kitchen table instead of the bamboo "occasional" table—a mere stand for the aspidistra—which she considered proper for a top floor back. And even now there was endless nagging because Gordon would never allow his table to be "tidied up." The table was in a permanent mess. It was almost covered with a muddle of papers, perhaps two hundred sheets of sermon paper, grimy and dog-eared, and all written on and crossed out and written on again—a sort of sordid labyrinth of papers to which only Gordon possessed the key. There was a film of dust over everything, and there were several foul little trays containing tobacco ash and the twisted stubs of cigarettes. Except for a few books on the mantelpiece, this table, with its mess of papers, was the sole mark Gordon's personality had left on the room.

It was beastly cold. Gordon thought he would light the oil lamp. He lifted it—it felt very light; the spare oil can also was empty—no oil till Friday. He applied a match; a dull yellow flame crept unwillingly round the wick. It might burn for a couple of hours, with any luck. As Gordon threw away the match his eye fell upon the aspidistra in its grass-green pot. It was a peculiarly mangy specimen. It had only seven leaves and never seemed to put forth any new ones. Gordon had a sort of secret feud with the aspidistra. Many a time he had furtively attempted to kill it—starving it of water, grinding hot cigarette-ends against its stem, even mixing salt with its earth. But the beastly things are practically immortal. In almost any circumstances they can preserve a wilting, diseased existence. Gordon stood up and deliberately wiped his kerosiny fingers on the aspidistra leaves.

At this moment Mrs. Wisbeach's voice rang shrewishly up the stairs:

"Mister Com-stock!"

Gordon went to the door. "Yes?" he called down.

"Your supper's been waiting for you this ten minutes. Why can't you come down and have it, 'stead of keeping me waiting for the washing up?"

Gordon went down. The dining-room was on the first floor, at the back, opposite Flaxman's room. It was a cold, close-smelling room, twilit even at midday. There were more aspidistras in it than Gordon had ever accurately counted. They were all over the place—on the sideboard, on the floor, on "occasional" tables; in the window there was a sort of florist's stand of them, blocking out the light. In the half-darkness, with aspidistras all about you, you had the feeling of being in some sunless aquarium amid the dreary foliage of water-flowers. Gordon's supper was set out, waiting for him, in the circle of white light that the cracked gas-jet cast upon the table cloth. He sat down with his back to the fireplace (there was an aspidistra in the grate instead of a fire) and ate his plate of cold beef and his two slices of crumbly white bread, with Canadian butter, mousetrap cheese and Pan Yan pickle, and drank a glass of cold but musty water.

When he went back to his room the oil-lamp had got going, more or less. It was hot enough to boil a kettle by, he thought. And now for the great event of the evening—his illicit cup of tea. He made himself a cup of tea almost every night, in the deadliest secrecy. Mrs. Wisbeach refused to give her lodgers tea with their supper, because she "couldn't be bothered with hotting up extra water," but at the same time making tea in your bedroom was strictly forbidden. Gordon looked with disgust at the muddled papers on the table. He told himself defiantly that he wasn't going to do any work to-night. He would have a cup of tea and smoke up his remaining cigarettes, and read *King Lear* or *Sherlock Holmes*. His books were on the mantelpiece beside the alarm clock—Shakespeare in the Everyman edition, *Sherlock Holmes*, Villon's poems, *Roderick Random*, *Les Fleurs du Mal*, a pile of French novels. But he read nothing nowadays, except Shakespeare and *Sherlock Holmes*. Meanwhile, that cup of tea.

Gordon went to the door, pushed it ajar and listened. No sound of Mrs. Wisbeach. You had to be very careful; she was quite capable of sneaking upstairs and catching you in the act. This tea-making was the major household offense, next to bringing a woman in. Quietly he bolted the door, dragged his cheap suitcase from under the bed and unlocked it. From it he extracted a sixpenny Woolworth's kettle, a packet of Lyons' tea, a tin of condensed milk, a teapot and a cup. They were all packed in newspaper to prevent them from chinking.

He had his regular procedure for making tea. First he half filled the kettle with water from the jug and set it on the oil-stove. Then he knelt down and spread out a piece of newspaper. Yesterday's tea-leaves were still in the pot, of course. He shook them out on to the newspaper, cleaned out the pot with his thumb and folded the leaves into a bundle. Presently he would smuggle them downstairs. That was always the most risky part—getting rid of the used tea-leaves. It was like the difficulty murderers have in disposing of the body. As for the cup, he always washed it in his hand basin in the morning. A squalid business. It sickened him, sometimes. It was queer how furtively you had to live in Mrs. Wisbeach's house. You had the feeling that she was always watching you; and indeed, she was given to tiptoeing up and downstairs at all hours, in hope of catching the lodgers up to mischief. It was one of those houses where you cannot even go to the w.c. in peace because of the feeling that somebody is listening to you.

Gordon unbolted the door again and listened intently. No

one stirring. Ah! A clatter of crockery far below. Mrs. Wisbeach was washing up the supper things. Probably safe to go down, then.

He tiptoed down, clutching the damp bundle of tea-leaves against his breast. The w.c. was on the second floor. At the angle of the stairs he halted, listened a moment longer. Ah! Another clatter of crockery.

All clear! Gordon Comstock, poet ("of exceptional promise," *The Times Lit. Supp.* had said), hurriedly slipped into the the w.c., flung his tea-leaves down the waste-pipe and pulled the plug. Then he hurried back to his room, rebolted the door, and, with precautions against noise, brewed himself a fresh pot of tea.

The room was passably warm by now. The tea and a cigarette worked their short-lived magic. He began to feel a little less bored and angry. Should he do a spot of work after all? He ought to work, of course. He always hated himself afterwards when he had wasted a whole evening. Half unwillingly, he shoved his chair up to the table. It needed an effort even to disturb that frightful jungle of papers. He pulled a few grimy sheets towards him, spread them out and looked at them. God, what a mess! Written on, scored out, written over, scored out again, till they were like poor old hacked cancer-patients after twenty operations. But the handwriting, where it was not crossed out, was delicate and "scholarly." With pain and trouble Gordon had acquired that "scholarly" hand, so different from the beastly copperplate they had taught him at school.

Perhaps he *would* work; for a little while, anyway. He rummaged in the litter of papers. Where was that passage he had been working on yesterday? The poem was an immensely long one—that is, it was going to be immensely long when it was finished—two thousand lines or so, in rhyme royal, describing a day in London. *London Pleasures,* its name was. It was a huge, ambitious project—the kind of thing that should only be undertaken by people with endless leisure. Gordon had not grasped that fact when he began the poem; he grasped it now, however. How lightheartedly he had begun it, two years

30

ago! When he had chucked up everything and descended into the slime of poverty, the conception of this poem had been at least a part of his motive. He had felt so certain, then, that he was equal to it. But somehow, almost from the start, *London Pleasures* had gone wrong. It was too big for him, that was the truth. It had never really progressed, it had simply fallen apart into a series of fragments. And out of two years' work that was all that he had to show—just fragments, incomplete in themselves and impossible to join together. On every one of those sheets of paper there was some hacked scrap of verse which had been written and rewritten and rewritten over intervals of months. There were not five hundred lines that you could say were definitely finished. And he had lost the power to add to it any longer; he could only tinker with this passage or that, groping now here, now there, in its confusion. It was no longer a thing that he created, it was merely a nightmare with which he struggled.

For the rest, in two whole years he had produced nothing except a handful of short poems—perhaps a score in all. It was so rarely that he could attain the peace of mind in which poetry, or prose for that matter, has got to be written. The times when he "could not" work grew commoner and commoner. Of all types of human being, only the artist takes it upon him to say that he "cannot" work. But it is quite true; there *are* times when one cannot work. Money again, always money! Lack of money means discomfort, means squalid worries, means shortage of tobacco, means ever-present consciousness of failure—above all, it means loneliness. How can you be anything but lonely on two quid a week? And in loneliness no decent book was ever written. It was quite certain that *London Pleasures* would never be the poem he had conceived—it was quite certain, indeed, that it would never even be finished. And in the moments when he faced facts Gordon himself was aware of this.

Yet all the same, and all the more for that very reason, he went on with it. It was something to cling to. It was a way of hitting back at his poverty and his loneliness. And after all, there were times when the mood of creation returned, or seemed to return. It returned to-night, for just a little while—just as long as it takes to smoke two cigarettes. With smoke tickling his lungs, he abstracted himself from the mean and actual world. He drove his mind into the abyss where poetry is written. The gas-jet sang soothingly overhead. Words became vivid and momentous things. A couplet, written a year ago and left as finished, caught his eye with a note of doubt. He repeated it to himself, over and over. It was wrong, somehow. It had seemed all right, a year ago; now, on the other hand, it seemed subtly vulgar. He rummaged among the sheets of foolscap till he found one that had nothing written on the back, turned it over, wrote the couplet out anew, wrote a dozen different versions of it, repeated each of them over and over to himself. Finally there was none that satisfied him. The couplet would have to go. It was cheap and vulgar. He found the original sheet of paper and scored the couplet out with thick lines. And in doing this there was a sense of achievement, of time not wasted, as though the destruction of much labour were in some way an act of creation.

Suddenly a double knock deep below made the whole house rattle. Gordon started. His mind fled upwards from the abyss. The post! *London Pleasures* was forgotten.

His heart fluttered. Perhaps Rosemary *had* written. Besides, there were those two poems he had sent to the magazines. One of them, indeed, he had almost given up as lost; he had sent it to an American paper, the *Californian Review*, months ago. Probably they wouldn't even bother to send it back. But the other was with an English paper, the *Primrose Quarterly*. He had wild hopes of that one. The *Primrose Quarterly* was one of those poisonous literary papers in which the fashionable Nancy Boy and the professional Roman Catholic walk bras dessus, bras dessous. It was also by a long way the most influential literary paper in England. You were a made man once you had had a poem in it. In his heart Gordon knew that the *Primrose Quarterly* would never print his poems. He wasn't up to their standard. Still, miracles sometimes happen; or, if not miracles, accidents. After all, they'd had his poem six weeks. Would they keep it six weeks if they didn't mean to accept it? He tried to quell the insane hope. But at the worst there was a chance that Rosemary had written. It was four whole days since she had written. She wouldn't do it, perhaps, if she knew how it disappointed him. Her letters—long, ill-spelt letters, full of absurd jokes and protestations of love for him—meant far more to him than she could ever understand. They were a reminder that there was still somebody in the world who cared for him. They even made up for the times when some beast had sent back one of his poems; and, as a matter of fact, the magazines always did send back his poems, except *Antichrist*, whose editor, Ravelston, was his personal friend.

There was shuffling below. It was always some minutes before Mrs. Wisbeach brought the letters upstairs. She liked to paw them about, feel them to see how thick they were, read their postmarks, hold them up to the light and speculate on their contents, before yielding them to their rightful owners. She exercised a sort of droit du seigneur over letters. Coming to her house, they were, she felt, at least partially hers. If you had gone to the front door and collected your own letters she would have resented it bitterly. On the other hand, she also resented the labour of carrying them upstairs. You would hear her footsteps very slowly ascending, and then, if there was a letter for you, there would be loud aggrieved breathing on the landing—this to let you know that you had put Mrs. Wisbeach out of breath by dragging her up all those stairs. Finally, with a little impatient grunt, the letters would be shoved under your door.

Mrs. Wisbeach was coming up the stairs. Gordon listened. The footsteps paused on the first floor. A letter for Flaxman. They ascended, paused again on the second floor. A letter for the engineer. Gordon's heart beat painfully. A letter, please God, a letter! More footsteps. Ascending or descending? They were coming nearer, surely! Ah, no, no! The sound grew fainter. She was going down again. The footsteps died away. No letters.

He took up his pen again. It was a quite futile gesture. She hadn't written after all! The little beast! He had not the

33

smallest intention of doing any more work. Indeed, he could not. The disappointment had taken all the heart out of him. Only five minutes ago his poem had still seemed to him a living thing; now he knew it unmistakably for the worthless tripe that it was. With a kind of nervous disgust he bundled the scattered sheets together, stacked them in an untidy heap and dumped them on the other side of the table, under the aspidistra. He could not even bear to look at them any longer.

He got up. It was too early to go to bed; at least, he was not in the mood for it. He pined for a bit of amusement—something cheap and easy. A seat in the pictures, cigarettes, beer. Useless! No money to pay for any of them. He would read *King Lear* and forget this filthy century. Finally, however, it was *The Adventures of Sherlock Holmes* that he took from the mantelpiece. *Sherlock Holmes* was his favourite of all books, because he knew it by heart. The oil in the lamp was giving out and it was getting beastly cold. Gordon dragged the quilt from his bed, wrapped it round his legs and sat down to read. His right elbow on the table, his hands under his coat to keep them warm, he read through "The Adventure of the Speckled Band." The little gas-mantle sighed above, the circular flame of the oil-lamp burned low, a thin bracket of fire, giving out no more heat than a candle.

Down in Mrs. Wisbeach's lair the clock struck half past ten. You could always hear it striking at night. Ping-ping, ping-ping—a note of doom! The ticking of the alarm clock on the mantelpiece became audible to Gordon again, bringing with it the consciousness of the sinister passage of time. He looked about him. Another evening wasted. Hours, days, years slipping by. Night after night, always the same. The lonely room, the womanless bed; dust, cigarette ash, the aspidistra leaves. And he was thirty, nearly. In sheer self-punishment he dragged forth a wad of *London Pleasures*, spread out the grimy sheets and looked at them as one looks at a skull for a memento mori. *London Pleasures*, by Gordon Comstock, author of *Mice*. His magnum opus. The fruit (fruit, indeed!) of two years' work—that labyrinthine mess of words! And to-

34

night's achievement—two lines crossed out; two lines backward instead of forward.

The lamp made a sound like a tiny hiccup and went out. With an effort Gordon stood up and flung the quilt back on to his bed. Better get to bed, perhaps, before it got any colder. He wandered over towards the bed. But wait. Work to-morrow. Wind the clock, set the alarm. Nothing accomplished, nothing done, has earned a night's repose.

It was some time before he could find the energy to undress. For a quarter of an hour, perhaps, he lay on the bed fully dressed, his hands under his head. There was a crack on the ceiling that resembled the map of Australia. Gordon contrived to work off his shoes and socks without sitting up. He held up one foot and looked at it. A smallish, delicate foot. Ineffectual, like his hands. Also, it was very dirty. It was nearly ten days since he had had a bath. Becoming ashamed of the dirtiness of his feet, he sagged into a sitting position and undressed himself, throwing his clothes on to the floor. Then he turned out the gas and slid between the sheets, shuddering, for he was naked. He always slept naked. His last suit of pyjamas had gone west more than a year ago.

The clock downstairs struck eleven. As the first coldness of the sheets wore off, Gordon's mind went back to the poem he had begun that afternoon. He repeated in a whisper the single stanza that was finished:

> *"Sharply the menacing wind sweeps over*
> *The bending poplars, newly bare,*
> *And the dark ribbons of the chimneys*
> *Veer downward; flicked by whips of air,*
> *Torn posters flutter."*

The octosyllables flicked to and fro. Click-click, click-click! The awful, mechanical emptiness of it appalled him. It was like some futile little machine ticking over. Rhyme to rhyme, click-click, click-click. Like the nodding of a clockwork doll. Poetry! The last futility. He lay awake, aware of his own futility, of his thirty years, of the blind alley into which he had led his life.

The clock struck twelve. Gordon had stretched his legs out straight. The bed had grown warm and comfortable. The upturned beam of a car, somewhere in the street parallel to Willowbed Road, penetrated the blind and threw into silhouette a leaf of the aspidistra, shaped like Agamemnon's sword.

Chapter Three

GORDON COMSTOCK" was a pretty bloody name, but then Gordon came of a pretty bloody family. The "Gordon" part of it was Scotch, of course. The prevalence of such names nowadays is merely a part of the Scotchification of England that has been going on these last fifty years. "Gordon," "Colin," "Malcolm," "Donald"—these are the gifts of Scotland to the world, along with golf, whisky, porridge and the works of Barrie and Stevenson.

The Comstocks belonged to the most dismal of all classes, the middle-middle class, the landless gentry. In their miserable poverty they had not even the snobbish consolation of regarding themselves as an "old" family fallen on evil days, for they were not an "old" family at all, merely one of those families which rose on the wave of Victorian prosperity and then sank again faster than the wave itself. They had had at most fifty years of comparative wealth, corresponding with the lifetime of Gordon's grandfather, Samuel Comstock— Gran'pa Comstock, as Gordon was taught to call him, though the old man died four years before he was born.

Gran'pa Comstock was one of those people who even from the grave exert a powerful influence. In life he was a tough old scoundrel. He plundered the proletariat and the foreigner of fifty thousand pounds, he built himself a red-brick mansion as durable as a pyramid, and he begot twelve children, of whom eleven survived. Finally he died quite suddenly, of a cerebral hæmorrhage. In Kensal Green his children placed over him a monolith with the following inscription:

"In ever loving memory of
Samuel Ezekiel Comstock,
A faithful husband, a tender father and
An upright and godly man,
Who was born on July 9th, 1828, and
Departed this life September 5th, 1901,
This stone is erected by
His sorrowing children.
He sleeps in the arms of Jesus."

No need to repeat the blasphemous comments which everyone who had known Gran'pa Comstock made on that last
sentence. But it is worth pointing out that the chunk of
granite on which it was inscribed weighed close on five tons
and was quite certainly put there with the intention, though
not the conscious intention, of making sure that Gran'pa
Comstock shouldn't get up from underneath it. If you want
to know what a dead man's relatives really think of him, a
good rough test is the weight of his tombstone.

The Comstocks, as Gordon knew them, were a peculiarly
dull, shabby, dead-alive, ineffectual family. They lacked vitality to an extent that was surprising. That was Gran'pa
Comstock's doing, of course. By the time when he died all his
children were grown up and some of them were middle-aged,
and he had long ago succeeded in crushing out of them any
spirit they might ever have possessed. He had lain upon them
as a garden roller lies upon daisies, and there was no chance
of their flattened personalities ever expanding again. One
and all they turned out listless, gutless, unsuccessful sort of
people. None of the boys had proper professions, because
Gran'pa Comstock had been at the greatest pains to drive all
of them into professions for which they were totally unsuited.
Only one of them—John, Gordon's father—had even braved
Gran'pa Comstock to the extent of getting married during
the latter's lifetime. It was impossible to imagine any of them
making any sort of mark in the world, or creating anything,
or destroying anything, or being happy, or vividly unhappy,
or fully alive, or even earning a decent income. They just

38

drifted along in an atmosphere of semi-genteel failure. They were one of those depressing families, so common among the middle-middle classes, in which *nothing ever happens.*

From his earliest childhood Gordon's relatives had depressed him horribly. When he was a little boy he still had great numbers of uncles and aunts living. They were all more or less alike —grey, shabby, joyless people, all rather sickly in health and all perpetually harassed by money-worries which fizzled along without ever reaching the sensational explosion of bankruptcy. It was noticeable even then that they had lost all impulse to reproduce themselves. Really vital people, whether they have money or whether they haven't, multiply almost as automatically as animals. Gran'pa Comstock, for instance, himself one of a litter of twelve, had produced eleven progeny. Yet all those eleven produced only two progeny between them, and those two—Gordon and his sister Julia—had produced, by 1934, not even one. Gordon, last of the Comstocks, was born in 1905, an unintended child; and thereafter, in thirty long, long years, there was not a single birth in the family, only deaths. And not only in the matter of marrying and begetting, but in every possible way, *nothing ever happened* in the Comstock family. Every one of them seemed doomed, as though by a curse, to a dismal, shabby, hole-and-corner existence. None of them ever *did* anything. They were the kind of people who in every conceivable activity, even if it is only getting on to a bus, are automatically elbowed away from the heart of things. All of them, of course, were hopeless fools about money. Gran'pa Comstock had finally divided his money among them more or less equally, so that each received, after the sale of the red-brick mansion, round about five thousand pounds. And no sooner was Gran'pa Comstock underground than they began to fritter their money away. None of them had the guts to lose it in sensational ways such as squandering it on women or at the races; they simply dribbled it away and dribbled it away, the women in silly investments and the men in futile little business ventures that petered out after a year or two, leaving a net loss. More than half of them went unmarried to their graves. Some of the women did make rather undesirable middle-aged marriages after their father was dead, but the men, because of their incapacity to earn a proper living, were the kind who "can't afford" to marry. None of them, except Gordon's Aunt Angela, ever had so much as a home to call their own; they were the kind of people who live in godless "rooms" and tomb-like boarding-houses. And year after year they died off and died off, of dingy but expensive little diseases that swallowed up the last penny of their capital. One of the women, Gordon's Aunt Charlotte, wandered off into the Mental Home at Clapham in 1916. The Mental Homes of England, how chock-a-block they stand! And it is above all derelict spinsters of the middle-middle classes who keep them going. By 1934 only three of that generation survived; Aunt Charlotte already mentioned, and Aunt Angela, who by some happy chance had been induced to buy a house and a tiny annuity in 1912, and Uncle Walter, who dingily existed on the few hundred pounds that were left out of his five thousand and by running short-lived "agencies" for this and that.

Gordon grew up in the atmosphere of cut-down clothes and stewed neck of mutton. His father, like the other Comstocks, was a depressed and therefore depressing person, but he had some brains and a slight literary turn. And seeing that his mind was of the literary type and he had a shrinking horror of anything to do with figures, it had seemed only natural to Gran'pa Comstock to make him into a chartered accountant. So he practised, ineffectually, as a chartered accountant, and was always buying his way into partnerships which were dissolved after a year or two, and his income fluctuated, sometimes rising to five hundred a year and sometimes falling to two hundred, but always with a tendency to decrease. He died in 1922, aged only fifty-six, but worn out—he had suffered from a kidney disease for a long time past.

Since the Comstocks were genteel as well as shabby, it was considered necessary to waste huge sums on Gordon's "education." What a fearful thing it is, this incubus of "education"! It means that in order to send his son to the right kind of school (that is, a public school or an imitation of one) a middle-class man is obliged to live for years on end in a style that would be scorned by a jobbing plumber. Gordon was sent to wretched, pretentious schools whose fees were round about £120 a year. Even these fees, of course, meant fearful sacrifices at home. Meanwhile Julia, who was five years older than he, received as nearly as possible no education at all. She was, indeed, sent to one or two poor, dingy little boarding schools, but she was "taken away" for good when she was sixteen. Gordon was "the boy" and Julia was "the girl," and it seemed natural to everyone that "the girl" should be sacrificed to "the boy." Moreover, it had early been decided in the family that Gordon was "clever." Gordon, with his wonderful "cleverness," was to win scholarships, make a brilliant success in life and retrieve the family fortunes—that was the theory, and no one believed in it more firmly than Julia. Julia was a tall, ungainly girl, much taller than Gordon, with a thin face and a neck just a little too long—one of those girls who even at their most youthful remind one irresistibly of a goose. But her nature was simple and affectionate. She was a self-effacing, home-keeping, ironing, darning and mending kind of girl, a natural spinster-soul. Even at sixteen she had "old maid" written all over her. She idolised Gordon. All through his childhood she watched over him, nursed him, spoiled him, went in rags so that he might have the right clothes to go to school in, saved up her wretched pocket-money to buy him Christmas presents and birthday presents. And of course he repaid her, as soon as he was old enough, by despising her because she was not pretty and not "clever."

Even at the third-rate schools to which Gordon was sent nearly all the boys were richer than himself. They soon found out his poverty, of course, and gave him hell because of it. Probably the greatest cruelty one can inflict on a child is to send it to school among children richer than itself. A child conscious of poverty will suffer snobbish agonies such as a grown-up person can scarcely even imagine. In those days, especially at his preparatory school, Gordon's life had been one long conspiracy to keep his end up and pretend that his parents were richer than they were. Ah, the humiliations of those days! That

41

awful business, for instance, at the beginning of each term, when you had to "give in" to the headmaster, publicly, the money you had brought back with you; and the contemptuous, cruel sniggers from the other boys when you didn't "give in" ten bob or more. And the time when the others found out that Gordon was wearing a ready-made suit which had cost thirty-five shillings! The times that Gordon dreaded most of all were when his parents came down to see him. Gordon, in those days still a believer, used actually to pray that his parents wouldn't come down to school. His father, especially, was the kind of father you couldn't help being ashamed of; a cadaverous, despondent man, with a bad stoop, his clothes dismally shabby and hopelessly out of date. He carried about with him an atmosphere of failure, worry and boredom. And he had such a dreadful habit, when he was saying good-bye, of tipping Gordon half a crown right in front of the other boys, so that everyone could see that it was only half a crown and not, as it ought to have been, ten bob! Even twenty years afterwards the memory of that school made Gordon shudder.

The first effect of all this was to give him a crawling reverence for money. In those days he actually hated his poverty-stricken relatives—his father and mother, Julia, everybody. He hated them for their dingy homes, their dowdiness, their joyless attitude to life, their endless worrying and groaning over threepences and sixpences. By far the commonest phrase in the Comstock household was, "We can't afford it." In those days he longed for money as only a child can long. Why *shouldn't* one have decent clothes and plenty of sweets and go to the pictures as often as one wanted to? He blamed his parents for their poverty as though they had been poor on purpose. Why couldn't they be like other boys' parents? They *preferred* being poor, it seemed to him. That is how a child's mind works.

But as he grew older he grew—not less unreasonable, exactly, but unreasonable in a different way. By this time he had found his feet at school and was less violently oppressed. He never was very successful at school—he did no work and won no scholarships—but he managed to develop his brain

42

along the lines that suited it. He read the books which the headmaster denounced from the pulpit, and developed unorthodox opinions about the C. of E., patriotism and the Old Boys' tie. Also he began writing poetry. He even, after a year or two, began to send poems to the *Athenæum*, the *New Age* and the *Weekly Westminster;* but they were invariably rejected. Of course there were other boys of similar type with whom he associated. Every public school has its small self-conscious intelligentsia. And at that moment, in the years just after the War, England was so full of revolutionary opinion that even the public schools were infected by it. The young, even those who had been too young to fight, were in a bad temper with their elders, as well they might be; practically everyone with any brains at all was for the moment a revolutionary. Meanwhile the old—those over sixty, say—were running in circles like hens, squawking about "subversive ideas." Gordon and his friends had quite an exciting time with their "subversive ideas." For a whole year they ran an unofficial monthly paper called the *Bolshevik*, duplicated with a jellygraph. It advocated Socialism, free love, the dismemberment of the British Empire, the abolition of the Army and Navy, and so on and so forth. It was great fun. Every intelligent boy of sixteen is a Socialist. At that age one does not see the hook sticking out of the rather stodgy bait.

In a crude, boyish way, he had begun to get the hang of this money-business. At an earlier age than most people he grasped that *all* modern commerce is a swindle. Curiously enough, it was the advertisements in the Underground stations that first brought it home to him. He little knew, as the biographers say, that he himself would one day have a job in an advertising firm. But there was more to it than the mere fact that business is a swindle. What he realised, and more clearly as time went on, was that money-worship has been elevated into a religion. Perhaps it is the only real religion—the only really *felt* religion—that is left to us. Money is what God used to be. Good and evil have no meaning any longer except failure and success. Hence the profoundly significant phrase, to *make good*. The decalogue has been reduced to two commandments. One for the employers—the elect, the money-priest-hood as it were—"Thou shalt make money"; the other for the employed—the slaves and underlings—"Thou shalt not lose thy job." It was about this time that he came across *The Ragged Trousered Philanthropists* and read about the starving carpenter who pawns everything but sticks to his aspidistra. The aspidistra became a sort of symbol for Gordon after that. The aspidistra, flower of England! It ought to be on our coat of arms instead of the lion and the unicorn. There will be no revolution in England while there are aspidistras in the windows.

He did not hate and despise his relatives now—or not so much, at any rate. They still depressed him greatly—those poor old withering aunts and uncles, of whom two or three had already died, his father, worn out and spiritless, his mother, faded, nervy and "delicate" (her lungs were none too strong), Julia, already, at one-and-twenty, a dutiful, resigned drudge who worked twelve hours a day and never had a decent frock. But he grasped now what was the matter with them. It was not *merely* the lack of money. It was rather that, having no money, they still lived mentally in the money-world—the world in which money is virture and poverty is crime. It was not poverty but the down-dragging of *respectable* poverty that had done for them. They had accepted the money-code, and by that code they were failures. They had never had the sense to lash out and just *live,* money or no money, as the lower classes do. How right the lower classes are! Hats off to the factory lad who with fourpence in the world puts his girl in the family way! At least he's got blood and not money in his veins.

Gordon thought it all out, in the naïve selfish manner of a boy. There are two ways to live, he decided. You can be rich, or you can deliberately refuse to be rich. You can possess money, or you can despise money; the one fatal thing is to worship money and fail to get it. He took it for granted that he himself would never be able to make money. It hardly even occurred to him that he might have talents which could be turned to account. That was what his schoolmasters had done for him; they had rubbed it into him that he was a sedi-

44

tious little nuisance and not likely to "succeed" in life. He accepted this. Very well, then, he would refuse the whole business of "succeeding"; he would make it his especial purpose *not* to "succeed." Better to reign in hell than serve in heaven; better to serve in hell than serve in heaven, for that matter. Already, at sixteen, he knew which side he was on. He was *against* the money-god and all his swinish priesthood. He had declared war on money; but secretly, of course.

It was when he was seventeen that his father died, leaving about two hundred pounds. Julia had been at work for some years now. During 1918 and 1919 she had worked in a Government office, and after that she took a course of cookery and got a job in a nasty, ladylike little teashop near Earl's Court Underground Station. She worked a seventy-two hour week and was given her lunch and tea and twenty-five shillings; out of this she contributed twelve shillings a week, often more, to the household expenses. Obviously the best thing to do, now that Mr. Comstock was dead, would have been to take Gordon away from school, find him a job and let Julia have the two hundred pounds to set up a teashop of her own. But here the habitual Comstock folly about money stepped in. Neither Julia nor her mother would hear of Gordon leaving school. With the strange idealistic snobbishness of the middle classes, they were willing to go to the workhouse sooner than let Gordon leave school before the statutory age of eighteen. The two hundred pounds, or more than half of it, must be used in completing Gordon's "education." Gordon let them do it. He had declared war on money, but that did not prevent him from being damnably selfish. Of course he dreaded this business of going to work. What boy wouldn't dread it? Pen-pushing in some filthy office—God! His uncles and aunts were already talking dismally about "getting Gordon settled in life." They saw everything in terms of "good" jobs. Young Smith had got such a "good" job in a bank, and young Jones had got such a "good" job in an insurance office. It made him sick to hear them. They seemed to want to see every young man in England nailed down in the coffin of a "good" job.

Meanwhile, money had got to be earned. Before her marriage Gordon's mother had been a music teacher, and even since then she had taken pupils, sporadically, when the family were in lower water than usual. She now decided that she would start giving lessons again. It was fairly easy to get pupils in the suburbs—they were living in Acton—and with the music fees and Julia's contribution they could probably "manage" for the next year or two. But the state of Mrs. Comstock's lungs was now something more than "delicate." The doctor who had attended her husband before his death had put his stethoscope to her chest and looked serious. He had told her to take care of herself, keep warm, eat nourishing food, and, above all, avoid fatigue. The fidgeting, tiring job of giving piano lessons was, of course, the worst possible thing for her. Gordon knew nothing of this. Julia knew, however. It was secret between the two women, carefully kept from Gordon.

A year went by. Gordon spent it rather miserably, more and more embarrassed by his shabby clothes and lack of pocket-money, which made girls an object of terror to him. However, the *New Age* accepted one of his poems that year. Meanwhile, his mother sat on comfortless piano stools in draughty drawing-rooms, giving lessons at two shillings an hour. And then Gordon left school, and fat, interfering Uncle Walter, who had business connections in a small way, came forward and said that a friend of a friend of his could get Gordon ever such a "good" job in the accounts department of a red lead firm. It was really a splendid job—a wonderful opening for a young man. If Gordon buckled to work in the right spirit he might be a Big Pot one of these days. Gordon's soul squirmed. Suddenly, as weak people do, he stiffened, and, to the horror of the whole family, refused even to try for the job.

There were fearful rows, of course. They could not under-stand him. It seemed to them a kind of blasphemy to refuse such a "good" job when you got the chance of it. He kept reiterating that he didn't want *that kind* of job. Then what *did* he want? they all demanded. He wanted to "write," he told them sullenly. But how could he possibly make a living by "writing"? they demanded again. And of course he couldn't answer. At the back of his mind was the idea that he could somehow live by writing poetry; but that was too absurd even to be mentioned. But at any rate, he wasn't going into business, into the money-world. He would have a job, but not a "good" job. None of them had the vaguest idea what he meant. His mother wept, even Julia "went for" him, and all round him there were uncles and aunts (he still had six or seven of them left) feebly volleying and incompetently thundering. And after three days a dreadful thing happened. In the middle of supper his mother was seized by a violent fit of coughing, put her hand to her breast, fell forward and began bleeding at the mouth.

Gordon was terrified. His mother did not die, as it happened, but she looked deathly as they carried her upstairs. Gordon rushed for the doctor. For several days his mother lay at death's door. It was the draughty drawing-rooms and the trudging to and fro in all weathers that had done it. Gordon hung helplessly about the house, a dreadful feeling of guilt mingling with his misery. He did not exactly know, but he half divined, that his mother had killed herself in order to pay his school fees. After this he could not go on opposing her any longer. He went to Uncle Walter and told him that he would take that job in the red lead firm, if they would give it him. So Uncle Walter spoke to his friend, and the friend spoke to his friend, and Gordon was sent for and interviewed by an old gentleman with badly fitting false teeth, and finally was given a job, on probation. He started on twenty-five bob a week. And with this firm he remained six years.

They moved away from Acton and took a flat in a desolate red block of flats somewhere in the Paddington district. Mrs. Comstock had brought her piano, and when she had got some of her strength back she gave occasional lessons. Gordon's wages were gradually raised, and the three of them "managed," more or less. It was Julia and Mrs. Comstock who did most of the "managing." Gordon still had a boy's selfishness about money. At the office he got on not absolutely badly. It was said of him that he was worth his wages but wasn't the type that Makes Good. In a way the utter contempt that he had for his work made things easier for him. He could put up with this meaningless office-life, because he never for an instant thought of it as permanent. Somehow, sometime, God knew how or when, he was going to break free of it. After all, there was always his "writing." Some day, perhaps, he might be able to make a living of sorts by "writing"; and you'd feel you were free of the money-stink if you were a "writer," would you not? The types he saw all around him, especially the older men, made him squirm. That was what it meant to worship the money-god! To settle down, to Make Good, to sell your soul for a villa and an aspidistra! To turn into the typical little bowler-hatted sneak—Strube's "little man"—the little docile cit who slips home by the six-fifteen to a supper of cottage pie and stewed tinned pears, half an hour's listening-in to the B.B.C. Symphony Concert, and then perhaps a spot of licit sexual intercourse if his wife "feels in the mood!" What a fate! No, it isn't like that that one was meant to live. One's got to get right out of it, out of the money-stink. It was a kind of plot that he was nursing. He was as though dedicated to this war against money. But it was still a secret. The people at the office never suspected him of unorthodox ideas. They never even found out that he wrote poetry—not that there was much to find out, for in six years he had less than twenty poems printed in the magazines. To look at, he was just the same as any other City clerk—just a soldier in the strap-hanging army that sways eastward at morning, westward at night, in the carriages of the Underground.

He was twenty-four when his mother died. The family was breaking up. Only four of the older generation of Comstocks were left now—Aunt Angela, Aunt Charlotte, Uncle Walter and another uncle who died a year later. Gordon and Julia gave up the flat. Gordon took a furnished room in Doughty Street (he felt it vaguely literary, living in Bloomsbury), and Julia moved to Earl's Court, to be near the shop. Julia was nearly thirty now, and looked much older. She was thinner than ever, though healthy enough, and there was grey in her hair. She still worked twelve hours a day, and in six years her wages had only risen by ten shillings a week. The horribly ladylike lady who kept the teashop was a semi-friend as well as an employer, and thus could sweat and bully Julia to the tune of "dearest" and "darling." Four months after his mother's death Gordon suddenly walked out of his job. He gave the firm no reasons. They imagined that he was going to "better himself," and—luckily, as it turned out—gave him quite good references. He had not even thought of looking for another job. He wanted to burn his boats. From now on he would breathe free air, free of the money-stink. He had not consciously waited for his mother to die before doing this; still, it was his mother's death that had nerved him to it.

Of course there was another and more desolating row in what was left of the family. They thought Gordon must have gone mad. Over and over again he tried, quite vainly, to explain to them why he would not yield himself to the servitude of a "good" job. "But what are you going to live on? What are you going to live on?" was what they all wailed at him. He refused to think seriously about it. Of course, he still harboured the notion that he could make a living of sorts by "writing." By this time he had got to know Ravelston, editor of *Antichrist*, and Ravelston, besides printing his poems, managed to get him books to review occasionally. His literary prospects were not so bleak as they had been six years ago. But still, it was not the desire to "write" that was his real motive. To get out of the money-world—that was what he wanted. Vaguely he looked forward to some kind of moneyless, anchorite existence. He had a feeling that if you genuinely despise money you can keep going somehow, like the birds of the air. He forgot that the birds of the air don't pay room-rent. The poet starving in a garret—but starving, somehow, not uncomfortably—that was his vision of himself.

The next seven months were devastating. They scared him and almost broke his spirit. He learned what it means to live for weeks on end on bread and margarine, to try to "write" when you are half starved, to pawn your clothes, to sneak trembling up the stairs when you owe three weeks' rent and your landlady is listening for you. Moreover, in those seven months he wrote practically nothing. The first effect of poverty is that it kills thought. He grasped, as though it were a new

49

discovery, that you do not escape from money merely by being moneyless. On the contrary, you are the hopeless slave of money until you have enough of it to live on—a "competence," as the beastly middle-class phrase goes. Finally he was turned out of his room, after a vulgar row. He was three days and four nights in the street. It was bloody. Three mornings, on the advice of another man he met on the Embankment, he spent in Billingsgate, helping to shove fish-barrows up the twisty little hills from Billingsgate into Eastcheap. "Twopence an up" was what you got, and the work knocked hell out of your thigh muscles. There were crowds of people on the same job, and you had to wait your turn; you were lucky if you made eighteenpence between four in the morning and nine. After three days of it Gordon gave up. What was the use? He was beaten. There was nothing for it but to go back to his family, borrow some money and find another job.

But now, of course, there was no job to be had. For months he lived by cadging on the family. Julia kept him going till the last penny of her tiny savings was gone. It was abominable. Here was the outcome of all his fine attitudes! He had renounced ambition, made war on money, and all it led to was cadging from his sister! And Julia, he knew, felt his failure far more than she felt the loss of her savings. She had had such hopes of Gordon. He alone of all the Comstocks had had it in him to "succeed." Even now she believed that somehow, some day, he was going to retrieve the family fortunes. He was so "clever"—surely he could make money if he tried! For two whole months Gordon stayed with Aunt Angela in her little house at Highgate—poor, faded, mummified Aunt Angela, who even for herself had barely enough to eat. All this time he searched desperately for work. Uncle Walter could not help him. His influence in the business world, never large, was now practically nil. At last, however, in a quite unexpected way, the luck turned. A friend of a friend of Julia's employer's brother managed to get Gordon a job in the accounts department of the New Albion Publicity Company.

The New Albion was one of those publicity firms which have sprung up everywhere since the War—the fungi, as you might

50

say, that sprout from a decaying capitalism. It was a smallish rising firm and took every class of publicity it could get. It designed a certain number of large-scale posters for oatmeal stout, self-raising flour and so forth, but its main line was millinery and cosmetic advertisements in the women's illustrated papers, besides minor ads in twopenny weeklies, such as Whiterose Pills for Female Disorders, Your Horoscope Cast by Professor Raratongo, The Seven Secrets of Venus, New Hope for the Ruptured, Earn Five Pounds a Week in your Spare Time, and Cyprolax Hair Lotion Banishes all Unpleasant Intruders. There was a large staff of commercial artists, of course. It was here that Gordon first made the acquaintance of Rosemary. She was in the "studio" and helped to design fashion plates. It was a long time before he actually spoke to her. At first he knew her merely as a remote personage, small, dark, with swift movements, distinctly attractive but rather intimidating. When they passed one another in the corridors she eyed him ironically, as though she knew all about him and considered him a bit of a joke; nevertheless she seemed to look at him a little oftener than was necessary. He had nothing to do with her side of the business. He was in the accounts department, a mere clerk on three quid a week.

The interesting thing about the New Albion was that it was so completely modern in spirit. There was hardly a soul in the firm who was not perfectly well aware that publicity—advertising—is the dirtiest ramp that capitalism has yet produced. In the red lead firm there had still lingered certain notions of commercial honour and usefulness. But such things would have been laughed at in the New Albion. Most of the employees were the hard-boiled, Americanised, go-getting type—the type to whom nothing in the world is sacred, except money. They had their cynical code worked out. The public are swine; advertising is the rattling of a stick inside a swill-bucket. And yet beneath their cynicism there was the final naïveté, the blind worship of the money-god. Gordon studied them unobtrusively. As before, he did his work passably well and his fellow-employees looked down on him. Nothing had changed in his inner mind. He still despised and repudiated

51

the money-code. Somehow, sooner or later, he was going to escape from it; even now, after his late fiasco, he still plotted to escape. He was *in* the money-world, but not *of* it. As for the types about him, the little bowler-hatted worms who never turned, and the go-getters, the American business-college gutter-crawlers, they rather amused him than not. He liked studying their slavish keep-your-job mentality. He was the chiel amang them takin' notes.

One day a curious thing happened. Somebody chanced to see a poem of Gordon's in a magazine, and put it about that they "had a poet in the office." Of course Gordon was laughed at, not ill-naturedly, by the other clerks. They nicknamed him "the bard" from that day forth. But though amused, they were also faintly contemptuous. It confirmed all their ideas about Gordon. A fellow who wrote poetry wasn't exactly the type to Make Good. But the thing had an unexpected sequel. About the time when the clerks grew tired of chaffing Gordon, Mr. Erskine, the managing director, who had hitherto taken only the minimum notice of him, suddenly sent for him and interviewed him.

Mr. Erskine was a large, slow-moving man with a broad, healthy, expressionless face. From his appearance and the slowness of his speech you would have guessed with confidence that he had something to do with either agriculture or cattle-breeding. His wits were as slow as his movements, and he was the kind of man who never hears anything until everybody else has stopped talking about it. How such a man came to be in charge of an advertising agency, only the strange gods of capitalism know. But he was quite a likeable person. He had not that sniffish, buttoned-up spirit that usually goes with an ability to make money. And in a way his fat-wittedness stood him in good stead. Being insensible to popular prejudice, he could assess people on their merits; consequently, he was rather good at choosing talented employees. The news that Gordon had written poems, so far from shocking him, vaguely impressed him. They wanted literary talent in the New Albion. Having sent for Gordon, he studied him in a somnolent, sidelong way and asked him a number of inconclusive questions.

52

He never listened to Gordon's answers, but punctuated his questions with a noise that sounded like "Hm, hm, hm." Wrote poetry, did he? Oh yes? Hm. And had it printed in the papers? Hm, hm. Suppose they paid you for that kind of thing? Not much, eh? No, suppose not. Hm, hm. Poetry? Hm. A bit difficult, that must be. Getting the lines the same length, and all that. Hm, hm. Write anything else? Stories, and so forth? Hm. Oh yes? Very interesting. Hm!

Then, without further questions, he promoted Gordon to a special post as secretary—in effect, apprentice—to Mr. Clew, the New Albion's head copywriter. Like every other advertising agency, the New Albion was constantly in search of copywriters with a touch of imagination. It is a curious fact, but it is much easier to find competent draughtsmen than to find people who can think of slogans like "Q.T. Sauce Keeps Hubby Smiling" and "Kiddies clamour for their Breakfast Crisps." Gordon's wages were not raised for the moment, but the firm had their eye on him. With luck he might be a full-fledged copywriter in a year's time. It was an unmistakable chance to Make Good.

For six months he was working with Mr. Clew. Mr. Clew was a harassed man of about forty, with wiry hair into which he often plunged his fingers. He worked in a stuffy little office whose walls were entirely papered with his past triumphs in the form of posters. He took Gordon under his wing in a friendly way, showed him the ropes and was even ready to listen to his suggestions. At that time they were working on a line of magazine ads for April Dew, the great new deodorant which the Queen of Sheba Toilet Requisites Co. (this was Flaxman's firm, curiously enough) were putting on the market. Gordon started on the job with secret loathing. But now there was a quite unexpected development. It was that Gordon showed, almost from the start, a remarkable talent for copywriting. He could compose an ad as though he had been born to it. The vivid phrase that sticks and rankles, the neat little para. that packs a world of lies into a hundred words— they came to him almost unsought. He had always had a gift for words, but this was the first time he had used it successfully.

Mr. Clew thought him very promising. Gordon watched his own development, first with surprise, then with amusement, and finally with a kind of horror. *This,* then was what he was coming to! Writing lies to tickle the money out of fools' pockets! There was a beastly irony, too, in the fact that he, who wanted to be a "writer," should score his sole success in writing ads for deodorants. However, that was less unusual than he imagined. Most copywriters, they say, are novelists manqués; or is it the other way about?

The Queen of Sheba were very pleased with their ads. Mr. Erskine also was pleased. Gordon's wages were raised by ten shillings a week. And it was now that Gordon grew frightened. Money was getting him after all. He was sliding down, down, into the money-sty. A little more and he would be stuck in it for life. It is queer how these things happen. You set your face against success, you swear never to Make Good—you honestly believe that you couldn't Make Good even if you wanted to; and then something happens along, some mere chance, and you find yourself Making Good almost automatically. He saw that now or never was the time to escape. He had got to get out of it—out of the money-world, irrevocably, before he was too far involved.

But this time he wasn't going to be starved into submission. He went to Ravelston and asked his help. He told him that he wanted some kind of job; not a "good" job, but a job that would keep his body without wholly buying his soul. Ravelston understood perfectly. The distinction between a job and a "good" job did not have to be explained to him; nor did he point out to Gordon the folly of what he was doing. That was the great thing about Ravelston. He could always see another person's point of view. It was having money that did it, no doubt; for the rich can afford to be intelligent. Moreover, being rich himself, he could find jobs for other people. After only a fortnight he told Gordon of something that might suit him. A Mr. McKechnie, a rather dilapidated second-hand bookseller with whom Ravelston dealt occasionally, was looking for an assistant. He did not want a trained assistant who would expect full wages; he wanted somebody who looked

54

like a gentleman and could talk about books—somebody to impress the more bookish customers. It was the very reverse of a "good" job. The hours were long, the pay was wretched—two pounds a week—and there was no chance of advancement. It was a blind-alley job. And, of course, a blind-alley job was the very thing Gordon was looking for. He went and saw Mr. McKechnie, a sleepy, benign old Scotchman with a red nose and a white beard stained by snuff, and was taken on without demur. At this time, too, his volume of poems, *Mice,* was going to press. The seventh publisher to whom he had sent it had accepted it. Gordon did not know that this was Ravelston's doing. Ravelston was a personal friend of the publisher. He was always arranging this kind of thing, stealthily, for obscure poets. Gordon thought the future was opening before him. He was a made man—or, by Smilesian, aspidistral standards, *un*made.

He gave them a month's notice at the office. It was a painful business altogether. Julia, of course, was more distressed than ever at this second abandonment of a "good" job. By this time Gordon had got to know Rosemary. She did not try to prevent him from throwing up his job. It was against her code to interfere—"You've got to live your own life," was always her attitude. But she did not in the least understand why he was doing it. The thing that most upset him, curiously enough, was his interview with Mr. Erskine. Mr. Erskine was genuinely kind. He did not want Gordon to leave the firm, and said so frankly. With a sort of elephantine politeness he refrained from calling Gordon a young fool. He did, however, ask him why he was leaving. Somehow, Gordon could not bring himself to avoid answering or to say—the only thing Mr. Erskine would have understood—that he was going after a better-paid job. He blurted out shamefacedly that he "didn't think business suited him" and that he "wanted to go in for writing." Mr. Erskine was noncommittal. Writing, eh? Hm. Much money in that sort of thing nowadays? Not much, eh? Hm. No, suppose not. Hm. Gordon, feeling and looking ridiculous, mumbled that he had "got a book just coming out." A book of poems,

55

he added, with difficulty in pronouncing the word. Mr. Erskine regarded him sidelong before remarking:

"Poetry, eh? Hm. Poetry? Make a living out of that sort of thing, do you think?"

"Well—not a living, exactly. But it would help."

"Hm—well! You know best, I expect. If you want a job any time, come back to us. I dare say we could find room for you. We can do with your sort here. Don't forget."

Gordon left with a hateful feeling of having behaved perversely and ungratefully. But he had got to do it; he had got to get out of the money-world. It was queer. All over England young men were eating their hearts out for lack of jobs, and here was he, Gordon, to whom the very word "job" was faintly nauseous, having jobs thrust unwanted upon him. It was an example of the fact that you can get anything in this world if you genuinely don't want it. Moreover, Mr. Erskine's words stuck in his mind. Probably he had meant what he said. Probably there *would* be a job waiting for Gordon if he chose to go back. So his boats were only half burned. The New Albion was a doom before him as well as behind.

But how happy he had been, just at first, in Mr. McKechnie's bookshop! For a little while—a very little while—he had the illusion of being really out of the money-world. Of course the book-trade was a swindle, like all other trades; but how different a swindle! Here was no hustling and Making Good, no gutter-crawling. No go-getter could put up for ten minutes with the stagnant air of the book-trade. As for the work, it was very simple. It was mainly a question of being in the shop ten hours a day. Mr. McKechnie wasn't a bad old stick. He was a Scotchman, of course, but Scottish is as Scottish does. At any rate he was reasonably free from avarice—his most distinctive trait semed to be laziness. He was also a teetotaller and belonged to some Nonconformist sect or other, but this did not affect Gordon. Gordon had been at the shop about a month when *Mice* was published. No less than thirteen papers reviewed it! And *The Times Lit. Supp.* said that it showed "exceptional promise." It was not till months later that he realised what a hopeless failure *Mice* had really been.

And it was only now, when he was down to two quid a week and had practically cut himself off from the prospect of earning more that he grasped the real nature of the battle he was fighting. The devil of it is that the glow of renunciation never lasts. Life on two quid a week ceases to be a heroic gesture and becomes a dingy habit. Failure is as great a swindle as success. He had thrown up his "good" job and renounced "good" jobs for ever. Well, that was necessary. He did not want to go back on it. But it was no use pretending that because his poverty was self-imposed he had escaped the ills that poverty drags in its train. It was not a question of hardship. You don't suffer real physical hardship on two quid a week, and if you did it wouldn't matter. It is in the brain and the soul that lack of money damages you. Mental deadness, spiritual squalor—they seem to descend upon you inescapably when your income drops below a certain point. Faith, hope, money—only a saint could have the first two without having the third.

He was growing more mature. Twenty-seven, twenty-eight, twenty-nine. He had reached the age when the future ceases to be a rosy blur and becomes actual and menacing. The spectacle of his surviving relatives depressed him more and more. As he grew older he felt himself more akin to them. That was the way he was going! A few years more, and he would be like that, just like that! He felt this even with Julia, whom he saw oftener than his uncle and aunt. In spite of various resolves never to do it again, he still borrowed money off Julia periodically. Julia's hair was greying fast; there was a deep line scored down each of her thin red cheeks. She had settled her life into a routine in which she was not unhappy. There was her work at the shop, her "sewing" at nights in her Earl's Court bed-sitting-room (second floor, back, nine bob a week unfurnished), her occasional forgatherings with spinster friends as lonely as herself. It was the typical submerged life of the penniless unmarried woman; she accepted it, hardly realising that her destiny could ever have been different. Yet in her way she suffered, more for Gordon than for herself. The gradual decay of the family, the way they had

57

died off and died off and left nothing behind, was a sort of tragedy in her mind. Money, money! "None of us ever seems to make any money!" was her perpetual lament. And of them all, Gordon alone had had the chance to make money; and Gordon had chosen not to. He was sinking effortless into the same rut of poverty as the others. After the first row was over, she was too decent to "go for" him again because he had thrown up his job at the New Albion. But his motives were quite meaningless to her. In her wordless feminine way she knew that the sin against money is the ultimate sin.

And as for Aunt Angela and Uncle Walter—oh dear, oh dear! What a couple! It made Gordon feel ten years older every time he looked at them.

Uncle Walter, for example. Uncle Walter was very depressing. He was sixty-seven, and what with his various "agencies" and the dwindling remnants of his patrimony his income might have been nearly three pounds a week. He had a tiny little cabin of an office off Cursitor Street, and he lived in a very cheap boarding-house in Holland Park. That was quite according to precedent; all the Comstock men drifted naturally into boarding-houses. When you looked at poor old uncle, with his large tremulous belly, his bronchitic voice, his broad, pale, timidly pompous face, rather like Sargent's portrait of Henry James, his entirely hairless head, his pale, pouchy eyes and his ever-drooping moustache, to which he tried vainly to give an upward twirl—when you looked at him, you found it totally impossible to believe that he had ever been young. Was it conceivable that such a being had ever felt life tingle in his veins? Had he ever climbed a tree, taken a header off a spring-board, or been in love? Had he ever had a brain in working order? Even back in the early 'nineties, when he was arithmetically young, had he ever made any kind of stab at life? A few furtive half-hearted frolics, perhaps. A few whiskies in dull bars, a visit or two to the Empire promenade, a little whoring on the Q.T.; the sort of dingy, drabby fornications that you can imagine happening between Egyptian mummies after the museum is closed for

58

the night. And after that the long, long quiet years of business failure, loneliness, and stagnation in godless boarding-houses.

And yet uncle in his old age was probably not unhappy. He had one hobby of never-failing interest, and that was his diseases. He suffered, by his own account, from every disease in the medical dictionary, and was never weary of talking about them. Indeed, it seemed to Gordon that none of the people in his uncle's boarding-house—he had been there occasionally—ever did talk about anything except their diseases. All over the darkish drawing-room, ageing, discoloured people sat about in couples, discussing symptoms. Their conversation was like the dripping of stalactite to stalagmite. Drip, drip. "How is your lumbago?" says stalactite to stalagmite. "I find my Kruschen Salts are doing me good," says stalagmite to stalactite. Drip, drip, drip.

And then there was Aunt Angela, aged sixty-nine. Gordon tried not even to think of Aunt Angela oftener than he could help.

Poor, dear, good, kind, depressing Aunt Angela!

Poor, shrivelled, parchment-yellow, skin-and-bone Aunt Angela! There in her miserable little semi-detached house in Highgate—Briarbrae, its name was—there in her palace in the northern mountains, there dwelleth she, Angela the Ever-virgin, of whom no man either living or among the shades can say truly that upon her lips he hath pressed the dear caresses of a lover. All alone she dwelleth, and all day long she fareth to and fro, and in her hand is the feather-mop fashioned from the tail feathers of the contumacious turkey, and with it she polisheth the dark-leaved aspidistras and flicketh the hated dust from the resplendent never-to-be-used Crown Derby china tea-service. And ever and anon she comforteth her dear heart with draughts of the dark brown tea, both Flowery Orange and Pekoe Points, which the small-bearded sons of Coromandel have ferried to her across the wine-dark sea. Poor, dear, good, kind, but on the whole unlovable Aunt Angela! Her annuity was ninety-eight pounds a year (thirty-eight bob a week, but she retained the middle-class habit of thinking of her income as a yearly and not a weekly thing), and out of that, twelve and sixpence a week went on house rates. She would probably have starved occasionally if Julia had not smuggled her packets of cakes and bread and butter from the shop—always, of course, presented as "Just a few little things that it seemed a pity to throw away," with the solemn pretence that Aunt Angela didn't really need them.

Yet she too had her pleasures, poor old auntie. She had become a great novel-reader in her old age, the public library being only ten minutes' walk from Briarbrae. During his lifetime, on some whim or other, Gran'pa Comstock had forbidden his daughters to read novels. Consequently, having only begun to read novels in 1902, Aunt Angela was always a couple of decades behind the current mode in fiction. But she plodded along in the rear, faint yet pursuing. In the nineteen-hundreds she was still reading Rhoda Broughton and Mrs. Henry Wood. In the War years she discovered Hall Caine and Mrs. Humphry Ward. In the nineteen-twenties she was reading Silas Hocking and H. Seton Merriman, and by the nineteen-thirties she had almost, but not quite, caught up with W. B. Maxwell and William J. Locke. Further she would never get. As for the post-War novelists, she had heard of them afar off, with their immorality and their blasphemies and their devastating "cleverness." But she would never live to read them. Walpole we know, and Hichens we read, but Hemingway, who are you?

Well, this was 1934, and that was what was left of the Comstock family. Uncle Walter, with his "agencies" and his diseases. Aunt Angela, dusting the Crown Derby china tea-service in Briarbrae. Aunt Charlotte, still preserving a vague, vegetable existence in the Mental Home. Julia, working a seventy-two-hour week and doing her "sewing" at nights by the tiny gas-fire in her bed-sitting-room. Gordon, nearly thirty, earning two quid a week in a fool's job, and struggling, as the sole demonstrable object of his existence, with a dreadful book that never got any further.

Possibly there were some other, more distantly related Comstocks, for Gran'pa Comstock had been one of a family of twelve. But if any survived they had grown rich and lost touch with their poor relations; for money is thicker than blood. As for Gordon's branch of the family, the combined income of the five of them, allowing for the lump sum that had been paid down when Aunt Charlotte entered the Mental Home, might have been six hundred a year. Their combined ages were two hundred and sixty-three years. None of them had ever been out of England, fought in war, been in prison, ridden a horse, travelled in an aeroplane, got married or given birth to a child. There seemed no reason why they should not continue in the same style until they died. Year in, year out, *nothing ever happened* in the Comstock family.

Chapter Four

Sharply the menacing wind sweeps over
The bending poplars, newly bare.

As a matter of fact, though, there was not a breath of wind that afternoon. It was almost as mild as spring. Gordon repeated to himself the poem he had begun yesterday, in a cadenced whisper, simply for the pleasure of the sound of it. He was pleased with the poem at this moment. It was a good poem—or would be when it was finished, anyway. He had forgotten that last night it had almost made him sick.

The plane trees brooded motionless, dimmed by faint wreaths of mist. A tram boomed in the valley far below. Gordon walked up Malkin Hill, rustling instep-deep through the dry, drifted leaves. All down the pavement they were strewn, crinkly and golden, like the rustling flakes of some American breakfast cereal; as though the queen of Brobdingnag had upset her packet of Truweet Breakfast Crisps down the hillside.

Jolly, the windless winter days! Best time of all the year—or so Gordon thought at this moment. He was as happy as you can be when you haven't smoked all day and have only three-halfpence and a Joey in the world. This was Thursday, early-closing day and Gordon's afternoon off. He was going to the house of Paul Doring, the critic, who lived in Coleridge Grove and gave literary tea-parties.

It had taken him an hour or more to get himself ready. Social life is so complicated when your income is two quid a week. He had had a painful shave in cold water immediately after dinner. He had put on his best suit—three years old but just passable when he remembered to press the trousers under his mattress. He had turned his collar inside out and tied his tie so that the torn place didn't show. With the point of a match he had scraped enough blacking from the tin to polish his shoes. He had even borrowed a needle from Lorenheim and darned his socks—a tedious job, but better than inking the places where your ankle shows through. Also he had procured an empty Gold Flake packet and put into it a single cigarette extracted from the penny-in-the-slot-machine. That was just for the look of the thing. You can't, of course, go to other people's houses with *no* cigarettes. But if you have even one it's all right, because when people see one cigarette in a packet they assume that the packet has been full. It is fairly easy to pass the thing off as an accident.

"Have a cigarette?" you say casually to someone.

"Oh—thanks."

You push the packet open and then register surprise. "Hell! I'm down to my last. And I could have sworn I had a full packet."

"Oh, I won't take your last. Have one of *mine*," says the other.

"Oh—thanks."

And after that, of course, your host and hostess press cigarettes upon you. But you must have *one* cigarette, just for honour's sake.

Sharply the menacing wind sweeps over. He would finish that poem presently. He could finish it whenever he chose. It was queer, how the mere prospect of going to a literary tea-party bucked him up. When your income is two quid a week you at least aren't jaded by too much human contact. Even to see the inside of somebody else's house is a kind of treat. A padded armchair under your bum, and tea and cigarettes and the smell of women—you learn to appreciate such things when you are starved of them. In practice, though, Doring's parties never in the least resembled what Gordon looked forward to. Those wonderful, witty, erudite conversations that he imag-

63

ined beforehand—they never happened or began to happen. Indeed there was never anything that could properly be called conversation at all; only the stupid clacking that goes on at parties everywhere, in Hampstead or Hong Kong. No one really worth meeting ever came to Doring's parties. Doring was such a very mangy lion himself that his followers were hardly even worthy to be called jackals. Quite half of them were those hen-witted middle-aged women who have lately escaped from good Christian homes and are trying to be literary. The star exhibits were troops of bright young things who dropped in for half an hour, formed circles of their own and talked sniggeringly about other bright young things to whom they referred by nicknames. For the most part Gordon found himself hanging about on the edges of conversations. Doring was kind in a slapdash way and introduced him to everybody as "Gordon Comstock—*you* know; the poet. He wrote that dashed clever book of poems called *Mice. You* know." But Gordon had never yet encountered anybody who *did* know. The bright young things summed him up at a glance and ignored him. He was thirtyish, moth-eaten and obviously penniless. And yet, in spite of the invariable disappointment, how eagerly he looked forward to those literary tea-parties! They were a break in his loneliness, anyway. That is the devilish thing about poverty, the ever-recurrent thing—loneliness. Day after day with never an intelligent person to talk to; night after night back to your godless room, always alone. Perhaps it sounds rather fun if you are rich and sought-after; but how different it is when you do it from necessity!

Sharply the menacing wind sweeps over. A stream of cars hummed easily up the hill. Gordon eyed them without envy. Who wants a car, anyway? The pink doll-faces of upper-class women gazed at him through the car window. Bloody nit-witted lapdogs. Pampered bitches dozing on their chains. Better the lone wolf than the cringing dog. He thought of the Tube stations at early morning. The black hordes of clerks scurrying underground like ants into a hole; swarms of little ant-like men, each with dispatch-case in right hand, newspaper in left hand, and the fear of the sack like a maggot in his heart. How it eats at them, that secret fear! Especially on winter days, when they hear the menace of the wind. Winter, the sack, the workhouse, the Embankment benches! Ah!

> *Sharply the menacing wind sweeps over*
> *The bending poplars, newly bare,*
> *And the dark ribbons of the chimneys*
> *Veer downward; flicked by whips of air,*
> *Torn posters flutter; coldly sound*
> *The boom of trams and the rattle of hooves,*
> *And the clerks who hurry to the station*
> *Look, shuddering, over the eastern rooves,*
> *Thinking——*

What do they think? Winter's coming. Is my job safe? The sack means the workhouse. Circumcise ye your foreskins, saith the Lord. Suck the blacking off the boss's boots. Yes!

> *Thinking each one, "Here comes the winter!*
> *Please God I keep my job this year!"*
> *And bleakly, as the cold strikes through*
> *Their entrails like an icy spear,*
> *They think——*

"Think" again. No matter. What do they think? Money, money! Rent, rates, taxes, school bills, season tickets, boots for the children. And the life insurance policy and the skivvy's wages. And, my God, suppose the wife gets in the family way again! And did I laugh loud enough when the boss made that joke yesterday? And the next instalment on the vacuum cleaner.

Neatly, taking a pleasure in his neatness, with the sensation of dropping piece after piece of a jigsaw puzzle into place, he fashioned another stanza:

> *They think of rent, rates, season tickets,*
> *Insurance, coal, the skivvy's wages,*
> *Boots, school bills, and the next instalment*
> *Upon the two twin beds from Drage's.*

Not bad, not bad at all. Finish it presently. Four or five more stanzas. Ravelston would print it.

A starling sat in the naked boughs of a plane tree, crooning self-pitifully as starlings do on warm winter days when they believe spring is in the air. At the foot of the tree a huge sandy cat sat motionless, mouth open, gazing upwards with rapt desire, plainly expecting that the starling would drop into its mouth. Gordon repeated to himself the four finished stanzas of his poem. It was *good*. Why had he thought last night that it was mechanical, weak and empty? He was a poet. He walked more upright, arrogantly almost, with the pride of a poet. Gordon Comstock, author of *Mice*. "Of exceptional promise," *The Times Lit. Supp.* had said. Author also of *London Pleasures*. For that too would be finished quite soon. He knew now that he could finish it when he chose. Why had he ever despaired of it? Three months it might take; soon enough to come out in the summer. In his mind's eye he saw the "slim" white buckram shape of *London Pleasures;* the excellent paper, the wide margins, the good Caslon type, the refined dust-jacket. And the reviews in all the best papers. "An outstanding achievement"—*The Times Lit. Supp.* "A welcome relief from the Sitwell school"—*Scrutiny*.

Coleridge Grove was a damp, shadowy, secluded road, a blind alley and therefore void of traffic. Literary associations of the wrong kind (Coleridge was rumoured to have lived there for six weeks in the summer of 1821) hung heavy upon it. You could not look at its antique decaying houses, standing back from the road in dank gardens under heavy trees, without feeling an atmosphere of outmoded "culture" envelop you. In some of those houses, undoubtedly, Browning Societies still flourished, and ladies in art serge sat at the feet of extinct poets talking about Swinburne and Walter Pater. In spring the gardens were sprinkled with purple and yellow crocuses, and later with harebells, springing up in little Wendy rings among the anæmic grass; and even the trees, it seemed to Gordon, played up to their environment and twisted themselves into whimsy Rackhamesque attitudes. It was queer that a prosperous hack critic like Paul Doring should live in such

66

a place. For Doring was an astonishingly bad critic. He re-
viewed novels for the *Sunday Post* and discovered the great
English novel with Walpolean regularity once a fortnight.
You would have expected him to live in a flat on Hyde Park
Corner. Perhaps it was a kind of penance that he had imposed
upon himself, as though by living in the refined discomfort of
Coleridge Grove he propitiated the injured gods of literature.

Gordon came round the corner, turning over in his mind a
line from *London Pleasures*. And then suddenly he stopped
short. There was something wrong about the look of the
Dorings' gate. What was it? Ah, of course! There were no cars
waiting outside.

He paused, walked on a step or two and stopped again,
like a dog that smells danger. It was all wrong. There *ought*
to be some cars. There were always quite a lot of people at
the Dorings' parties, and half of them came in cars. Why had
nobody else arrived? Could he be too early? But no! They had
said half past three and it was at least twenty to four.

He hastened towards the gate. Already he felt practically
sure that the party *had* been put off. A chill like the shadow
of a cloud had fallen across him. Suppose the Dorings weren't
at home! Suppose the party had been put off! And this thought,
though it dismayed him, did not strike him as in the least im-
probable. It was his special bugbear, the especial childish dread
he carried about with him, to be invited to people's houses
and then find them not at home. Even when there was no
doubt about the invitation he always half expected that there
would be some hitch or other. He was never quite certain
of his welcome. He took it for granted that people would
snub him and forget about him. Why not, indeed? He had
no money. When you have no money your life is one long
series of snubs.

He swung the iron gate open. It creaked with a lonely
sound. The dank mossy path was bordered with chunks of
some Rackhamesque pinkish stone. Gordon inspected the
house-front narrowly. He was so used to this kind of thing.
He had developed a sort of Sherlock Holmes technique for
finding out whether a house was inhabited or not. Ah! Not

much doubt about it this time. The house had a deserted look. No smoke coming from the chimneys, no windows lighted. It must be getting darkish indoors—surely they would have lighted the lamps? And there was not a single foot-mark on the steps; that settled it. Nevertheless with a sort of desperate hope he tugged at the bell. An old-fashioned wire bell, of course. In Coleridge Grove it would have been considered low and unliterary to have an electric bell.

Clang, clang, clang! went the bell.

Gordon's last hope vanished. No mistaking the hollow clangour of a bell echoing through an empty house. He seized the handle again and gave it a wrench that almost broke the wire. A frightful, clamorous peal answered him. But it was useless, quite useless. Not a foot stirred within. Even the servants were out. At this moment he became aware of a lace cap, some dark hair and a pair of youthful eyes regarding him furtively from the basement of the house next door. It was a servant-girl who had come out to see what all the noise was about. She caught his eye and gazed into the middle distance. He looked a fool and knew it. One always does look a fool when one rings the bell of an empty house. And suddenly it came to him that that girl knew all about him—knew that the party had been put off and that everyone except Gordon had been told of it—knew that it was because he had no money that he wasn't worth the trouble of telling. *She* knew. Servants always know.

He turned and made for the gate. Under the servant's eye he had to stroll casually away, as though this were a small disappointment that scarcely mattered. But he was trembling so with anger that it was difficult to control his movements. The sods! The bloody sods! To have played a trick like that on him. To have invited him, and then changed the day and not even bothered to tell him! There might be other explanations—he just refused to think of them. The sods, the bloody sods! His eye fell upon one of the Rackhamesque chunks of stone. How he'd love to pick that thing up and bash it through the window! He grasped the rusty gate-bar so hard that he hurt his hand and almost tore it. The physical pain did him good. It counteracted the agony at his heart. It was not merely that he had been cheated of an evening spent in human company, though that was much. It was the feeling of helplessness, of insignificance, of being set aside, ignored—a creature not worth worrying about. They'd changed the day and hadn't even bothered to tell him. Told everybody else, but not him. That's how people treat you when you've no money! Just wantonly, cold-bloodedly insult you. It was likely enough, indeed, that the Dorings had honestly forgotten, meaning no harm; it was even possible that he himself had mistaken the date. But no! He wouldn't think of it. The Dorings had done it on purpose. Of *course* they had done it on purpose! Just hadn't troubled to tell him, because he had no money and consequently didn't matter. The sods!

He walked rapidly away. There was a sharp pain in his breast. Human contact, human voices! But what was the good of wishing? He'd have to spend the evening alone, as usual. His friends were so few and lived so far away. Rosemary would still be at work; besides, she lived at the back of beyond, in West Kensington, in a women's hostel guarded by female dragons. Ravelston lived nearer, in the Regent's Park district. But Ravelston was a rich man and had many engagements; the chances were always against his being at home. Gordon could not even ring him up, because he hadn't the necessary two pennies; only three halfpence and the Joey. Besides, how could he go and see Ravelston when he had no money? Ravelston would be sure to say "Let's go to a pub," or something! He couldn't let Ravelston pay for his drinks. His friendship with Ravelston was only possible on the understanding that he paid his share of everything.

He took out his single cigarette and lighted it. It gave him no pleasure to smoke, walking fast; it was a mere reckless gesture. He did not take much notice of where he was going. All he wanted was to tire himself, to walk and walk till the stupid physical fatigue had obliterated the Dorings' snub. He moved roughly southward—through the wastes of Camden Town, down Tottenham Court Road. It had been dark for some time now. He crossed Oxford Street, threaded through

69

Covent Garden, found himself in the Strand and crossed the river by Waterloo Bridge. With night the cold had descended. As he walked his anger grew less violent, but his mood could not fundamentally improve. There was a thought that kept haunting him—a thought from which he fled, but which was not to be escaped. It was the thought of his poems. His empty, silly, futile poems! How could he ever have believed in them? To think that actually he had imagined, so short a time ago, that even *London Pleasures* might one day come to something! It made him sick to think of his poems now. It was like remembering last night's debauch. He knew in his bones that he was no good and his poems were no good. *London Pleasures* would never be finished. If he lived to be a thousand he would never write a line worth reading. Over and over, in self-hatred, he repeated those four stanzas of the poem he had been making up. Christ, what tripe! Rhyme to rhyme—tinkle, tinkle, tinkle! Hollow as an empty biscuit tin. *That* was the kind of muck he had wasted his life on.

He had walked a long way, five or seven miles perhaps. His feet were hot and swollen from the pavements. He was somewhere in Lambeth, in a slummy quarter where the narrow, puddled streets plunged into blackness at fifty yards' distance. The few lamps, mist-ringed, hung like isolated stars, illumining nothing save themselves. He was getting devilishly hungry. The coffee-shops tempted him with their steamy windows and their chalked signs: "Good Cup of Tea, 2d. No Urns Used." But it was no use, he couldn't spend his Joey. He went under some echoing railway arches and up the alley on to Hungerford Bridge. On the miry water, lit by the glare of skysigns, the muck of East London was racing inland. Corks, lemons, barrel-staves, a dead dog, hunks of bread. Gordon walked along the Embankment to Westminster. The wind made the plane trees rattle. *Sharply the menacing wind sweeps over.* He winced. That tripe again! Even now, though it was December, a few poor draggled old wrecks were settling down on the benches, tucking themselves up in sort of parcels of newspaper. Gordon looked at them callously. On the bum, they called it. He would come to it himself some day. Better so, perhaps? He never felt any pity for the genuine poor. It is the black-coated poor, the middle-middle class, who need pitying.

He walked up to Trafalgar Square. Hours and hours to kill. The National Gallery? Ah, shut long ago, of course. It would be. It was a quarter past seven. Three, four, five hours before he could sleep. He walked seven times round the square, slowly. Four times clockwise, three times widdershins. His feet were sore and most of the benches were empty, but he would not sit down. If he halted for an instant the longing for tobacco would come upon him. In the Charing Cross Road the tea-shops called like sirens. Once the glass door of a Lyons swung open, letting out a wave of hot cake-scented air. It almost overcame him. After all, why *not* go in? You could sit there for nearly an hour. A cup of tea twopence, two buns a penny each. He had fourpence halfpenny, counting the Joey. But no! That bloody Joey! The girl at the cash desk would titter. In a vivid vision he saw the girl at the cash desk, as she handled his threepenny-bit, grin sidelong at the girl behind the cake-counter. They'd *know* it was your last threepence. No use. Shove on. Keep moving.

In the deadly glare of the Neon lights the pavements were densely crowded. Gordon threaded his way, a small shabby figure, with pale face and unkempt hair. The crowd slid past him; he avoided and was avoided. There is something horrible about London at night; the coldness, the anonymity, the aloofness. Seven million people, sliding to and fro, avoiding contact, barely aware of one another's existence, like fish in an aquarium tank. The street swarmed with pretty girls. By scores they streamed past him, their faces averted or unseeing; cold nymph-creatures, dreading the eyes of the male. It was queer how many of them seemed to be alone, or with another girl. Far more women alone than women with men, he noted. That too was money. How many girls alive wouldn't be manless sooner than take a man who's moneyless?

The pubs were open, oozing sour whiffs of beer. People were trickling by ones and twos into the picture-houses. Gordon halted outside a great garish picture-house, under the weary eye of the commissionaire, to examine the photographs.

71

Greta Garbo in *The Painted Veil*. He yearned to go inside, not for Greta's sake, but just for the warmth and the softness of the velvet seat. He hated the pictures, of course, seldom went there even when he could afford it. Why encourage the art that is destined to replace literature? But still, there is a kind of soggy attraction about it. To sit on the padded seat in the warm smoke-scented darkness, letting the flickering drivel on the screen gradually overwhelm you—feeling the waves of its silliness lap you round till you seem to drown, intoxicated, in a viscous sea—after all, it's the kind of drug we need. The right drug for friendless people. As he approached the Palace Theatre a tart on sentry-go under the porch marked him down, stepped forward and stood in his path. A short, stocky Italian girl, very young, with big black eyes. She looked agreeable, and, what tarts so seldom are, merry. For a moment he checked his step, even allowed himself to catch her eye. She looked up at him, ready to break out into a broad-lipped smile. Why not stop and talk to her? She looked as though she might understand him. But no! No money! He looked away and side-stepped her with the cold haste of a man whom poverty makes virtuous. How furious she'd be if he stopped and then she found he had no money! He pressed on. Even to talk costs money.

Up Tottenham Court Road and Camden Road it was a dreary drudge. He walked slower, dragging his feet a little. He had done ten miles over pavements. More girls streamed past, unseeing. Girls alone, girls with youths, girls with other girls, girls alone. Their cruel youthful eyes went over him and through him as though he had not existed. He was too tired to resent it. His shoulders surrendered to their weariness; he slouched, not trying any longer to preserve his upright carriage and his you-be-damned air. They flee from me that sometime did me seek. How could you blame them? He was thirty, moth-eaten and without charm. Why should any girl ever look at him again?

He reflected that he must go home at once if he wanted any food—for Ma Wisbeach refused to serve meals after nine o'clock. But the thought of his cold womanless bedroom sickened him. To climb the stairs, light the gas, flop down at the table with hours to kill and nothing to do, nothing to read, nothing to smoke—no, *not* endurable. In Camden Town the pubs were full and noisy, though this was only Thursday. Three women, red-armed, squat as the beer mugs in their hands, stood outside a pub door, talking. From within came hoarse voices, fag-smoke, the fume of beer. Gordon thought of the Crichton Arms. Flaxman might be there. Why not risk it? A half of bitter, threepence halfpenny. He had fourpence halfpenny counting the Joey. After all, a Joey *is* legal tender.

He felt dreadfully thirsty already. It had been a mistake to let himself think of beer. As he approached the Crichton, he heard voices singing. The great garish pub seemed to be more brightly lighted than usual. There was a concert or something going on inside. Twenty ripe male voices were chanting in unison:

> *"Fo-or ree's a jorrigoo' fellow,*
> *For ree's a jorrigoo' fellow,*
> *For ree's a jorrigoo' fe-ELL-OW——*
> *And toori oori us!"*

At least, that was what it sounded like. Gordon drew nearer, pierced by a ravishing thirst. The voices were so soggy, so infinitely beery. When you heard them you saw the scarlet faces of prosperous plumbers. There was a private room behind the bar where the Buffaloes held their secret conclaves. Doubtless it was they who were singing. They were giving some kind of commemorative booze to their president, secretary, Grand Herbivore or whatever he is called. Gordon hesitated outside the saloon bar. Better go to the public bar, perhaps. Draught beer in the public, bottled beer in the saloon. He went round to the other side of the pub. The beer-choked voices followed him:

> *"With a toori oori ay,*
> *An' a toori oori ay!*

> *"Fo-or ree's a jorrigoo' fellow,*
> *For ree's a jorrigoo' fellow——"*

He felt quite faint for a moment. But it was fatigue and hunger as well as thirst. He could picture the cosy room where those Buffaloes were singing; the roaring fire, the big shiny table, the bovine photographs on the wall. Could picture also, as the singing ceased, twenty scarlet faces disappearing into pots of beer. He put his hand into his pocket and made sure that the threepenny-bit was still there. After all, why not? In the public bar, who would comment? Slap the Joey down on the bar and pass it off as a joke. "Been saving that up from the Christmas pudding—ha, ha!" Laughter all round. Already he seemed to have the metallic taste of draught beer on his tongue.

He fingered the tiny disc, irresolute. The Buffaloes had tuned up again:

> *"With a toori oori ay,*
> *An' a toori oori ay!*

> *"Fo-or* ree's *a jorrigoo' fellow——"*

Gordon moved back to the saloon bar. The window was frosted, and also steamy from the heat inside. Still, there were chinks where you could see through. He peeped in. Yes, Flaxman was there.

The saloon bar was crowded. Like all rooms seen from the outside, it looked ineffably cosy. The fire that blazed in the grate danced, mirrored, in the brass spittoons. Gordon thought he could almost smell the beer through the glass. Flaxman was propping up the bar with two fish-faced pals who looked like insurance-touts of the better type. One elbow on the bar, his foot on the rail, a beer-streaked glass in the other hand, he was swapping backchat with the blonde cutie barmaid. She was standing on a chair behind the bar, ranging the bottled beer and talking saucily over her shoulder. You couldn't hear what they were saying, but you could guess. Flaxman let fall some memorable witticism. The fish-faced men bellowed with obscene laughter. And the blonde cutie, tittering down at him, half shocked and half delighted, wriggled her neat little bum.

Gordon's heart sickened. To be in there, just to be in there!

74

In the warmth and light, with people to talk to, with beer and cigarettes and a girl to flirt with! After all, why *not* go in? You could borrow a bob off Flaxman. Flaxman would lend it you all right. He pictured Flaxman's careless assent—"What ho, chappie! How's life? What? A bob? Sure! Take two. Catch, chappie!"—and the florin flicked along the beer-wet bar. Flaxman was a decent sort, in his way.

Gordon put his hand against the swing door. He even pushed it open a few inches. The warm fog of smoke and beer slipped through the crack. A familiar, reviving smell; nevertheless as he smelled it his nerve failed him. No! Impossible to go in. He turned away. He couldn't go shoving into that saloon bar with only fourpence halfpenny in his pocket. Never let other people buy your drinks for you! The first commandment of the moneyless. He made off, down the dark pavement.

> *"For ree's a jorrigoo' fe-ELL-OW—*
> *And toori oori us!*

> *"With a toori oori ay!*
> *An' a——"*

The voices, diminishing with distance, rolled after him, bearing faint tidings of beer. Gordon took the threepenny-bit from his pocket and sent it skimming away into the darkness.

He was going home, if you could call it "going." At any rate he was gravitating in that direction. He did not want to go home, but he had got to sit down. His legs ached and his feet were bruised, and that vile bedroom was the sole place in London where he had purchased the right to sit down. He slipped in quietly, but, as usual, not quite so quietly that Mrs. Wisbeach failed to hear him. She gave him a brief nosy glance round the corner of her door. It would be a little after nine. She might get him a meal if he asked her. But she would grizzle and make a favour of it, and he would go to bed hungry sooner than face that.

He started up the stairs. He was half way up the first flight when a double knock behind made him jump. The post! Perhaps a letter from Rosemary!

Forced from outside, the letter flap lifted, and with an effort,

75

like a heron regurgitating a flatfish, vomited a bunch of letters on to the mat. Gordon's heart bounded. There were six or seven of them. Surely among all that lot there must be one for himself! Mrs. Wisbeach, as usual, had darted from her lair at the sound of the postman's knock. As a matter of fact, in two years Gordon had never once succeeded in getting hold of a letter before Mrs. Wisbeach laid hands on it. She gathered the letters jealously to her breast, and then, holding them up one at a time, scanned their addresses. From her manner you could gather that she suspected each one of them of containing a writ, an improper love letter or an ad for Amen Pills.

"One for you, Mr. Comstock," she said sourly, handing him a letter.

His heart shrank and paused in its beat. A long-shaped envelope. Not from Rosemary, therefore. Ah! It was addressed in his own handwriting. From the editor of a paper, then. He had two poems "out" at present. One with the *Californian Review,* the other with the *Primrose Quarterly.* But this wasn't an American stamp. And the *Primrose* had had his poem at least six weeks! Good God, supposing they'd accepted it!

He had forgotten Rosemary's existence. He said "Thanks!", stuck the letter in his pocket and started up the stairs with outward calm, but no sooner was he out of Mrs. Wisbeach's sight than he bounded up three steps at a time. He had got to be alone to open that letter. Even before he reached the door he was feeling for his matchbox, but his fingers were trembling so that in lighting the gas he chipped the mantle. He sat down, took the letter from his pocket, and then quailed. For a moment he could not nerve himself to open it. He held it up to the light and felt it to see how thick it was. His poem had been two sheets. Then, calling himself a fool, he ripped the envelope open. Out tumbled his own poem, and with it a neat—oh, so neat!—little printed slip of imitation parchment:

"The Editor regrets that he is unable to make use of the enclosed contribution."

The slip was decorated with a design of funereal laurel leaves.

Gordon gazed at the thing with wordless hatred. Perhaps no snub in the world is so deadly as this, because none is so unanswerable. Suddenly he loathed his own poem and was acutely ashamed of it. He felt it the weakest, silliest poem ever written. Without looking at it again he tore it into small bits and flung them into the wastepaper basket. He would put that poem out of mind for ever. The rejection slip, however, he did not tear up yet. He fingered it, feeling its loathly sleekness. Such an elegant little thing, printed in admirable type. You could tell at a glance that it came from a "good" magazine —a snooty highbrow magazine with the money of a publishing house behind it. Money, money! Money and culture! It was a stupid thing that he had done. Fancy sending a poem to a paper like the *Primrose!* As though they'd accept poems from people like *him*. The mere fact that the poem wasn't typed would tell them what kind of person he was. He might as well have dropped a card on Buckingham Palace. He thought of the people who wrote for the *Primrose;* a coterie of moneyed highbrows—those sleek, refined young animals who suck in money and culture with their mother's milk. The idea of trying to horn in among that pansy crowd! But he cursed them all the same. The sods! The bloody sods! "The Editor regrets!" Why be so bloody mealy-mouthed about it? Why not say outright, "We don't want your bloody poems. We only take poems from chaps we were at Cambridge with. You proletarians keep your distance"? The bloody, hypocritical sods!

At last he crumpled up the rejection slip, threw it away and stood up. Better get to bed while he had the energy to undress. Bed was the only place that was warm. But wait. Wind the clock, set the alarm. He went through the familiar action with a sense of deadly staleness. His eye fell upon the aspidistra. Two years he had inhabited this vile room; two mortal years in which nothing had been accomplished. Seven hundred wasted days, all ending in the lonely bed. Snubs, failures, insults, all of them unavenged. Money, money, all is money!

77

Because he had no money the Dorings snubbed him, because he had no money the *Primrose* had turned down his poem, because he had no money Rosemary wouldn't sleep with him. Social failure, artistic failure, sexual failure—they are all the same. And lack of money is at the bottom of them all.

He must hit back at somebody or something. He could not go to bed with that rejection slip as the last thing in his mind. He thought of Rosemary. It was five days now since she had written. If there had been a letter from her this evening even that rap over the knuckles from the *Primrose Quarterly* would have mattered less. She declared that she loved him, and she wouldn't sleep with him, wouldn't even write to him! She was the same as all the others. She despised him and forgot about him because he had no money and therefore didn't matter. He would write her an enormous letter, telling her what it felt like to be ignored and insulted, making her see how cruelly she had treated him.

He found a clean sheet of paper and wrote in the top right-hand corner:

"31 Willowbed Road, N.W., December 1st, 9.30 p.m."

But having written that much, he found that he could write no more. He was in the defeated mood when even the writing of a letter is too great an effort. Besides, what was the use? She would never understand. No woman ever understands. But he must write something. Something to wound her—that was what he most wanted, at this moment. He meditated for a long time, and at last wrote, exactly in the middle of the sheet:

"You have broken my heart."

No address, no signature. Rather neat it looked, all by itself, there in the middle of the sheet, in his small "scholarly" handwriting. Almost like a little poem in itself. This thought cheered him up a little.

He stuck the letter in an envelope and then went out and posted it at the post office on the corner, spending his last three halfpence on a penny stamp and a halfpenny stamp out of the slot machine.

78

Chapter Five

WE'RE printing that poem of yours in next month's *Antichrist,*" said Ravelston from his first-floor window.

Gordon, on the pavement below, affected to have forgotten the poem Ravelston was speaking about; he remembered it intimately, of course, as he remembered all his poems.

"Which poem?" he said.

"The one about the dying prostitute. We thought it was rather successful."

Gordon laughed a laugh of gratified conceit, and managed to pass it off as a laugh of sardonic amusement.

"Aha! A dying prostitute! That's rather what you might call one of my subjects. I'll do you one about an aspidistra next time."

Ravelston's over-sensitive, boyish face, framed by nice dark-brown hair, drew back a little from the window.

"It's intolerably cold," he said. "You'd better come up and have some food, or something."

"No, you come down. I've had dinner. Let's go to a pub and have some beer."

"All right, then. Half a minute while I get my shoes on."

They had been talking for some minutes, Gordon on the pavement, Ravelston leaning out of the window above. Gordon had announced his arrival not by knocking at the door but by throwing a pebble against the window pane. He never, if he could help it, set foot inside Ravelston's flat. There was something in the atmosphere of the flat that upset him and made him feel mean, dirty and out of place. It was so overwhelmingly, though unconsciously, upper-class. Only in the street or in a pub could he feel himself approximately Ravelston's equal. It would have astonished Ravelston to learn that his four-roomed flat, which he thought of as a poky little place, had this effect upon Gordon. To Ravelston, living in the wilds of Regent's Park was practically the same thing as living in the slums; he had chosen to live there, en bon socialiste, precisely as your social snob will live in a mews in Mayfair for the sake of the "W.1" on his notepaper. It was part of a life-long attempt to escape from his own class and become, as it were, an honorary member of the proletariat. Like all such attempts, it was foredoomed to failure. No rich man ever succeeds in disguising himself as a poor man; for money, like murder, will out.

On the street door there was a brass plate inscribed:

P. W. H. Ravelston

ANTICHRIST

Ravelston lived on the first floor, and the editorial offices of *Antichrist* were downstairs. *Antichrist* was a middle- to high-brow monthly, Socialist in a vehement but ill-defined way. In general, it gave the impression of being edited by an ardent Nonconformist who had transferred his allegiance from God to Marx, and in doing so had got mixed up with a gang of vers libre poets. This was not really Ravelston's character; merely he was softer-hearted than an editor ought to be, and consequently was at the mercy of his contributors. Practically anything got printed in *Antichrist* if Ravelston suspected that its author was starving.

Ravelston appeared a moment later, hatless and pulling on a pair of gauntlet gloves. You could tell him at a glance for a rich young man. He wore the uniform of the moneyed intelligentsia; an old tweed coat—but it was one of those coats which have been made by a good tailor and grow more aristocratic as they grow older—very loose grey flannel bags, a grey pullover, much-worn brown shoes. He made a point of going everywhere, even to fashionable houses and expensive restaurants, in these clothes, just to show his contempt for upper-class conventions; he did not fully realise that it is only the upper classes who can do these things. Though he was a year older than Gordon he looked much younger. He was very tall, with a lean, wide-shouldered body and the typical lounging grace of the upper-class youth. But there was something curiously apologetic in his movements and in the expression of his face. He seemed always in the act of stepping out of somebody else's way. When expressing an opinion he would rub his nose with the back of his left forefinger. The truth was that in every moment of his life he was apologising, tacitly, for the largeness of his income. You could make him uncomfortable as easily by reminding him that he was rich as you could make Gordon by reminding him that he was poor.

"You've had dinner, I gather?" said Ravelston, in his rather Bloomsbury voice.

"Yes, ages ago. Haven't you?"

"Oh, yes, certainly. Oh, quite!"

It was twenty past eight and Gordon had had no food since midday. Neither had Ravelston. Gordon did not know that Ravelston was hungry, but Ravelston knew that Gordon was hungry, and Gordon knew that Ravelston knew it. Nevertheless, each saw good reason for pretending not to be hungry. They seldom or never had meals together. Gordon would not let Ravelston buy his meals for him, and for himself he could not afford to go to restaurants, not even to a Lyons or an A.B.C. This was Monday and he had five and ninepence left. He might afford a couple of pints at a pub, but not a proper meal. When he and Ravelston met it was always agreed, with silent manœuvrings, that they should do nothing that involved spending money, beyond the shilling or so one spends in a pub. In this way the fiction was kept up that there was no serious difference in their incomes.

Gordon sidled closer to Ravelston as they started down the pavement. He would have taken his arm, only of course one can't do that kind of thing. Beside Ravelston's taller, comelier figure he looked frail, fretful and miserably shabby. He adored Ravelston and was never quite at ease in his presence. Ravelston had not merely a charm of manner, but also a kind of fundamental decency, a graceful attitude to life, which Gordon scarcely encountered elsewhere. Undoubtedly it was bound up with the fact that Ravelston was rich. For money buys all virtues. Money suffereth long and is kind, is not puffed up, doth not behave unseemly, seeketh not her own. But in some ways Ravelston was not even like a moneyed person. The fatty degeneration of the spirit which goes with wealth had missed him, or he had escaped it by a conscious effort. Indeed his whole life was a struggle to escape it. It was for this reason that he gave up his time and a large part of his income to editing an unpopular Socialist monthly. And apart from *Antichrist*, money flowed from him in all directions. A tribe of cadgers ranging from poets to pavement-artists browsed upon him unceasingly. For himself he lived upon eight hundred a year or thereabouts. Even of this income he was acutely ashamed. It was not, he realised, exactly a proletarian income; but he had never learned to get along on less. Eight hundred a year was a minimum living wage to him, as two pounds a week was to Gordon.

"How is your work getting on?" said Ravelston presently.

"Oh, as usual. It's a drowsy kind of job. Swapping backchat with old hens about Hugh Walpole. I don't object to it."

"I meant your own work—your writing. Is *London Pleasures* getting on all right?"

"Oh, Christ! Don't speak of it. It's turning my hair grey."

"Isn't it going forward at all?"

"My books don't go forward. They go backward."

Ravelston sighed. As editor of *Antichrist*, he was so used to encouraging despondent poets that it had become a second nature to him. He did not need telling why Gordon "couldn't" write, and why all poets nowadays "can't" write, and why when they do write it is something as arid as the rattling of a pea inside a big drum. He said with sympathetic gloom:

"Of course I admit this isn't a hopeful age to write poetry in."

"You bet it isn't."

Gordon kicked his heel against the pavement. He wished that *London Pleasures* had not been mentioned. It brought

82

back to him the memory of his mean, cold bedroom and the grimy papers littered under the aspidistra. He said abruptly:

"This writing business! What b——s it all is! Sitting in a corner torturing a nerve which won't even respond any longer. And who wants poetry nowadays? Training performing fleas would be useful by comparison."

"Still, you oughtn't to let yourself be discouraged. After all, you do produce something, which is more than one can say for a lot of poets nowadays. There was *Mice*, for instance."

"Oh, *Mice*! It makes me spew to think of it."

He thought with loathing of that sneaky little foolscap octavo. Those forty or fifty drab, dead little poems, each like a little abortion in its labelled jar. "Exceptional promise," *The Times Lit. Supp.* had said. A hundred and fifty-three copies sold and the rest remaindered. He had one of those movements of contempt and even horror which every artist has at times when he thinks of his own work.

"It's dead," he said. "Dead as a blasted fœtus in a bottle."

"Oh, well, I suppose that happens to most books. You can't expect an enormous sale for poetry nowadays. There's too much competition."

"I didn't mean that. I meant the poems themselves are dead. There's no life in them. Everything I write is like that. Lifeless, gutless. Not necessarily ugly or vulgar; but dead—just dead." The word "dead" re-echoed in his mind, setting up its own train of thought. He added: "My poems are dead because I'm dead. You're dead. We're all dead. Dead people in a dead world."

Ravelston murmured agreement, with a curious air of guilt. And now they were off upon their favourite subject—Gordon's favourite subject, anyway; the futility, the bloodiness, the deathliness of modern life. They never met without talking for at least half an hour in this vein. But it always made Ravelston feel rather uncomfortable. In a way, of course, he knew—it was precisely this that *Antichrist* existed to point out—that life under a decaying capitalism is deathly and meaningless. But this knowledge was only theoretical. You can't really *feel* that kind of thing when your income is eight hundred a year. Most of the time, when he wasn't thinking of coal-miners, Chinese junk-coolies and the unemployed in Middlesbrough, he felt that life was pretty good fun. Moreover, he had the naïve belief that in a little while Socialism is going to put things right. Gordon always seemed to him to exaggerate. So there was subtle disagreement between them, which Ravelston was too good-mannered to press home.

But with Gordon it was different. Gordon's income was two pounds a week. Therefore the hatred of modern life, the desire to see our money-civilisation blown to hell by bombs, was a thing he genuinely felt. They were walking southward, down a darkish, meanly decent residential street with a few shuttered shops. From a hoarding on the blank end of a house the yard-wide face of Corner Table simpered, pallid in the lamplight. Gordon caught a glimpse of a withering aspidistra in a lower window. London! Mile after mile of mean lonely houses, let off in flats and single rooms; not homes, not communities, just clusters of meaningless lives drifting in a sort of drowsy chaos to the grave! He saw men as corpses walking. The thought that he was merely objectifying his own inner misery hardly troubled him. His mind went back to Wednesday afternoon, when he had desired to hear the enemy aeroplanes zooming over London. He caught Ravelston's arm and paused to gesticulate at the Corner Table poster.

"Look at that bloody thing up there! Look at it, just look at it! Doesn't it make you spew?"

"It's æsthetically offensive, I grant. But I don't see that it matters very greatly."

"Of course it matters—having the town plastered with things like that."

"Oh, well, it's merely a temporary phenomenon. Capitalism in its last phase. I doubt whether it's worth worrying about."

"But there's more in it than that. Just look at that fellow's face gaping down at us! You can see our whole civilisation written there. The imbecility, the emptiness, the desolation! You can't look at it without thinking of French letters and

84

machine guns. Do you know that the other day I was actually wishing war would break out? I was longing for it—praying for it, almost."

"Of course, the trouble is, you see, that about half the young men in Europe are wishing the same thing."

"Let's hope they are. Then perhaps it'll happen."

"My dear old chap, no! Once is enough, surely."

Gordon walked on, fretfully. "This life we live nowadays! It's not life, it's stagnation, death-in-life. Look at all these bloody houses, and the meaningless people inside them! Sometimes I think we're all corpses. Just rotting upright."

"But where you make your mistake, don't you see, is in talking as if all this was incurable. This is only something that's got to happen before the proletariat take over."

"Oh, Socialism! Don't talk to me about Socialism."

"You ought to read Marx, Gordon, you really ought. Then you'd realise that this is only a phase. It can't go on for ever."

"Can't it? It *feels* as if it was going on for ever."

"It's merely that we're at a bad moment. We've got to die before we can be reborn, if you take my meaning."

"We're dying right enough. I don't see much signs of our being reborn."

Ravelston rubbed his nose. "Oh, well, we must have faith, I suppose. And hope."

"We must have money, you mean," said Gordon gloomily.

"Money?"

"It's the price of optimism. Give me five quid a week and *I'd* be a Socialist, I dare say."

Ravelston looked away, discomfited. This money-business! Everywhere it came up against you! Gordon wished he had not said it. Money is the one thing you must never mention when you are with people richer than yourself. Or if you do, then it must be money in the abstract, money with a big "M," not the actual concrete money that's in your pocket and isn't in mine. But the accursed subject drew him like a magnet. Sooner or later, especially when he had a few drinks inside him, he invariably began talking with self-pitiful detail about the bloodiness of life on two quid a week. Sometimes, from sheer nervous impulse to say the wrong thing, he would come out with some squalid confession—as, for instance, that he had been without tobacco for two days, or that his underclothes were in holes and his overcoat up the spout. But nothing of that sort should happen to-night, he resolved. They veered swiftly away from the subject of money and began talking in a more general way about Socialism. Ravelston had been trying for years to convert Gordon to Socialism, without even succeeding in interesting him in it. Presently they passed a low-looking pub on a corner in a side-street. A sour cloud of beer seemed to hang about it. The smell revolted Ravelston. He would have quickened his pace to get away from it. But Gordon paused, his nostrils tickled.

"Christ! I could do with a drink," he said.

"So could I," said Ravelston gallantly.

Gordon shoved open the door of the public bar, Ravelston following. Ravelston persuaded himself that he was fond of pubs, especially low-class pubs. Pubs are genuinely proletarian. In a pub you can meet the working class on equal terms—or that's the theory, anyway. But in practice Ravelston never went into a pub unless he was with somebody like Gordon, and he always felt like a fish out of water when he got there. A foul yet coldish air enveloped them. It was a filthy, smoky room, low-ceilinged, with a sawdusted floor and plain deal tables ringed by generations of beer-pots. In one corner four monstrous women with breasts the size of melons were sitting drinking porter and talking with bitter intensity about someone called Mrs. Croop. The landlady, a tall grim woman with a black fringe, looking like the madame of a brothel, stood behind the bar, her powerful forearms folded, watching a game of darts which was going on between four labourers and a postman. You had to duck under the darts as you crossed the room. There was a moment's hush and people glanced inquisitively at Ravelston. He was so obviously a gentleman. They didn't see his type very often in the public bar.

Ravelston pretended not to notice that they were staring at him. He lounged towards the bar, pulling off a glove to

86

feel for the money in his pocket. "What's yours?" he said casually.

But Gordon had already shoved his way ahead and was tapping a shilling on the bar. Always pay for the first round of drinks! It was his point of honour. Ravelston made for the only vacant table. A navvy leaning on the bar turned on his elbow and gave him a long, insolent stare. "A —— toff!" he was thinking. Gordon came back balancing two pint glasses of dark common ale. They were thick cheap glasses, thick as jam jars almost, and dim and greasy. A thin yellow froth was subsiding on the beer. The air was thick with gunpowdery tobacco-smoke. Ravelston caught sight of a well-filled spittoon near the bar and averted his eyes. It crossed his mind that this beer had been sucked up from some beetle-ridden cellar through yards of slimy tube, and that the glasses had never been washed in their lives, only rinsed in beery water. Gordon was very hungry. He could have done with some bread and cheese, but to order any would have been to betray the fact that he had had no dinner. He took a deep pull at his beer and lighted a cigarette, which made him forget his hunger a little. Ravelston also swallowed a mouthful or so and set his glass gingerly down. It was typical London beer, sickly and yet leaving a chemical after-taste. Ravelston thought of the wines of Burgundy. They went on arguing about Socialism.

"You know, Gordon, it's really time you started reading Marx," said Ravelston, less apologetically than usual, because the vile taste of the beer had annoyed him.

"I'd sooner read Mrs. Humphry Ward," said Gordon.

"But don't you see, your attitude is so unreasonable. You're always tirading against Capitalism, and yet you won't accept the only possible alternative. One can't put things right in a hole-and-corner way. One's got to accept either Capitalism or Socialism. There's no way out of it."

"I tell you I can't be bothered with Socialism. The very thought of it makes me yawn."

"But what's your objection to Socialism, anyway?"

"There's only one objection to Socialism, and that is that nobody wants it."

87

"Oh, surely it's rather absurd to say that!"

"That's to say, nobody who could see what Socialism would really mean."

"But what *would* Socialism mean, according to your idea of it?"

"Oh! Some kind of Aldous Huxley *Brave New World;* only not so amusing. Four hours a day in a model factory, tightening up bolt number 6003. Rations served out in greaseproof paper at the communal kitchen. Community-hikes from Marx Hostel to Lenin Hostel and back. Free abortion-clinics on all the corners. All very well in its way, of course. Only we don't want it."

Ravelston sighed. Once a month, in *Antichrist,* he repudiated this version of Socialism. "Well, what *do* we want, then?"

"God knows. All we know is what we don't want. That's what's wrong with us nowadays. We're stuck, like Buridan's donkey. Only there are three alternatives instead of two, and all three of them make us spew. Socialism's only one of them."

"And what are the other two?"

"Oh, I suppose suicide and the Catholic Church."

Ravelston smiled, anticlerically shocked. "The Catholic Church! Do you consider that an alternative?"

"Well, it's a standing temptation to the intelligentsia, isn't it?"

"Not what *I* should call the intelligentsia. Though there was Eliot, of course," Ravelston admitted.

"And there'll be plenty more, you bet. I dare say it's fairly cosy under Mother Church's wing. A bit insanitary, of course —but you'd feel safe there, anyway."

Ravelston rubbed his nose reflectively. "It seems to me that's only another form of suicide."

"In a way. But so's Socialism. At least it's a counsel of despair. But I couldn't commit suicide, real suicide. It's too meek and mild. I'm not going to give up my share of earth to anyone else. I'd want to do in a few of my enemies first."

Ravelston smiled again. "And who are your enemies?"

"Oh, anyone with over five hundred a year."

A momentary uncomfortable silence fell. Ravelston's income,

after payment of income tax, was probably two thousand a year. This was the kind of thing Gordon was always saying. To cover the awkwardness of the moment, Ravelston took up his glass, steeled himself against the nauseous taste and swallowed about two-thirds of his beer—enough, at any rate, to give the impression that he had finished it.

"Drink up!" he said with would-be heartiness. "It's time we had the other half of that."

Gordon emptied his glass and let Ravelston take it. He did not mind letting Ravelston pay for the drinks now. He had paid the first round and honour was satisfied. Ravelston walked self-consciously to the bar. People began staring at him again as soon as he stood up. The navvy, still leaning against the bar over his untouched pot of beer, gazed at him with quiet insolence. Ravelston resolved that he would drink no more of this filthy common ale.

"Two double whiskies, would you, please?" he said apologetically.

The grim landlady stared. "What?" she said.

"Two double whiskies, please."

"No whisky 'ere. We don't sell spirits. Beer 'ouse, we are."

The navvy smiled flickeringly under his moustache. "—— ignorant toff!" he was thinking. "Asking for whisky in a —— beer 'ouse!" Ravelston's pale face flushed slightly. He had not known till this moment that some of the poorer pubs cannot afford a spirit licence.

"Bass, then, would you? Two pint bottles of Bass."

There were no pint bottles. They had to have four half pints. It was a very poor house. Gordon took a deep, satisfying swallow of Bass. More alcoholic than the draught beer, it fizzed and prickled in his throat, and because he was hungry it went a little to his head. He felt at once more philosophic and more self-pitiful. He had made up his mind not to begin belly-aching about his poverty; but now he was going to begin after all. He said abruptly:

"This is all b——s that we've been talking."

"What's all b——s?"

"All this about Socialism and Capitalism and the state of the

89

modern world and God knows what. I don't give a —— for the state of the modern world. If the whole of England was starving except myself and the people I care about, I wouldn't give a damn."

"Don't you exaggerate just a little?"

"No. All this talk we make—we're only objectifying our own feelings. It's all dictated by what we've got in our pockets. I go up and down London saying it's a city of the dead, and our civilisation's dying, and I wish war would break out, and God knows what; and all it means is that my wages are two quid a week and I wish they were five."

Ravelston, once again reminded obliquely of his income, stroked his nose slowly with the knuckle of his left forefinger.

"Of course, I'm with you up to a point. After all, it's only what Marx said. Every ideology is a reflection of economic circumstances."

"Ah, but you only understand it out of Marx! You don't know what it means to have to crawl along on two quid a week. It isn't a question of hardship—it's nothing so decent as hardship. It's the bloody, sneaking, squalid meanness of it. Living alone for weeks on end because when you've no money you've no friends. Calling yourself a writer and never even producing anything because you're always too washed out to write. It's a sort of filthy sub-world one lives in. A sort of spiritual sewer."

He had started now. They were never together long without Gordon beginning to talk in this strain. It was the vilest manners. It embarrassed Ravelston horribly. And yet somehow Gordon could not help it. He had got to retail his troubles to somebody, and Ravelston was the only person who understood. Poverty, like every other dirty wound, has got to be exposed occasionally. He began to talk in obscene detail of his life in Willowbed Road. He dilated on the smell of slops and cabbage, the clotted sauce-bottles in the dining-room, the vile food, the aspidistras. He described his furtive cups of tea and his trick of throwing the used tea-leaves down the w.c. Ravelston, guilty and miserable, sat staring at his glass and revolving it slowly between his hands. Against his right

90

breast he could feel, a square accusing shape, the pocket-book in which, as he knew, eight pound notes and two ten-bob notes nestled against his fat green cheque-book. How awful these details of poverty are! Not that what Gordon was describing was real poverty. It was at worst the fringe of poverty. But what of the real poor? What of the unemployed in Middlesbrough, seven in a room on twenty-five bob a week? When there are people living like that, how dare one walk the world with pound notes and cheque-books in one's pocket?

"It's bloody," he murmured several times, impotently. In his heart he wondered—it was his invariable reaction—whether Gordon would accept a tenner if you offered to lend it to him.

They had another drink, which Ravelston again paid for, and went out into the street. It was almost time to part. Gordon never spent more than an hour or two with Ravelston. One's contacts with rich people, likes one's visits to high altitudes, must always be brief. It was a moonless, starless night, with a damp wind blowing. The night air, the beer and the watery radiance of the lamps induced in Gordon a sort of dismal clarity. He perceived that it is quite impossible to explain to any rich person, even to anyone so decent as Ravelston, the essential bloodiness of poverty. For this reason it became all the more important to explain it. He said suddenly:

"Have you read Chaucer's *Man of Lawe's Tale?*"

"The *Man of Lawe's Tale?* Not that I remember. What's it about?"

"I forget. I was thinking of the first six stanzas. Where he talks about poverty. The way it gives everyone the right to stamp on you! The way everyone *wants* to stamp on you! It makes people *hate* you, to know that you've no money. They insult you just for the pleasure of insulting you and knowing that you can't hit back."

Ravelston was pained. "Oh, no, surely not! People aren't so bad as all that."

"Ah, but you don't know the things that happen!"

Gordon did not want to be told that "people aren't so bad." He clung with a sort of painful joy to the notion that because he was poor everyone must *want* to insult him. It fitted in

91

with his philosophy of life. And suddenly, with the feeling that he could not stop himself, he was talking of the thing that had been rankling in his mind for two days past—the snub he had had from the Dorings on Thursday. He poured the whole story out quite shamelessly. Ravelston was amazed. He could not understand what Gordon was making such a fuss about. To be disappointed at missing a beastly literary tea-party seemed to him absurd. He would not have gone to a literary tea-party if you had paid him. Like all rich people, he spent far more time in avoiding human society than in seeking it. He interrupted Gordon:

"Really, you know, you ought not to take offence so easily. After all, a thing like that doesn't really matter."

"It isn't the thing itself that matters, it's the spirit behind it. The way they snub you as a matter of course, just because you've got no money."

"But quite possibly it was all a mistake, or something. Why should anyone want to snub you?"

" 'If thou be poure, thy brother hateth thee,' " quoted Gordon perversely.

Ravelston, deferential even to the opinions of the dead, rubbed his nose. "Does Chaucer say that? Then I'm afraid I disagree with Chaucer. People don't hate you, exactly."

"They do. And they're quite right to hate you. You *are* hateful. It's like those ads for Listerine. 'Why is he always alone? Halitosis is ruining his career.' Poverty is spiritual halitosis."

Ravelston sighed. Undoubtedly Gordon was perverse. They walked on, arguing, Gordon vehemently, Ravelston deprecatingly. Ravelston was helpless against Gordon in an argument of this kind. He felt that Gordon exaggerated, and yet he never liked to contradict him. How could he? He was rich and Gordon was poor. And how can you argue about poverty with someone who is genuinely poor?

"And then the way women treat you when you've no money!" Gordon went on. "That's another thing about this accursed money-business—women!"

Ravelston nodded rather gloomily. This sounded to him

more reasonable than what Gordon had been saying before. He thought of Hermione Slater, his own girl. They had been lovers two years but had never bothered to get married. It was "too much fag," Hermione always said. She was rich, of course, or rather her people were. He thought of her shoulders, wide, smooth and young, that seemed to rise out of her clothes like a mermaid rising from the sea; and her skin and hair, which were somehow warm and sleepy, like a wheatfield in the sun. Hermione always yawned at the mention of Socialism, and refused even to read *Antichrist*. "Don't talk to me about the lower classes," she used to say. "I hate them. They *smell*." And Ravelston adored her.

"Of course women *are* a difficulty," he admitted.

"They're more than a difficulty, they're a bloody curse. That is, if you've got no money. A woman hates the sight of you if you've got no money."

"I think that's putting it a little too strongly. Things aren't so crude as all that."

Gordon did not listen. "What rot it is to talk about Socialism or any other ism when women are what they are! The only thing a woman ever wants is money; money for a house of her own and two babies and Drage furniture and an aspidistra. The only sin they can imagine is not wanting to grab money. No woman ever judges a man by anything except his income. Of course she doesn't put it to herself like that. She says he's *such a nice man*—meaning that he's got plenty of money. And if you haven't got money you aren't *nice*. You're dishonoured, somehow. You've sinned. Sinned against the aspidistra."

"You talk a great deal about aspidistras," said Ravelston.

"They're a dashed important subject," said Gordon.

Ravelston rubbed his nose and looked away uncomfortably.

"Look here, Gordon, you don't mind my asking—have you got a girl of your own?"

"Oh, Christ! Don't speak of her!"

He began, nevertheless, to talk about Rosemary. Ravelston had never met Rosemary. At this moment Gordon could not even remember what Rosemary was like. He could not remember how fond he was of her and she of him, how

93

happy they always were together on the rare occasions when they could meet, how patiently she put up with his almost intolerable ways. He remembered nothing save that she would not sleep with him and that it was now a week since she had even written. In the dank night air, with beer inside him, he felt himself a forlorn, neglected creature. Rosemary was "cruel" to him—that was how he saw it. Perversely, for the mere pleasure of tormenting himself and making Ravelston uncomfortable, he began to invent an imaginary character for Rosemary. He built up a picture of her as a callous creature who was amused by him and yet half despised him, who played with him and kept him at arm's length, and who would nevertheless fall into his arms if only he had a little more money. And Ravelston, who had never met Rosemary, did not altogether disbelieve him. He broke in:

"But I say, Gordon, look here. This girl, Miss—Miss Waterlow, did you say her name was?—Rosemary; doesn't she care for you at all, really?"

Gordon's conscience pricked him, though not very deeply. He could not say that Rosemary did not care for him.

"Oh, yes, she does care for me. In her own way, I dare say she cares for me quite a lot. But not enough, don't you see. She can't, while I've got no money. It's all money."

"But surely money isn't so important as all that? After all, there *are* other things."

"What other things? Don't you see that a man's whole personality is bound up with his income? His personality *is* his income. How can you be attractive to a girl when you've got no money? You can't wear decent clothes, you can't take her out to dinner or to the theatre or away for week-ends, you can't carry a cheery, interesting atmosphere about with you. And it's rot to say that kind of thing doesn't matter. It does. If you haven't got money there isn't even anywhere where you can meet. Rosemary and I never meet except in the streets or in picture galleries. She lives in some foul women's hostel, and my bitch of a landlady won't allow women in the house. Wandering up and down beastly wet

94

streets—that's what Rosemary associates me with. Don't you see how it takes the gilt off everything?"

Ravelston was distressed. It must be pretty bloody when you haven't even the money to take your girl out. He tried to nerve himself to say something, and failed. With guilt, and also with desire, he thought of Hermione's body, naked, like a ripe warm fruit. With any luck she would have dropped in at the flat this evening. Probably she was waiting for him now. He thought of the unemployed in Middlesbrough. Sexual starvation is awful among the unemployed. They were nearing the flat. He glanced up at the windows. Yes, they were lighted up. Hermione must be there. She had her own latchkey.

As they approached the flat Gordon edged closer to Ravelston. Now the evening was ending, and he must part from Ravelston, whom he adored, and go back to his foul lonely bedroom. And all evenings ended in this way; the return through dark streets to the lonely room, the womanless bed. And Ravelston would say "Come up, won't you?" and Gordon, in duty bound, would say, "No." Never stay too long with those you love—another commandment of the moneyless.

They halted at the foot of the steps. Ravelston laid his gloved hand on one of the iron spearheads of the railing.

"Come up, won't you?" he said without conviction.

"No, thanks. It's time I was getting back."

Ravelston's fingers tightened round the spearhead. He pulled as though to go up, but did not go. Uncomfortably, looking over Gordon's head into the distance, he said:

"I say, Gordon, look here. You won't be offended if I say something?"

"What?"

"I say, you know, I hate that business about you and your girl. Not being able to take her out, and all that. It's bloody, that kind of thing."

"Oh, it's nothing, really."

As soon as he heard Ravelston say that it was "bloody," he knew that he had been exaggerating. He wished that he had not talked in that silly self-pitiful way. One says these things,

95

with the feeling that one cannot help saying them, and afterwards one is sorry.

"I dare say I exaggerate," he said.

"I say, Gordon, look here. Let me lend you ten quid. Take the girl out to dinner a few times. Or away for the week-end, or something. It might make all the difference. I hate to think——"

Gordon frowned bitterly, almost fiercely. He had stepped a pace back, as though from a threat or an insult. The terrible thing was that the temptation to say "Yes" had almost overwhelmed him. There was so much that ten quid would do! He had a fleeting vision of Rosemary and himself at a restaurant table—a bowl of grapes and peaches, a bowing hovering waiter, a wine bottle dark and dusty in its wicker cradle.

"No fear!" he said.

"I do wish you would. I tell you I'd *like* to lend it you."

"Thanks. But I prefer to keep my friends."

"Isn't that rather—well, rather a bourgeois kind of thing to say?"

"Do you think it would be *borrowing* if I took ten quid off you? I couldn't pay it back in ten years."

"Oh, well! It wouldn't matter so very much." Ravelston looked away. Out it had got to come—the disgraceful, hateful admission that he found himself forced so curiously often to make! "You know, I've got quite a lot of money."

"I know you have. That's exactly why I won't borrow off you."

"You know, Gordon, sometimes you're just a little bit—well, pigheaded."

"I dare say. I can't help it."

"Oh, well! Good night, then."

"Good night."

Ten minutes later Ravelston rode southward in a taxi, with Hermione. She had been waiting for him, asleep or half asleep in one of the monstrous armchairs in front of the sitting-room fire. Whenever there was nothing particular to do, Hermione always fell asleep as promptly as an animal, and the more she slept the healthier she became. As he came across to her she woke and stretched herself with voluptuous, sleepy writhings, half smiling, half yawning up at him, one cheek and bare arm rosy in the firelight. Presently she mastered her yawns to greet him:

"Hullo, Philip! Where have you been all this time? I've been waiting ages."

"Oh, I've been out with a fellow. Gordon Comstock. I don't expect you know him. The poet."

"Poet! How much did he borrow off you?"

"Nothing. He's not that kind of person. He's rather a fool about money, as a matter of fact. But he's very gifted in his way."

"You and your poets! You look tired, Philip. What time did you have dinner?"

"Well—as a matter of fact I didn't have any dinner."

"Didn't have any dinner! Why?"

"Oh, well, you see—I don't know if you'll understand. It was a kind of accident. It was like this."

He explained. Hermione burst out laughing and dragged herself into a more upright position.

"Philip! You *are* a silly old ass! Going without your dinner, just so as not to hurt that little beast's feelings! You must have some food at once. And of course your char's gone home. Why don't you keep some proper servants, Philip? I hate this hole-and-corner way you live. We'll go out and have supper at Modigliani's."

"But it's after ten. They'll be shut."

"Nonsense! They're open till two. I'll ring up for a taxi. I'm not going to have you starving yourself."

In the taxi she lay against him, still half asleep, her head pillowed on his breast. He thought of the unemployed in Middlesbrough, seven in a room on twenty-five bob a week. But the girl's body was heavy against him, and Middlesbrough was very far away. Also he was damnably hungry. He thought of his favourite corner table at Modigliani's, and of that vile pub with its hard benches, stale beer-stink and brass spittoons. Hermione was sleepily lecturing him.

"Philip, why do you have to live in such a dreadful way?"

"But I don't live in a dreadful way."

"Yes, you do. Pretending you're poor when you're not, and living in that poky flat with no servants, and going about with all these beastly people."

"What beastly people?"

"Oh, people like this poet friend of yours. All those people who write for your paper. They only do it to cadge from you. Of course I know you're a Socialist. So am I. I mean we're all Socialists nowadays. But I don't see why you have to give all your money away and make friends with the lower classes. You can be a Socialist *and* have a good time, that's what I say."

"Hermione, dear, please don't call them the lower classes!"

"Why not? They *are* the lower classes, aren't they?"

"It's such a hateful expression. Call them the working class, can't you?"

"The working class, if you like, then. But they smell just the same."

"You oughtn't to say that kind of thing," he protested weakly.

"Do you know, Philip, sometimes I think you *like* the lower classes."

"Of course I like them."

"How disgusting. How absolutely disgusting."

She lay quiet, content to argue no longer, her arms round him, like a sleepy siren. The woman-scent breathed out of her, a powerful wordless propaganda against all altruism and all justice. Outside Modigliani's they had paid off the taxi and were moving for the door when a big, lank wreck of a man seemed to spring up from the paving-stones in front of them. He stood across their path like some fawning beast, with dreadful eagerness and yet timorously, as though afraid that Ravelston would strike him. His face came close up to Ravelston's—a dreadful face, fish-white and scrubby-bearded to the eyes. The words "A cup of tea, guv'nor!" were breathed through carious teeth. Ravelston shrank from him in disgust. He could not help it. His hand moved automatically to his pocket. But in the same instant Hermione caught him by the arm and hauled him inside the restaurant.

"You'd give away every penny you've got if I let you," she said.

They went to their favourite table in the corner. Hermione played with some grapes, but Ravelston was very hungry. He ordered the grilled rumpsteak he had been thinking of, and half a bottle of Beaujolais. The fat, white-haired Italian waiter, an old friend of Ravelston's, brought the smoking steak. Ravelston cut it open. Lovely, its red-blue heart! In Middlesbrough the unemployed huddle in frowzy beds, bread and marg and milkless tea in their bellies. He settled down to his steak with all the shameful joy of a dog with a stolen leg of mutton.

Gordon walked rapidly homewards. It was cold. The fifth of December—real winter now. Circumcise ye your foreskins, saith the Lord. The damp wind blew spitefully through the naked trees. *Sharply the menacing wind sweeps over*. The poem he had begun on Wednesday, of which six stanzas were now finished, came back into his mind. He did not dislike it at this moment. It was queer how talking with Ravelston always bucked him up. The mere contact with Ravelston seemed to reassure him somehow. Even when their talk had been unsatisfactory, he came away with the feeling that, after all, he wasn't quite a failure. Half aloud he repeated the six finished stanzas. They were not bad, not bad at all.

But intermittently he was going over in his mind the things he had said to Ravelston. He stuck to everything he had said. The humiliation of poverty! That's what they can't understand and won't understand. Not hardship—you don't suffer hardship on two quid a week, and if you did it wouldn't matter— but just humiliation, the awful, bloody humiliation. The way it gives everyone the right to stamp on you. The way everyone *wants* to stamp on you. Ravelston wouldn't believe it. He had too much decency, that was why. He thought you could be poor and still be treated like a human being. But Gordon knew better. He went into the house repeating to himself that he knew better.

There was a letter waiting for him on the hall tray. His

heart jumped. All letters excited him nowadays. He went up the stairs three at a time, shut himself in and lit the gas. The letter was from Doring.

"DEAR COMSTOCK,—What a pity you didn't turn up on Saturday. There were some people I wanted you to meet. We did tell you it was Saturday and not Thursday this time, didn't we? My wife says she's certain she told you. Anyway, we're having another party on the twenty-third, a sort of before-Christmas party, about the same time. Won't you come then? Don't forget the date this time.

"Yours
"PAUL DORING."

A painful convulsion happened below Gordon's ribs. So Doring was pretending that it was all a mistake—was pretending not to have insulted him! True, he could not actually have gone there on Saturday, because on Saturday he had to be at the shop; still, it was the intention that counted.

His heart sickened as he re-read the words "Some people I wanted you to meet." Just like his bloody luck! He thought of the people he might have met—editors of highbrow magazines, for instance. They might have given him books to review or asked to see his poems or Lord knew what. For a moment he was dreadfully tempted to believe that Doring had spoken the truth. Perhaps after all they *had* told him it was Saturday and not Thursday. Perhaps if he searched his memory he might remember about it—might even find the letter itself lying about among his muddle of papers. But no! He wouldn't think of it. He fought down the temptation. The Dorings *had* insulted him on purpose. He was poor, therefore they had insulted him. If you are poor, people will insult you. It was his creed. Stick to it!

He went across to the table, tearing Doring's letter into small bits. The aspidistra stood in its pot, dull green, ailing, pathetic in its sickly ugliness. As he sat down, he pulled it towards him and looked at it meditatively. There was the intimacy of hatred between the aspidistra and him. "I'll beat you yet, you b——," he whispered to the dusty leaves.

100

Then he rummaged among his papers until he found a clean sheet, took his pen and wrote in his small, neat hand, right in the middle of the sheet:

"DEAR DORING,—With reference to your letter: Go and —— yourself.
"Yours truly
"GORDON COMSTOCK."

He stuck it into an envelope, addressed it and at once went out to get stamps from the slot machine. Post it to-night: these things look different in the morning. He dropped it into the pillar-box. So there was another friend gone west.

Chapter Six

THIS woman business! What a bore it is! What a pity we can't cut it right out, or at least be like the animals—minutes of ferocious lust and months of icy chastity. Take a cock pheasant, for example. He jumps up on the hens' backs without so much as a with your leave or by your leave. And no sooner is it over than the whole subject is out of his mind. He hardly even notices his hens any longer; he ignores them, or simply pecks them if they come too near his food. He is not called upon to support his offspring, either. Lucky pheasant! How different from the lord of creation, always on the hop between his memory and his conscience!

To-night Gordon wasn't even pretending to do any work. He had gone out again immediately after supper. He walked southward, rather slowly, thinking about women. It was a mild, misty night, more like autumn than winter. This was Tuesday and he had four and fourpence left. He could go down to the Crichton if he chose. Doubtless Flaxman and his pals were already boozing there. But the Crichton, which had seemed like paradise when he had no money, bored and disgusted him when it was in his power to go there. He hated the stale, beery place, and the sights, sounds, smells, all so blatantly and offensively male. There were no women there; only the barmaid with her lewd smile which seemed to promise everything and promised nothing.

Women, women! The mist that hung motionless in the air turned the passers-by into ghosts at twenty yards' distance; but in the little pools of light about the lamp-posts there were glimpses of girls' faces. He thought of Rosemary, of women in general, and of Rosemary again. All afternoon he had been thinking of her. It was with a kind of resentment that he thought of her small, strong body, which he had never yet seen naked. How damned unfair it is that we are filled to the brim with these tormenting desires and then forbidden to satisfy them! Why should one, merely because one has no money, be deprived of *that?* It seems so natural, so necessary, so much a part of the inalienable rights of a human being. As he walked down the dark street, through the cold yet languorous air, there was a strangely hopeful feeling in his breast. He half believed that somewhere ahead in the darkness a woman's body was waiting for him. But also he knew that no woman was waiting, not even Rosemary. It was eight days now since she had even written to him. The little beast! Eight whole days without writing! When she knew how much her letters meant to him! How manifest it was that she didn't care for him any longer, that he was merely a nuisance to her with his poverty and his shabbiness and his everlasting pestering of her to say she loved him! Very likely she would never write again. She was sick of him—sick of him because he had no money. What else could you expect? He had no hold over her. No money, therefore no hold. In the last resort, what holds a woman to a man, except money?

A girl came down the pavement alone. He passed her in the light of the lamp-post. A working-class girl, eighteen years old it might be, hatless, with wildrose face. She turned her head quickly when she saw him looking at her. She dreaded to meet his eyes. Beneath the thin silky raincoat she was wearing, belted at the waist, her youthful flanks showed supple and trim. He could have turned and followed her, almost. But what was the use? She'd only run away or call a policeman. My golden locks time hath to silver turned, he thought. He was thirty and moth-eaten. What woman worth having would ever look at him again?

This woman business! Perhaps you'd feel differently about it if you were married? But he had taken an oath against marriage long ago. Marriage is only a trap set for you by the money-god. You grab the bait; snap goes the trap; and there you are, chained by the leg to some "good" job till they cart you to Kensal Green. And what a life! Licit sexual intercourse in the shade of the aspidistra. Pram-pushing and sneaky adulteries. And the wife finding you out and breaking the cut-glass whisky decanter over your head.

Nevertheless he perceived that in a way it is necessary to marry. If marriage is bad, the alternative is worse. For a moment he wished that he were married; he pined for the difficulty of it, the reality, the pain. And marriage must be indissoluble, for better for worse, for richer for poorer, till death do you part. The old Christian ideal—marriage tempered by adultery. Commit adultery if you must, but at any rate have the decency to *call* it adultery. None of that American soul-mate slop. Have your fun and then sneak home, juice of the forbidden fruit dripping from your whiskers, and take the consequences. Cut-glass whisky decanters broken over your head, nagging, burnt meals, children crying, clash and thunder of embattled mothers-in-law. Better that, perhaps, than horrible freedom? You'd know, at least, that it was real life that you were living.

But anyway, how can you marry on two quid a week? Money, money, always money! The devil of it is, that outside marriage, no decent relationship with a woman is possible. His mind moved backwards, over his ten years of adult life. The faces of women flowed through his memory. Ten or a dozen of them there had been. Tarts, also. *Comme au long d'un cadavre un cadavre étendu.* And even when they were not tarts it had been squalid, always squalid. Always it had started in a sort of cold-blooded wilfulness and ended in some mean, callous desertion. That, too, was money. Without money, you can't be straightforward in your dealings with women. For without money, you can't pick and choose, you've got to take what women you can get; and then, necessarily, you've got to break free of them. Constancy, like all other virtues, has got to be paid for in money. And the mere fact that he had rebelled against the money code and wouldn't settle down in the prison of a "good" job—a thing no woman will ever understand—had brought a quality of impermanence, of deception, into all his affairs with women. Abjuring money, he ought to have abjured women too. Serve the money-god, or do without women—those are the only alternatives. And both were equally impossible.

From the side-street just ahead, a shaft of white light cut through the mist, and there was a bellowing of street hawkers. It was Luton Road, where they have the open-air market two evenings a week. Gordon turned to his left, into the market. He often came this way. The street was so crowded that you could only with difficulty thread your way down the cabbage-littered alley between the stalls. In the glare of hanging electric bulbs, the stuff on the stalls glowed with fine lurid colours—hacked, crimson chunks of meat, piles of oranges and green and white broccoli, stiff, glassy-eyed rabbits, live eels looping in enamel troughs, plucked fowls hanging in rows, sticking out their naked breasts like guardsmen naked on parade. Gordon's spirits revived a little. He liked the noise, the bustle, the vitality. Whenever you see a street-market you know that there's hope for England yet. But even here he felt his solitude. Girls were thronging everywhere, in knots of four or five, prowling desirously about the stalls of cheap underwear and swapping backchat and screams of laughter with the youths who followed them. None had eyes for Gordon. He walked among them as though invisible, save that their bodies avoided him when he passed them. Ah, look there! Involuntarily he paused. Over a pile of art-silk undies on a stall, three girls were bending, intent, their faces close together—three youthful faces, flower-like in the harsh light, clustering side by side like a truss of blossom on a Sweet William or phlox. His heart stirred. No eyes for him, of course! One girl looked up. Ah! Hurriedly, with an offended air, she looked away again. A delicate flush like a wash of aquarelle flooded her face. The hard, sexual stare in his eyes had frightened her. They flee from me that sometime did me seek! He walked on. If only Rosemary were here! He forgave her now for not writing to him. He could forgive her anything, if only she were here. He knew now how much she meant to him, because she alone of all women in the world was willing to save him from the humiliation of his loneliness.

At this moment he looked up, and saw something that made his heart jump. He changed the focus of his eyes abruptly. For a moment he thought he was imagining it. But no! It *was* Rosemary!

She was coming down the alley between the stalls, twenty or thirty yards away. It was as though his desire had called her into being. She had not seen him yet. She came towards him, a small debonair figure, picking her way nimbly through the crowd and the muck underfoot, her face scarcely visible because of a flat black hat which she wore cocked down over her eyes like a Harrow boy's straw hat. He started towards her and called her name.

"Rosemary! Hi, Rosemary!"

A blue-aproned man thumbing codfish on a stall turned to stare at him. Rosemary did not hear him because of the din. He called again.

"Rosemary! I say, Rosemary!"

They were only a few yards apart now. She started and looked up.

"Gordon! What are you doing here?"

"What are *you* doing here?"

"I was coming to see you."

"But how did you know I was here?"

"I didn't. I always come this way. I get out of the tube at Camden Town."

Rosemary sometimes came to see Gordon at Willowbed Road. Mrs. Wisbeach would inform him sourly that "there was a young woman to see him," and he would come downstairs and they would go out for a walk in the streets. Rosemary was never allowed indoors, not even into the hall. That was a rule of the house. You would have thought "young women" were plague-rats by the way Mrs. Wisbeach spoke of them. Gordon took Rosemary by the upper arm and made to pull her against him.

"Rosemary! Oh, what a joy to see you again! I was so vilely lonely. Why didn't you come before?"

106

She shook off his hand and stepped back out of his reach. Under her slanting hat-brim she gave him a glance that was intended to be angry.

"Let me go, now! I'm very angry with you. I very nearly didn't come after that beastly letter you sent me."

"What beastly letter?"

"You know very well."

"No, I don't. Oh, well, let's get out of this. Somewhere where we can talk. This way."

He took her arm, but she shook him off again, continuing, however, to walk at his side. Her steps were quicker and shorter than his. And walking beside him she had the appearance of something extremely small, nimble and young, as though he had had some lively little animal, a squirrel for instance, frisking at his side. In reality she was not very much smaller than Gordon, and only a few months younger. But no one would ever have described Rosemary as a spinster of nearly thirty, which in fact she was. She was a strong, agile girl, with stiff black hair, a small triangular face and very pronounced eyebrows. It was one of those small, peaky faces, full of character, which one sees in sixteenth-century portraits. The first time you saw her take her hat off you got a surprise, for on her crown three white hairs glittered among the black ones like silver wires. It was typical of Rosemary that she never bothered to pull the white hairs out. She still thought of herself as a very young girl, and so did everybody else. Yet if you looked closely the marks of time were plain enough on her face.

Gordon walked more boldly with Rosemary at his side. He was proud of her. People were looking at her, and therefore at him as well. He was no longer invisible to women. As always, Rosemary was rather nicely dressed. It was a mystery how she did it on four pounds a week. He liked particularly the hat she was wearing—one of those flat felt hats which were then coming into fashion and which caricatured a clergyman's shovel hat. There was something essentially frivolous about it. In some way difficult to be described, the angle at which it was cocked forward harmonised appealingly with the curve of Rosemary's behind.

"I like your hat," he said.

In spite of herself, a small smile flickered at the corner of her mouth.

"It *is* rather nice," she said, giving the hat a little pat with her hand.

She was still pretending to be angry, however. She took care that their bodies should not touch. As soon as they had reached the end of the stalls and were in the main street she stopped and faced him sombrely.

"What do you mean by writing me letters like that?" she said.

"Letters like what?"

"Saying I'd broken your heart."

"So you have."

"It looks like it, doesn't it!"

"I don't know. It certainly feels like it."

The words were spoken half jokingly, and yet they made her look more closely at him—at his pale, wasted face, his uncut hair, his general down-at-heel, neglected appearance. Her heart softened instantly, and yet she frowned. Why *won't* he take care of himself? was the thought in her mind. They had moved closer together. He took her by the shoulders. She let him do it, and, putting her small arms round him, squeezed him very hard, partly in affection, partly in exasperation.

"Gordon, you *are* a miserable creature!" she said.

"Why am I a miserable creature?"

"Why can't you look after yourself properly? You're a perfect scarecrow. Look at these awful old clothes you're wearing!"

"They're suited to my station. One can't dress decently on two quid a week, you know."

"But surely there's no need to go about looking like a rag-bag? Look at this button on your coat, broken in half!"

She fingered the broken button, and then suddenly lifted his discoloured Woolworth's tie aside. In some feminine way she had divined that he had no buttons on his shirt.

108

"Yes, *again!* Not a single button. You are awful, Gordon!"

"I tell you I can't be bothered with things like that. I've got a soul above buttons."

"But why not give them to *me* and let me sew them on for you? And, oh, Gordon! You haven't even shaved to-day. How absolutely beastly of you. You might at least take the trouble to shave every morning."

"I can't afford to shave every morning," he said perversely.

"What *do* you mean, Gordon? It doesn't cost money to shave, does it?"

"Yes, it does. Everything costs money. Cleanness, decency, energy, self-respect—everything. It's all money. Haven't I told you that a million times?"

She squeezed his ribs again—she was surprisingly strong—and frowned up at him, studying his face as a mother looks at some peevish child of which she is unreasonably fond.

"*What* a fool I am!" she said.

"In what way a fool?"

"Because I'm so fond of you."

"Are you fond of me?"

"Of course I am. You know I am. I adore you. It's idiotic of me."

"Then come somewhere where it's dark. I want to kiss you."

"Fancy being kissed by a man who hasn't even shaved!"

"Well, that'll be a new experience for you."

"No, it won't, Gordon. Not after knowing *you* for two years."

"Oh, well, come on, anyway."

They found an almost dark alley between the backs of houses. All their lovemaking was done in such places. The only place where they could ever be private was the streets. He pressed her shoulders against the rough damp bricks of the wall. She turned her face readily up to his and clung to him with a sort of eager violent affection, like a child. And yet all the while, though they were body to body, it was as though there were a shield between them. She kissed him as a child might have done, because she knew that he expected to be kissed. It was always like this. Only at very rare moments could he awake in her the beginnings of physical desire; and these she seemed afterwards to forget, so that he always had to begin at the beginning over again. There was something defensive in the feeling of her small, shapely body. She longed to know the meaning of physical love, but also she dreaded it. It would destroy her youth, the youthful, sexless world in which she chose to live.

He parted his mouth from hers in order to speak to her.

"Do you love me?" he said.

"Of course, silly. Why do you always ask me that?"

"I like to hear you say it. Somehow I never feel sure of you till I've heard you say it."

"But why?"

"Oh, well, you might have changed your mind. After all, I'm not exactly the answer to a maiden's prayer. I'm thirty, and moth-eaten at that."

"Don't be so absurd, Gordon! Anyone would think you were a hundred, to hear you talk. You know I'm the same age as you are."

"Yes, but not moth-eaten."

She rubbed her cheek against his, feeling the roughness of his day-old beard. Their bellies were close together. He thought of the two years he had wanted her and never had her. With his lips almost against her ear he murmured:

"Are you *ever* going to sleep with me?"

"Yes, some day I will. Not now. Some day."

"It's always 'some day.' It's been 'some day' for two years now."

"I know. But I can't help it."

He pressed her back against the wall, pulled off the absurd flat hat and buried his face in her hair. It was tormenting to be so close to her and all for nothing. He put a hand under her chin and lifted her small face up to his, trying to distinguish her features in the almost complete darkness.

"Say you will, Rosemary. There's a dear! Do!"

"You know I'm going to *some* time."

"Yes, but not *some* time—now. I don't mean this moment, but soon. When we get an opportunity. Say you will!"

110

"I can't. I can't promise."

"Say 'yes,' Rosemary. *Please* do!"

"No."

Still stroking her invisible face, he quoted:

> *"Veuillez le dire donc selon*
> *Que vous estes benigne et doulche,*
> *Car ce doulx mot n'est pas si long*
> *Qu'il vous face mal en la bouche."*

"What does that mean?"

He translated it.

"I can't, Gordon. I just can't."

"Say 'yes,' Rosemary, there's a dear. Surely it's as easy to say 'yes' as 'no' ?"

"No, it isn't. It's easy enough for you. You're a man. It's different for a woman."

"Say 'yes,' Rosemary! 'Yes'—it's such an easy word. Go on, now; say it. 'Yes!' "

"Anyone would think you were teaching a parrot to talk, Gordon."

"Oh, damn! Don't make jokes about it."

It was not much use arguing. Presently they came out into the street and walked on, southward. Somehow, from Rosemary's swift, neat movements, from her general air of a girl who knows how to look after herself and who yet treats life mainly as a joke, you could make a good guess at her upbringing and her mental background. She was the youngest child of one of those huge hungry families which still exist here and there in the middle classes. There had been fourteen children all told—the father was a country solicitor. Some of Rosemary's sisters were married, some of them were schoolmistresses or running typing bureaux; the brothers were farming in Canada, on tea-plantations in Ceylon, in obscure regiments of the Indian Army. Like all women who have had an eventful girlhood, Rosemary wanted to remain a girl. That was why, sexually, she was so immature. She had kept late into life the high-spirited sexless atmosphere of a big family. Also she had absorbed into her very bones the code of fair play and live-and-let-live. She was profoundly magnanimous, quite incapable of spiritual bullying. From Gordon, whom she adored, she put up with almost anything. It was the measure of her magnanimity that never once, in the two years that she had known him, had she blamed him for not attempting to earn a proper living.

Gordon was aware of all this. But at the moment he was thinking of other things. In the pallid circles of light about the lamp-posts, beside Rosemary's smaller, trimmer figure, he felt graceless, shabby and dirty. He wished very much that he had shaved that morning. Furtively he put a hand into his pocket and felt his money, half afraid—it was a recurrent fear with him—that he might have dropped a coin. However, he could feel the milled edge of a florin, his principal coin at the moment. Four and fourpence left. He couldn't possibly take her out to supper, he reflected. They'd have to trail dismally up and down the streets, as usual, or at best go to a Lyons for a coffee. Bloody! How can you have any fun when you've got no money? He said broodingly:

"Of course it all comes back to money."

This remark came out of the blue. She looked up at him in surprise.

"What do you mean, it all comes back to money?"

"I mean the way nothing ever goes right in my life. It's always money, money, money that's at the bottom of everything. And especially between me and you. That's why you don't really love me. There's a sort of film of money between us. I can feel it every time I kiss you."

"Money! What *has* money got to do with it, Gordon?"

"Money's got to do with everything. If I had more money you'd love me more."

"Of course, I wouldn't! Why should I?"

"You couldn't help it. Don't you see that if I had more money I'd be more worth loving? Look at me now! Look at my face, look at these clothes I'm wearing, look at everything else about me. Do you suppose I'd be like that if I had two thousand a year? If I had more money I should be a different person."

112

"If you were a different person I shouldn't love you."

"That's nonsense, too. But look at it like this. If we were married would you sleep with me?"

"What questions you do ask! Of course I would. Otherwise, where would be the sense of being married?"

"Well, then, suppose I was decently well off, *would* you marry me?"

"What's the good of talking about it, Gordon? You know we can't afford to marry."

"Yes, but *if* we could. Would you?"

"I don't know. Yes, I would, I dare say."

"There you are, then! That's what I said—money!"

"No, Gordon, no! That's not fair. You're twisting my words round."

"No, I'm not. You've got this money-business at the bottom of your heart. Every woman's got it. You wish I was in a *good* job now, don't you?"

"Not in the way you mean it. I'd like you to be earning more money—yes."

"And you think I ought to have stayed on at the New Albion, don't you? You'd like me to go back there now and write slogans for Q.T. Sauce and Truweet Breakfast Crisps. Wouldn't you?"

"No, I wouldn't. I *never* said that."

"You thought it, though. It's what any woman would think."

He was being horribly unfair, and he knew it. The one thing Rosemary had never said, the thing she was probably incapable of saying, was that he ought to go back to the New Albion. But for the moment he did not even want to be fair. His sexual disappointment still pricked him. With a sort of melancholy triumph he reflected that, after all, he was right. It was money that stood between them. Money, money, all is money! He broke into a half-serious tirade:

"Women! What nonsense they make of all our ideas! Because one can't keep free of women, and every woman makes one pay the same price. 'Chuck away your decency and make more money'—that's what women say. 'Chuck away your decency,

113

suck the blacking off the boss's boots and buy me a better fur coat than the woman next door.' Every man you can see has got some blasted woman hanging round his neck like a mermaid, dragging him down and down—down to some beastly little semi-detached villa in Putney, with hire-purchase furniture and a portable radio and an aspidistra in the window. It's women who make all progress impossible. Not that I believe in progress," he added rather unsatisfactorily.

"What absolute *nonsense* you do talk, Gordon! As though women were to blame for everything!"

"They are to blame, finally. Because it's the women who really believe in the money-code. The men obey it; they have to, but they don't believe in it. It's the women who keep it going. The women and their Putney villas and their fur coats and their babies and their aspidistras."

"It is *not* the women, Gordon! Women didn't invent money, did they?"

"It doesn't matter who invented it, the point is that it's women who worship it. A woman's got a sort of mystical feeling towards money. Good and evil in a woman's mind mean simply money and no money. Look at you and me. You won't sleep with me, simply and solely because I've got no money. Yes, that *is* the reason. (He squeezed her arm to silence her.) You admitted it only a minute ago. And if I had a decent income you'd go to bed with me to-morrow. It's not because you're mercenary. You don't want me to *pay* you for sleeping with me. It's not so crude as that. But you've got that deep-down mystical feeling that somehow a man without money isn't worthy of you. He's a weakling, a sort of half-man—that's how you feel. Hercules, god of strength and god of money—you'll find that in Lemprière. It's women who keep all mythologies going. Women!"

"Women!" echoed Rosemary on a different note. "I hate the way men are always talking about *women*. 'Women do this,' and '*Women* do that'—as though all women were exactly the same!"

"Of course all women are the same! What does any woman

want except a safe income and two babies and a semi-detached villa in Putney with an aspidistra in the window?"

"Oh, you and your aspidistras!"

"On the contrary, *your* aspidistras. You're the sex that cultivates them."

She squeezed his arm and burst out laughing. She was really extraordinarily good-natured. Besides, what he was saying was such palpable nonsense that it did not even exasperate her. Gordon's diatribes against women were in reality a kind of perverse joke; indeed, the whole sex-war is at bottom only a joke. For some reason it is great fun to pose as a feminist or an antifeminist according to your sex. As they walked on they began a violent argument upon the eternal and idiotic question of Man versus Woman. The moves in this argument—for they had it as often as they met—were always very much the same. Men are brutes and women are soulless, and women have always been kept in subjection and they jolly well ought to be kept in subjection, and look at Patient Griselda and look at Lady Astor, and what about polygamy and Hindu widows, and what about Mother Pankhurst's piping days when every decent woman wore mousetraps on her garters and couldn't look at a man without feeling her right hand itch for a castrating knife? Gordon and Rosemary never grew tired of this kind of thing. Each laughed with delight at the other's absurdities. There was a merry war between them. Even as they disputed, arm in arm, they pressed their bodies delightedly together. They were very happy. Indeed, they adored one another. Each was to the other a standing joke and an object infinitely precious. Presently a red and blue haze of Neon lights appeared in the distance. They had reached the beginning of the Tottenham Court Road. Gordon put his arm round her waist and turned her to the right, down a darkish side-street. They were so happy together that they had got to kiss. They stood clasped together under the lamp-post, still laughing, two enemies breast to breast. She rubbed her cheek against his.

"Gordon, you are such a dear old ass! I can't help loving you, scrubby jaw and all."

"Do you really?"

"Really and truly."

Her arms still round him, she leaned a little backwards, pressing her belly against his with a sort of innocent voluptuousness.

"Life *is* worth living, isn't it, Gordon?"

"Sometimes."

"If only we could meet a bit oftener! Sometimes I don't see you for weeks together."

"I know. It's bloody. If you knew how I hate my evenings alone!"

"One never seems to have time for anything. I don't even leave that beastly office till nearly seven. What do you do with yourself on Sundays, Gordon?"

"Oh, God! Moon about and look miserable, like everyone else."

"Why not let's go out for a walk in the country sometimes. Then we would have all day together. Next Sunday, for instance?"

The words chilled him. They brought back the thought of money, which he had succeeded in putting out of his mind for half an hour past. A trip into the country would cost money, far more than he could possibly afford. He said in a non-committal tone that transferred the whole thing to the realm of abstraction:

"Of course, it's not too bad in Richmond Park on Sundays. Or even on Hampstead Heath. Especially if you go in the mornings before the crowds get there."

"Oh, but let's go right out into the country! Somewhere in Surrey, for instance, or to Burnham Beeches. It's so lovely at this time of year, with all the dead leaves on the ground, and you can walk all day and hardly meet a soul. We'll walk for miles and miles and have dinner at a pub. It would be such fun. Do let's!"

Blast! The money-business was coming back. A trip even as far as Burnham Beeches would cost all of ten bob. He did some hurried mental arithmetic. Five bob he might manage, and Julia would "lend" him five; *give* him five, that was.

At the same moment he remembered his oath, constantly renewed and always broken, not to "borrow" money off Julia. He said in the same casual tone as before:

"It *would* be rather fun. I should think we might manage it. I'll let you know later in the week, anyway."

They came out of the side-street, still arm in arm. There was a pub on the corner. Rosemary stood on tiptoe, and, clinging to Gordon's arm to support herself, managed to look over the frosted lower half of the window.

"Look, Gordon, there's a clock in there. It's nearly half past nine. Aren't you getting frightfully hungry?"

"No," he said, instantly and untruthfully.

"I am. I'm simply starving. Let's go and have something to eat somewhere."

Money again! One moment more, and he must confess that he had only four and fourpence in the world—four and fourpence to last till Friday.

"I couldn't eat anything," he said. "I might manage a drink, I dare say. Let's go and have some coffee or something. I expect we'll find a Lyons open."

"Oh, don't let's go to a Lyons! I know such a nice little Italian restaurant, only just down the road. We'll have Spaghetti Napolitaine and a bottle of red wine. I adore spaghetti. Do let's!"

His heart sank. It was no good. He would have to own up. Supper at the Italian restaurant could not possibly cost less than five bob for the two of them. He said almost sullenly:

"It's about time I was getting home, as a matter of fact."

"Oh, Gordon! Already? Why?"

"Oh, well! If you *must* know, I've only got four and fourpence in the world. And it's got to last till Friday."

Rosemary stopped short. She was so angry that she pinched his arm with all her strength, meaning to hurt him and punish him.

"Gordon, you *are* an ass! You're a perfect idiot! You're the most unspeakable idiot I've ever seen!"

"Why am I an idiot?"

"Because what does it matter whether you've got any money? I'm asking *you* to have supper with *me*."

He freed his arm from hers and stood away from her. He did not want to look her in the face.

"What! Do you think I'd go to a restaurant and let you pay for my food?"

"But why not?"

"Because one can't do that sort of thing. It isn't done."

"It 'isn't done'! You'll be saying it's 'not cricket' in another moment. *What* 'isn't done'?"

"Letting you pay for my meals. A man pays for a woman, a woman doesn't pay for a man."

"Oh, Gordon! Are we living in the reign of Queen Victoria?"

"Yes, we are, as far as that kind of thing's concerned. Ideas don't change so quickly."

"But *my* ideas have changed."

"No, they haven't. You think they have, but they haven't. You've been brought up as a woman, and you can't help behaving like a woman, however much you don't want to."

"But what do you mean by *behaving like a woman*, anyway?"

"I tell you every woman's the same when it comes to a thing like this. A woman despises a man who's dependent on her and sponges on her. She may say she doesn't, she may *think* she doesn't, but she does. She can't help it. If I let you pay for my meals *you'd* despise me."

He had turned away. He knew how abominably he was behaving. But somehow he had got to say these things. The feeling that people—even Rosemary—*must* despise him for his poverty was too strong to be overcome. Only by rigid, jealous independence could he keep his self-respect. Rosemary was really distressed this time. She caught his arm and pulled him round, making him face her. With an insistent gesture, angrily and yet demanding to be loved, she pressed her breast against him.

"Gordon! I won't let you say such things. How can you say I'd ever despise you?"

"I tell you you couldn't help it if I let myself sponge on you."

"Sponge on me! What expressions you do use! How is it

118

sponging on me to let me pay for your supper just for once?"

He could feel the small breasts, firm and round, just beneath his own. She looked up at him, frowning and yet not far from tears. She thought him perverse, unreasonable, cruel. But her physical nearness distracted him. At this moment all he could remember was that in two years she had never yielded to him. She had starved him of the one thing that mattered. What was the good of pretending that she loved him when in the last essential she recoiled? He added with a kind of deadly joy:

"In a way you do despise me. Oh, yes, I know you're fond of me. But after all, you can't take me quite seriously. I'm a kind of joke to you. You're fond of me, and yet I'm not quite your equal—that's how you feel."

It was what he had said before, but with this difference, that now he meant it, or said it as if he meant it. She cried out with tears in her voice:

"I don't, Gordon, I don't! You *know* I don't!"

"You do. That's why you won't sleep with me. Didn't I tell you that before?"

She looked up at him an instant longer, and then buried her face in his breast as suddenly as though ducking from a blow. It was because she had burst into tears. She wept against his breast, angry with him, hating him, and yet clinging to him like a child. It was the childish way in which she clung to him, as a mere male breast to weep on, that hurt him most. With a sort of self-hatred he remembered the other women who in just this same way had cried against his breast. It seemed the only thing he could do with women, to make them cry. With his arm round her shoulders he caressed her clumsily, trying to console her.

"You've gone and made me cry!" she whimpered in self-contempt.

"I'm sorry! Rosemary, dear one! Don't cry, *please* don't cry."

"Gordon, dearest! *Why* do you have to be so beastly to me?"

"I'm sorry, I'm sorry! Sometimes I can't help it."

"But why? Why?"

She had got over her crying. Rather more composed, she drew away from him and felt for something to wipe her eyes. Neither of them had a handkerchief. Impatiently, she wrung the tears out of her eyes with her knuckles.

"How silly we always are! Now, Gordon, *be* nice for once. Come along to the restaurant and have some supper and let me pay for it."

"No."

"Just this once. Never mind about the old money-business. Do it just to please me."

"I tell you I can't do that kind of thing. I've got to keep my end up."

"But what do you mean, keep your end up?"

"I've made war on money, and I've got to keep the rules. The first rule is never to take charity."

"Charity! Oh, Gordon, I *do* think you're silly!"

She squeezed his ribs again. It was a sign of peace. She did not understand him, probably never would understand him; yet she accepted him as he was, hardly even protesting against his unreasonableness. As she put her face up to be kissed he noticed that her lips were salt. A tear had trickled here. He strained her against him. The hard defensive feeling had gone out of her body. She shut her eyes and sank against him and into him as though her bones had grown weak, and her lips parted and her small tongue sought for his. It was very seldom that she did that. And suddenly, as he felt her body yielding, he seemed to know with certainty that their struggle was ended. She was his now when he chose to take her. And yet perhaps she did not fully understand what it was that she was offering; it was simply an instinctive movement of generosity, a desire to reassure him—to smooth away that hateful feeling of being unlovable and unloved. She said nothing of this in words. It was the feeling of her body that seemed to say it. But even if this had been the time and the place he could not have taken her. At this moment he loved her but did not desire her. His desire could only return at some future time when there was no quarrel fresh in his mind and no

120

consciousness of four and fourpence in his pocket to daunt him.

Presently they separated their mouths, though still clinging closely together.

"How stupid it is, the way we quarrel, isn't it, Gordon? When we meet so seldom."

"I know. It's all my fault. I can't help it. Things rub me up. It's money at the bottom of it. Always money."

"Oh, money! You let it worry you too much, Gordon."

"Impossible. It's the only thing worth worrying about."

"But, anyway, we *will* go out into the country next Sunday, won't we? To Burnham Beeches or somewhere. It would be so nice if we could."

"Yes, I'd love to. We'll go early and be out all day. I'll raise the train fares somehow."

"But you'll let me pay my own fare, won't you?"

"No, I'd rather I paid them. But we'll go, anyway."

"And you really won't let me pay for your supper—just this once, just to show you trust me?"

"No, I can't. I'm sorry. I've told you why."

"Oh, dear! I suppose we shall have to say good night. It's getting late."

They stayed talking a long time, however, so long that Rosemary got no supper after all. She had to be back at her lodgings by eleven, or the she-dragons were angry. Gordon went to the top of the Tottenham Court Road and took the tram. It was a penny cheaper than taking the bus. On the wooden seat upstairs he was wedged against a small dirty Scotchman who read the football finals and oozed beer. Gordon was very happy. Rosemary was going to be his mistress. *Sharply the menacing wind sweeps over.* To the music of the tram's booming he whispered the seven completed stanzas of his poem. Nine stanzas there would be in all. It was *good*. He believed in it and in himself. He was a poet. Gordon Comstock, author of *Mice.* Even in *London Pleasures* he once again believed.

He thought of Sunday. They were to meet at nine o'clock at Paddington Station. Ten bob or so it would cost; he would raise the money if he had to pawn his shirt. And she was going to become his mistress; this very Sunday, perhaps, if the right chance offered itself. Nothing had been said. Only, somehow, it was agreed between them.

Please God it kept fine on Sunday! It was deep winter now. What luck if it turned out one of those splendid windless days—one of those days that might almost be summer, when you can lie for hours on the dead bracken and never feel cold! But you don't get many days like that; a dozen at most in every winter. As likely as not it would rain. He wondered whether they would get a chance to do it after all. They had nowhere to go, except the open air. There are so many pairs of lovers in London with "nowhere to go"; only the streets and the parks, where there is no privacy and it is always cold. It is not easy to make love in a cold climate when you have no money. The "never the time and the place" motif is not made enough of in novels.

Chapter Seven

T HE PLUMES of the chimneys floated perpendicular against
skies of smoky rose.

Gordon caught the 27 bus at ten past eight. The streets
were still locked in their Sunday sleep. On the doorsteps the
milk bottles waited ungathered like little white sentinels.
Gordon had fourteen shillings in hand—thirteen and nine,
rather, because the bus fare was threepence. Nine bob he
had set aside from his wages—God knew what that was going
to mean, later in the week!—and five he had borrowed from
Julia.

He had gone round to Julia's place on Thursday night.
Julia's room in Earl's Court, though only a second-floor back,
was not just a vulgar bedroom like Gordon's. It was a bed-
sitting with the accent on the sitting. Julia would have died
of starvation sooner than put up with such squalor as Gordon
lived in. Indeed every one of her scraps of furniture, collected
over intervals of years, represented a period of semistarvation.
There was a divan bed that could very nearly be mistaken for
a sofa, and a little round fumed oak table, and two "antique"
hardwood chairs, and an ornamental footstool and a chintz-
covered armchair—Drage's: thirteen monthly payments—in
front of the tiny gas-fire; and there were various brackets with
framed photos of father and mother and Gordon and Aunt
Angela, and a birchwood calendar—somebody's Christmas
present—with "It's a long lane that has no turning" done on
it in pokerwork. Julia depressed Gordon horribly. He was
always telling himself that he ought to go and see her oftener;

but in practice he never went near her except to "borrow" money.

When Gordon had given three knocks—three knocks for second floor—Julia took him up to her room and knelt down in front of the gas-fire.

"I'll light the fire again," she said. "You'd like a cup of tea, wouldn't you?"

He noted the "again." The room was beastly cold—no fire had been lighted in it this evening. Julia always "saved gas" when she was alone. He looked at her long narrow back as she knelt down. How grey her hair was getting! Whole locks of it were quite grey. A little more, and it would be "grey hair" tout court.

"You like your tea strong, don't you?" breathed Julia, hovering over the tea-caddy with tender, goose-like movements.

Gordon drank his cup of tea standing up, his eye on the birchwood calendar. Out with it! Get it over! Yet his heart almost failed him. The meanness of this hateful cadging! What would it all tot up to, the money he had "borrowed" from her in all these years?

"I say, Julia, I'm damned sorry—I hate asking you; but look here——"

"Yes, Gordon?" she said quietly. She knew what was coming.

"Look here, Julia, I'm damned sorry, but could you lend me five bob?"

"Yes, Gordon, I expect so."

She sought out the small, worn black leather purse that was hidden at the bottom of her linen drawer. He knew what she was thinking. It meant less for Christmas presents. That was the great event of her life nowadays—Christmas and the giving of presents: hunting through the glittering streets, late at night after the teashop was shut, from one bargain counter to another, picking out the trash that women are so curiously fond of. Handkerchief sachets, letter racks, teapots, manicure sets, birchwood calendars with mottoes in pokerwork. All through the year she was scraping from her wretched wages for "So and so's Christmas present," or "So and so's birthday present." And had she not, last Christmas, because Gordon was "fond of poetry," given him the *Selected Poems* of John Drinkwater in green morocco, which he had sold for half a crown? Poor Julia! Gordon made off with his five bob as soon as he decently could. Why is it that one can't borrow from a rich friend and can from a half-starved relative? But one's family, of course, "don't count."

On the top of the bus he did mental arithmetic. Thirteen and nine in hand. Two day-returns to Slough, five bob. Bus fares, say two bob more, seven bob. Bread and cheese and beer at a pub, say a bob each, nine bob. Tea, eightpence each, twelve bob. A bob for cigarettes, thirteen bob. That left ninepence for emergencies. They would manage all right. And how about the rest of the week? Not a penny for tobacco! But he refused to let it worry him. To-day would be worth it, anyway.

Rosemary met him on time. It was one of her virtues that she was never late, and even at this hour of the morning she was bright and debonair. She was rather nicely dressed, as usual. She was wearing her mock-shovel hat again, because he had said he liked it. They had the station practically to themselves. The huge grey place, littered and deserted, had a blowsy, unwashed air, as though it were still sleeping off a Saturday night debauch. A yawning porter in need of a shave told them the best way to get to Burnham Beeches, and presently they were in a third-class smoker, rolling westward, and the mean wilderness of London was opening out and giving way to narrow sooty fields dotted with ads for Carter's Little Liver Pills. The day was very still and warm. Gordon's prayer had come true. It was one of those windless days which you can hardly tell from summer. You could feel the sun behind the mist; it would break through presently, with any luck. Gordon and Rosemary were profoundly and rather absurdly happy. There was a sense of wild adventure in getting out of London, with the long day in "the country" stretching out ahead of them. It was months since Rosemary and a year since Gordon had set foot in "the country." They sat close together with the *Sunday Times* open across their knees; they did not read it, however, but watched the fields and cows and houses and the empty goods trucks and great sleeping factories rolling past. Both of them enjoyed the railway journey so much that they wished it had been longer.

At Slough they got out and travelled to Farnham Common in an absurd chocolate-coloured bus with no top. Slough was still half asleep. Rosemary remembered the way now that they had got to Farnham Common. You walked down a rutted road and came out on to stretches of fine, wet, tussocky grass dotted with little naked birches. The beech woods were beyond. Not a bough or a blade was stirring. The trees stood like ghosts in the still, misty air. Both Rosemary and Gordon exclaimed at the loveliness of everything. The dew, the stillness, the satiny stems of the birches, the softness of the turf under your feet! Nevertheless, at first they felt shrunken and out of place, as Londoners do when they get outside London. Gordon felt as though he had been living underground for a long time past. He felt etiolated and unkempt. He slipped behind Rosemary as they walked, so that she should not see his lined, colourless face. Also, they were out of breath before they had walked far, because they were only used to London walking, and for the first half hour they scarcely talked. They plunged into the woods and started westward, with not much idea of where they were making for—anywhere, so long as it was away from London. All round them the beech-trees soared, curiously phallic with their smooth skin-like bark and their flutings at the base. Nothing grew at their roots, but the dried leaves were strewn so thickly that in the distance the slopes looked like folds of copper-coloured silk. Not a soul seemed to be awake. Presently Gordon came level with Rosemary. They walked on hand in hand, swishing through the dry coppery leaves that had drifted into the ruts. Sometimes they came out on to stretches of road where they passed huge desolate houses—opulent country houses, once, in the carriage days, but now deserted and unsaleable. Down the road the mist-dimmed hedges wore that strange purplish brown, the colour of brown madder, the naked brushwood takes on in winter. There were a few birds about—jays, sometimes, passing between the trees with dipping flight, and pheasants that loitered across the road with long tails trailing, almost as tame as hens, as though knowing they were safe on Sunday. But in half an hour Gordon and Rosemary had not passed a human being. Sleep lay upon the countryside. It was hard to believe that they were only twenty miles out of London.

Presently they had walked themselves into trim. They had got their second wind and the blood glowed in their veins. It was one of those days when you feel you could walk a hundred miles if necessary. Suddenly, as they came out on to the road again, the dew all down the hedge glittered with a diamond flash. The sun had pierced the clouds. The light came slanting and yellow across the fields, and delicate unexpected colours sprang out in everything, as though some giant's child had been let loose with a new paintbox. Rosemary caught Gordon's arm and pulled him against her.

"Oh, Gordon, what a *lovely* day!"

"Lovely."

"And, oh, look, look! Look at all the rabbits in that field!"

Sure enough, at the other end of the field, innumerable rabbits were browsing, almost like a flock of sheep. Suddenly there was a flurry under the hedge. A rabbit had been lying there. It leapt from its nest in the grass with a flirt of dew and dashed away down the field, its white tail lifted. Rosemary threw herself into Gordon's arms. It was astonishingly warm, as warm as summer. They pressed their bodies together in a sort of sexless rapture, like children. Here in the open air he could see the marks of time quite clearly upon her face. She was nearly thirty, and looked it, and he was nearly thirty, and looked more; and it mattered nothing. He pulled off the absurd flat hat. The three white hairs gleamed on her crown. At the moment he did not wish them away. They were part of her and therefore lovable.

"What fun to be here alone with you! I'm so glad we came!"

"And, oh, Gordon, to think we've got all day together! And it might so easily have rained. How lucky we are!"

"Yes. We'll burn a sacrifice to the immortal gods, presently."

They were extravagantly happy. As they walked on they fell into absurd enthusiasms over everything they saw: over a jay's feather that they picked up, blue as lapis lazuli; over a stagnant pool like a jet mirror, with boughs reflected deep down in it; over the fungi that sprouted from the trees like monstrous horizontal ears. They discussed for a long time what would be the best epithet to describe a beech-tree. Both agreed that beeches look more like sentient creatures than other trees. It is because of the smoothness of their bark, probably, and the curious limb-like way in which the boughs sprout from the trunk. Gordon said that the little knobs on the bark were like the nipples of breasts and that the sinuous upper boughs, with their smooth sooty skin, were like the writhing trunks of elephants. They argued about similes and metaphors. From time to time they quarrelled vigorously, according to their custom. Gordon began to tease her by finding ugly similes for everything they passed. He said that the russet foliage of the hornbeams was like the hair of Burne-Jones maidens, and that the smooth tentacles of the ivy that wound about the trees were like the clinging arms of Dickens heroines. Once he insisted upon destroying some mauve toadstools because he said they reminded him of a Rackham illustration and he suspected fairies of dancing round them. Rosemary called him a soulless pig. She waded through a bed of drifted beech leaves that rustled about her, knee-deep, like a weightless red-gold sea.

"Oh, Gordon, these leaves! Look at them with the sun on them! They're like gold. They really are like gold."

"Fairy gold. You'll be going all Barrie in another moment. As a matter of fact, if you want an exact simile, they're just the colour of tomato soup."

"Don't be a pig, Gordon! Listen how they rustle. 'Thick as autumnal leaves that strow the brooks in Vallombrosa.' "

"Or like one of those American breakfast cereals. Truweet Breakfast Crisps. 'Kiddies clamour for their Breakfast Crisps.' "

"You are a beast!"

She laughed. They walked on hand in hand, swishing ankle-deep through the leaves and declaiming:

"Thick as the Breakfast Crisps that strow the plates
"In Welwyn Garden City!"

It was great fun. Presently they came out of the wooded
area. There were plenty of people abroad now, but not many
cars if you kept away from the main roads. Sometimes they
heard church bells ringing and made detours to avoid the
churchgoers. They began to pass through straggling villages
on whose outskirts pseudo-Tudor villas stood sniffishly apart,
amid their garages, their laurel shrubberies and their raw-
looking lawns. And Gordon had some fun railing against the
villas and the godless civilisation of which they were part—
a civilisation of stockbrokers and their lip-sticked wives, of
golf, whisky, ouija-boards and Aberdeen terriers called Jock.
So they walked another four miles or so, talking and frequently
quarrelling. A few gauzy clouds were drifting across the sky,
but there was hardly a breath of wind.

They were growing rather footsore and more and more
hungry. Of its own accord the conversation began to turn
upon food. Neither of them had a watch, but when they
passed through a village they saw that the pubs were open,
so that it must be after twelve o'clock. They hesitated outside a rather low-looking pub called the Bird in Hand. Gordon
was for going in; privately he reflected that in a pub like that
your bread and cheese and beer would cost you a bob at the
very most. But Rosemary said that it was a nasty-looking place,
which indeed it was, and they went on, hoping to find a
pleasanter pub at the other end of the village. They had
visions of a cosy bar-parlour, with an oak settle and perhaps
a stuffed pike in a glass case on the wall.

But there were no more pubs in the village, and presently
they were in open country again, with no houses in sight
and not even any signposts. Gordon and Rosemary began to
be alarmed. At two the pubs would shut, and then there
would be no food to be had, except perhaps a packet of
biscuits from some village sweetshop. At this thought a raven-
ing hunger took possession of them. They toiled exhaustedly
up an enormous hill, hoping to find a village on the other side.

There was no village, but far below a dark green river wound, with what seemed quite like a large town scattered along its edge and a grey bridge crossing it. They did not even know what river it was—it was the Thames, of course.

"Thank God!" said Gordon. "There must be plenty of pubs down there. We'd better take the first one we can find."

"Yes, do let's. I'm starving."

But when they neared the town it seemed strangely quiet. Gordon wondered whether the people were all at church or eating their Sunday dinners, until he realised that the place was quite deserted. It was Crickham-on-Thames, one of those riverside towns which live for the boating season and go into hibernation for the rest of the year. It straggled along the bank for a mile or more, and it consisted entirely of boat-houses and bungalows, all of them shut up and empty. There were no signs of life anywhere. At last, however, they came upon a fat, aloof, red-nosed man, with a ragged moustache, sitting on a camp-stool beside a jar of beer on the towpath. He was fishing with a twenty-foot roach pole, while on the smooth green water two swans circled about his float, trying to steal his bait as often as he pulled it up.

"Can you tell us where we can get something to eat?" said Gordon.

That fat man seemed to have been expecting this question and to derive a sort of private pleasure from it. He answered without looking at Gordon.

"*You* won't get nothing to eat. Not here you won't," he said.

"But dash it! Do you mean to say there isn't a pub in the whole place? We've walked all the way from Farnham Common."

The fat man sniffed and seemed to reflect, still keeping his eye on his float.

"I dessay you might try the Ravenscroft Hotel," he said. "About half a mile along, that is. I dessay they'd give you something; that is, they would if they was open."

"But *are* they open?"

"They might be and they might not," said the fat man comfortably.

130

"And can you tell us what time it is?" said Rosemary.

"It's jest gone ten parse one."

The two swans followed Gordon and Rosemary a little way along the towpath, evidently expecting to be fed. There did not seem much hope that the Ravenscroft Hotel would be open. The whole place had that desolate flyblown air of pleasure resorts in the off-season. The woodwork of the bungalows was cracking, the white paint was peeling off, the dusty windows showed bare interiors. Even the slot machines that were dotted along the bank were out of order. There seemed to be another bridge at the other end of the town. Gordon swore heartily.

"What bloody fools we were not to go into that pub when we had the chance!"

"Oh, dear! I'm simply *starving*. Had we better turn back, do you think?"

"It's no use, there were no pubs the way we came. We must keep on. I suppose the Ravenscroft Hotel's on the other side of that bridge. If that's a main road there's just a chance it'll be open. Otherwise we're sunk."

They dragged their way as far as the bridge. They were thoroughly footsore now. But behold! here at last was what they wanted, for just beyond the bridge, down a sort of private road, stood a biggish, smartish hotel, its back lawns running down to the river. It was obviously open. Gordon and Rosemary started eagerly towards it, and then paused, daunted.

"It looks frightfully expensive," said Rosemary.

It did look expensive. It was a vulgar pretentious place, all gilt and white paint—one of those hotels which have overcharging and bad service written on every brick. Beside the drive, commanding the road, a snobbish board announced in gilt lettering:

THE RAVENSCROFT HOTEL

Open to Non-residents.

LUNCHEONS — TEAS — DINNERS

DANCE HALL AND TENNIS COURTS

Parties catered for.

131

Two gleaming two-seater cars were parked in the drive. Gordon quailed. The money in his pocket seemed to shrink to nothing. This was the very opposite to the cosy pub they had been looking for. But he was very hungry. Rosemary tweaked at his arm.

"It looks a beastly place. I vote we go on."

"But we've got to get some food. It's our last chance. We shan't find another pub."

"The food's always so disgusting in these places. Beastly cold beef that tastes as if it had been saved up from last year. And they charge you the earth for it."

"Oh, well, we'll just order bread and cheese and beer. It always costs about the same."

"But they hate you doing that. They'll try to bully us into having a proper lunch, you'll see. We must be firm and just say bread and cheese."

"All right, we'll be firm. Come on."

They went in, resolved to be firm. But there was an expensive smell in the draughty hallway—a smell of chintz, dead flowers, Thames water and the rinsings of wine bottles. It was the characteristic smell of a riverside hotel. Gordon's heart sank lower. He knew the type of place this was. It was one of those desolate hotels which exist all along the motor roads and are frequented by stockbrokers airing their whores on Sunday afternoons. In such places you are insulted and overcharged almost as a matter of course. Rosemary shrank nearer to him. She too was intimidated. They saw a door marked "Saloon" and pushed it open, thinking it must be the bar. It was not a bar, however, but a large, smart, chilly room with corduroy-upholstered chairs and settees. You could have mistaken it for an ordinary drawing-room except that all the ashtrays advertised White Horse whisky. And round one of the tables the people from the cars outside—two blond, flat-headed, fattish men, over-youthfully dressed, and two disagreeable elegant young women—were sitting, having evidently just finished lunch. A waiter, bending over their table, was serving them with liqueurs.

Gordon and Rosemary had halted in the doorway. The

people at the table were already eyeing them with offensive upper-middle-class eyes. Gordon and Rosemary looked tired and dirty, and they knew it. The notion of ordering bread and cheese and beer had almost vanished from their minds. In such a place as this you couldn't possibly say "Bread and cheese and beer"; "Lunch" was the only thing you could say. There was nothing for it but "Lunch" or flight. The waiter was almost openly contemptuous. He had summed them up at a glance as having no money; but also he had divined that it was in their minds to fly and was determined to stop them before they could escape.

"Sare?" he demanded, lifting his tray off the table.

Now for it! Say "Bread and cheese and beer," and damn the consequences! Alas! his courage was gone. "Lunch" it would have to be. With a seeming-careless gesture he thrust his hand into his pocket. He was feeling his money to make sure that it was still there. Seven and elevenpence left, he knew. The waiter's eye followed the movement; Gordon had a hateful feeling that the man could actually see through the cloth and count the money in his pocket. In a tone as lordly as he could make it, he remarked:

"Can we have some lunch, please?"

"Luncheon, sare? Yes, sare. Zees way."

The waiter was a black-haired young man with a very smooth, well-featured, sallow face. His dress clothes were excellently cut, and yet unclean-looking, as though he seldom took them off. He looked like a Russian prince; probably he was an Englishman and had assumed a foreign accent because this was proper in a waiter. Defeated, Rosemary and Gordon followed him to the dining-room, which was at the back, giving on the lawn. It was exactly like an aquarium. It was built entirely of greenish glass, and it was so damp and chilly that you could almost have fancied yourself under water. You could both see and smell the river outside. In the middle of each of the small round tables there was a bowl of paper flowers, but at one side, to complete the aquarium effect, there was a whole florist's stand of evergreens, palms and aspidistras and so forth, like dreary water-plants. In summer such a room

133

might be pleasant enough; at present, when the sun had gone behind a cloud, it was merely dank and miserable. Rosemary was almost as much afraid of the waiter as Gordon was. As they sat down and he turned away for a moment she made a face at his back.

"I'm going to pay for my own lunch," she whispered to Gordon, across the table.

"No, you're not."

"What a horrible place! The food's sure to be filthy. I do wish we hadn't come."

"Sh!"

The waiter had come back with a flyblown printed menu. He handed it to Gordon and stood over him with the menacing air of a waiter who knows that you have not much money in your pocket. Gordon's heart pounded. If it was a table d'hôte lunch at three and sixpence or even half a crown, they were sunk. He set his teeth and looked at the menu. Thank God! It was à la carte. The cheapest thing on the list was cold beef and salad for one and sixpence. He said, or rather mumbled:

"We'll have some cold beef, please."

The waiter's delicate black eyebrows lifted. He feigned surprise.

"*Only* ze cold beef, sare?"

"Yes, that'll do to go on with, anyway."

"But you will not have *anysing* else, sare?"

"Oh, well. Bring us some bread, of course. And butter."

"But no soup to start wiz, sare?"

"No. No soup."

"Nor any fish, sare? Only ze cold beef?"

"Do we want any fish, Rosemary? I don't think we do. No. No fish."

"Nor any sweet to follow, sare? *Only* ze cold beef?"

Gordon had difficulty in controlling his features. He thought he had never hated anyone so much as he hated this waiter.

"We'll tell you afterwards if we want anything else," he said.

"And you will drink, sare?"

Gordon had meant to ask for beer, but he hadn't the courage

now. He had got to win back his prestige after this affair of the cold beef.

"Bring me the wine list," he said flatly.

Another flyblown list was produced. All the wines looked impossibly expensive. However, at the very top of the list there was some nameless table claret at two and nine a bottle. Gordon made hurried calculations. He could just manage two and nine. He indicated the wine with his thumbnail.

"Bring us a bottle of this," he said.

The waiter's eyebrows rose again. He essayed a stroke of irony.

"You will have ze *whole* bottle, sare? You would not prefare ze half bottle?"

"A whole bottle," said Gordon coldly.

All in a single delicate movement of contempt the waiter inclined his head, shrugged his left shoulder and turned away. Gordon could not stand it. He caught Rosemary's eye across the table. Somehow or other they had got to put that waiter in his place! In a moment the waiter came back, carrying the bottle of cheap wine by the neck, and half concealing it behind his coat tails, as though it were something a little indecent or unclean. Gordon had thought of a way to avenge himself. As the waiter displayed the bottle he put out a hand, felt it, and frowned.

"That's not the way to serve red wine," he said.

Just for a moment the waiter was taken aback. "Sare?" he said.

"It's stone cold. Take the bottle away and warm it."

"Very good, sare."

But it was not really a victory. The waiter did not look abashed. Was the wine worth warming? his raised eyebrow said. He bore the bottle away with easy disdain, making it quite clear to Rosemary and Gordon that it was bad enough to order the cheapest wine on the list without making this fuss about it afterwards.

The beef and salad were corpse-cold and did not seem like real food at all. They tasted like water. The rolls, also, though stale, were damp. The reedy Thames water seemed to have

135

got into everything. It was no surprise that when the wine was opened it tasted like mud. But it was alcoholic, that was the great thing. It was quite a surprise to find how stimulating it was, once you had got it past your gullet and into your stomach. After drinking a glass and a half Gordon felt very much better. The waiter stood by the door, ironically patient, his napkin over his arm, trying to make Gordon and Rosemary uncomfortable by his presence. At first he succeeded, but Gordon's back was towards him, and he disregarded him and presently almost forgot him. By degrees their courage returned. They began to talk more easily and in louder voices.

"Look," said Gordon. "Those swans have followed us all the way up here."

Sure enough, there were the two swans sailing vaguely to and fro over the dark green water. And at this moment the sun burst out again and the dreary aquarium of a dining-room was flooded with pleasant greenish light. Gordon and Rosemary felt suddenly warm and happy. They began chattering about nothing, almost as though the waiter had not been there, and Gordon took up the bottle and poured out two more glasses of wine. Over their glasses their eyes met. She was looking at him with a sort of yielding irony. "I'm your mistress," her eyes said; "what a joke!" Their knees were touching under the small table; momentarily she squeezed his knee between her own. Something leapt inside him; a warm wave of sensuality and tenderness crept up his body. He had remembered! She was his girl, his mistress. Presently, when they were alone, in some hidden place in the warm, windless air, he would have her naked body all for his own at last. True, all the morning he had known this, but somehow the knowledge had been unreal. It was only now that he grasped it. Without words said, with a sort of bodily certainty, he knew that within an hour she would be in his arms, naked. As they sat there in the warm light, their knees touching, their eyes meeting, they felt as though already everything had been accomplished. There was deep intimacy between them. They could have sat there for hours, just looking at one another and talking of trivial things that had meanings for them and

136

for nobody else. They did sit there for twenty minutes or more. Gordon had forgotten the waiter—had even forgotten, momentarily, the disaster of being let in for this wretched lunch that was going to strip him of every penny he had. But presently the sun went in, the room grew grey again, and they realised that it was time to go.

"The bill," said Gordon, turning half round.

The waiter made a final effort to be offensive.

"Ze bill, sare? But you do not wish any coffee, sare?"

"No, no coffee. The bill."

The waiter retired and came back with a folded slip on a salver. Gordon opened it. Six and threepence—and he had exactly seven and elevenpence in the world! Of course he had known approximately what the bill must be, and yet it was a shock now that it came. He stood up, felt in his pocket and took out all his money. The sallow young waiter, his salver on his arm, eyed the handful of money; plainly he divined that it was all Gordon had. Rosemary also had got up and come round the table. She pinched Gordon's elbow; this was a signal that she would like to pay her share. Gordon pretended not to notice. He paid the six and threepence, and, as he turned away, dropped another shilling on to the salver. The waiter balanced it for a moment on his hand, flicked it over and then slipped it into his waistcoat pocket with the air of covering up something unmentionable.

As they went down the passage, Gordon felt dismayed, helpless—dazed, almost. All his money gone at a single swoop! It was a ghastly thing to happen. If only they had not come to this accursed place! The whole day was ruined now—and all for the sake of a couple of plates of cold beef and a bottle of muddy wine! Presently there would be tea to think about, and he had only six cigarettes left, and there were the bus fares back to Slough and God knew what else; and he had just eightpence to pay for the lot! They got outside the hotel feeling as if they had been kicked out and the door slammed behind them. All the warm intimacy of a moment ago was gone. Everything seemed different now that they were outside. Their blood seemed to grow suddenly cooler in the open air.

Rosemary walked ahead of him, rather nervous, not speaking. She was half frightened now by the thing she had resolved to do. He watched her strong delicate limbs moving. There was her body that he had wanted so long; but now when the time had come it only daunted him. He wanted her to be his, he wanted to *have had* her, but he wished it were over and done with. It was an effort—a thing he had got to screw himself up to. It was strange that that beastly business of the hotel bill could have upset him so completely. The easy carefree mood of the morning was shattered; in its place there had come back the hateful, harassing, familiar thing—worry about money. In a minute he would have to own up that he had only eightpence left; he would have to borrow money off her to get them home; it would be squalid and shameful. Only the wine inside him kept up his courage. The warmth of the wine, and the hateful feeling of having only eightpence left, warred together in his body, neither getting the better of the other.

They walked rather slowly, but soon they were away from the river and on higher ground again. Each searched desperately for something to say and could think of nothing. He came level with her, took her hand and wound her fingers within his own. Like that they felt better. But his heart beat painfully, his entrails were constricted. He wondered whether she felt the same.

"There doesn't seem to be a soul about," she said at last.

"It's Sunday afternoon. They're all asleep under the aspidistra, after roast beef and Yorkshire."

There was another silence. They walked on fifty yards or so. With difficulty mastering his voice, he managed to say:

"It's extraordinarily warm. We might sit down for a bit if we can find a place."

"Yes, all right. If you like."

Presently they came to a small copse on the left of the road. It looked dead and empty, nothing growing under the naked trees. But at the corner of the copse, on the far side, there was a great tangled patch of sloe or blackthorn bushes. He put his arm round her without saying anything and

138

turned her in that direction. There was a gap in the hedge with some barbed wire strung across it. He held the wire up for her and she slipped nimbly under it. His heart leapt again. How supple and strong she was! But as he climbed over the wire to follow her, the eightpence—a sixpence and two pennies—clinked in his pocket, daunting him anew.

When they got to the bushes they found a natural alcove. On three sides were beds of thorn, leafless but impenetrable, and on the other side you looked downhill over a sweep of naked ploughed fields. At the bottom of the hill stood a low-roofed cottage, tiny as a child's toy, its chimneys smokeless. Not a creature was stirring anywhere. You could not have been more alone than in such a place. The grass was the fine mossy stuff that grows under trees.

"We ought to have brought a mackintosh," he said. He had knelt down.

"It doesn't matter. The ground's fairly dry."

He pulled her to the ground beside him, kissed her, pulled off the flat felt hat, lay upon her breast to breast, kissed her face all over. She lay under him, yielding rather than responding. She did not resist when his hand sought her breasts. But in her heart she was still frightened. She would do it—oh, yes! she would keep her implied promise, she would not draw back; but all the same she was frightened. And at heart he too was half reluctant. It dismayed him to find how little, at this moment, he really wanted her. The money-business still unnerved him. How can you make love when you have only eightpence in your pocket and are thinking about it all the time? Yet in a way he wanted her. Indeed, he could not do without her. His life would be a different thing when once they were really lovers. For a long time he lay on her breast, her head turned sideways, his face against her neck and hair, attempting nothing further.

Then the sun came out again. It was getting low in the sky now. The warm light poured over them as though a membrane across the sky had broken. It had been a little cold on the grass, really, with the sun behind the clouds; but now once again it was almost as warm as summer. Both of them sat up to exclaim at it.

"Oh, Gordon, look! Look how the sun's lighting everything up!"

As the clouds melted away a widening yellow beam slid swiftly across the valley, gilding everything in its path. Grass that had been dull green shone suddenly emerald. The empty cottage below sprang out into warm colours, purply-blue of tiles, cherry-red of brick. Only the fact that no birds were singing reminded you that it was winter. Gordon put his arm round Rosemary and pulled her hard against him. They sat cheek to cheek, looking down the hill. He turned her round and kissed her.

"You do like me, don't you?"

"Adore you, silly."

"And you're going to be nice to me, aren't you?"

"Nice to you?"

"Let me do what I want with you?"

"Yes, I expect so."

"Anything?"

"Yes, all right. Anything."

He pressed her back upon the grass. It was quite different now. The warmth of the sun seemed to have got into their bones. "Take your clothes off, there's a dear," he whispered. She did it readily enough. She had no shame before him. Besides, it was so warm and the place was so solitary that it did not matter how many clothes you took off. They spread her clothes out and made a sort of bed for her to lie on. Naked, she lay back, her hands behind her head, her eyes shut, smiling slightly, as though she had considered everything and were at peace in her mind. For a long time he knelt and gazed at her body. Its beauty startled him. She looked much younger naked than with her clothes on. Her face, thrown back, with eyes shut, looked almost childish. He moved closer to her. Once again the coins clinked in his pocket. Only eightpence left! Trouble coming presently. But he wouldn't think of it now. Get on with it, that's the great thing, get on

140

with it and damn the future! He put an arm beneath her and laid his body to hers.

"May I?—now?"

"Yes. All right."

"You're not frightened?"

"No."

"I'll be as gentle as I can with you."

"It doesn't matter."

A moment later:

"Oh, Gordon, no! No, no, no!"

"What? What is it?"

"No, Gordon, no! You mustn't! *No!*"

She put her hands against him and pushed him violently back. Her face looked remote, frightened, almost hostile. It was terrible to feel her push him away at such a moment. It was as though cold water had been dashed all over him. He fell back from her, dismayed, hurriedly rearranging his clothes.

"What is it? What's the matter?"

"Oh, Gordon! I thought you—oh, dear!"

She threw her arm over her face and rolled over on her side, away from him, suddenly ashamed.

"What is it?" he repeated.

"How could you be so *thoughtless?*"

"What do you mean—thoughtless?"

"Oh! you know what I mean!"

His heart shrank. He did know what she meant; but he had never thought of it till this moment. And of course—oh, yes!—he ought to have thought of it. He stood up and turned away from her. Suddenly he knew that he could go no further with this business. In a wet field on a Sunday afternoon—and in mid-winter at that! Impossible! It had seemed so right, so natural only a minute ago; now it seemed merely squalid and ugly.

"I didn't expect *this,*" he said bitterly.

"But I couldn't help it, Gordon! You ought to have—you know."

"You don't think I go in for that kind of thing, do you?"

141

"But what else can we do? I can't have a baby, can I?"

"You must take your chance."

"Oh, Gordon, how impossible you are!"

She lay looking up at him, her face full of distress, too overcome for the moment even to remember that she was naked. His disappointment had turned to anger. There you are, you see! Money again! Even in the most secret action of your life you don't escape it; you've still got to spoil everything with filthy cold-blooded precautions for money's sake. Money, money, always money! Even in the bridal bed, the finger of the money-god intruding! In the heights or in the depths, he is there. He walked a pace or two up and down, his hands in his pockets.

"Money again, you see!" he said. "Even at a moment like this it's got the power to stand over us and bully us. Even when we're alone and miles from anywhere, with not a soul to see us."

"What's *money* got to do with it?"

"I tell you it'd never even enter your head to worry about a baby if it wasn't for the money. You'd *want* the baby if it wasn't for that. You say you 'can't' have a baby. What do you mean, you 'can't' have a baby? You mean you daren't; because you'd lose your job and I've got no money and all of us would starve. This birth-control business! It's just another way they've found out of bullying us. And you want to acquiesce in it, apparently."

"But what am I to do, Gordon? What am I to do?"

At this moment the sun disappeared behind the clouds. It became perceptibly colder. After all, the scene was grotesque—the naked woman lying in the grass, the dressed man standing moodily by with his hands in his pockets. She'd catch her death of cold in another moment, lying there like that. The whole thing was absurd and indecent.

"But what else am I to do?" she repeated.

"I should think you might start by putting your clothes on," he said coldly.

He had only said it to avenge his irritation; but its result was to make her so painfully and obviously embarrassed that

142

he had to turn his back on her. She had dressed herself in a very few moments. As she knelt lacing up her shoes he heard her sniff once or twice. She was on the point of crying and was struggling to restrain herself. He felt horribly ashamed. He would have liked to throw himself on his knees beside her, put his arms round her and ask her pardon. But he could do nothing of the kind; the scene had left him lumpish and awkward. It was with difficulty that he could command his voice even for the most banal remark.

"Are you ready?" he said flatly.

"Yes."

They went back to the road, climbed through the wire and started down the hill without another word. Fresh clouds were rolling across the sun. It was getting much colder. Another hour and the early dusk would have fallen. They reached the bottom of the hill and came in sight of the Ravenscroft Hotel, scene of their disaster.

"Where are we going?" said Rosemary in a small sulky voice.

"Back to Slough, I suppose. We must cross the bridge and have a look at the signposts."

They scarcely spoke again till they had gone several miles. Rosemary was embarrassed and miserable. A number of times she edged closer to him, meaning to take his arm, but he edged away from her; and so they walked abreast with almost the width of the road between them. She imagined that she had offended him mortally. She supposed that it was because of his disappointment—because she had pushed him away at the critical moment—that he was angry with her; she would have apologised if he had given her a quarter of a chance. But as a matter of fact he was scarcely thinking of this any longer. His mind had turned away from that side of things. It was the money-business that was troubling him now—the fact that he had only eightpence in his pocket. In a very little while he would have to confess it. There would be the bus fares from Farnham to Slough, and tea in Slough, and cigarettes, and more bus fares and perhaps another meal when they got back to London; and just eightpence to cover the lot! He would have to borrow from Rosemary after all. And that was so damned humiliating. It is hateful to have to borrow money off someone you have just been quarrelling with. What nonsense it made of all his fine attitudes! There was he, lecturing her, putting on superior airs, pretending to be shocked because she took contraception for granted; and the next moment turning round and asking her for money! But there you are, you see, that's what money can do. There is no attitude that money or the lack of it cannot puncture.

By half past four it was almost completely dark. They tramped along misty roads where there was no illumination save the cracks of cottage windows and the yellow beam of an occasional car. It was getting beastly cold, too, but they had walked four miles and the exercise had warmed them. It was impossible to go on being unsociable any longer. They began to talk more easily, and by degrees they edged closer together. Rosemary took Gordon's arm. Presently she stopped him and swung him round to face her.

"Gordon, *why* are you so beastly to me?"

"How am I beastly to you?"

"Coming all this way without speaking a word!"

"Oh, well!"

"Are you still angry with me because of what happened just now?"

"No. I was never angry with you. *You're* not to blame."

She looked up at him, trying to divine the expression of his face in the almost pitch darkness. He drew her against him, and, as she seemed to expect it, tilted her face back and kissed her. She clung to him eagerly; her body melted against his. She had been waiting for this, it seemed.

"Gordon, you do love me, don't you?"

"Of course I do."

"Things went wrong somehow. I couldn't help it. I got frightened suddenly."

"It doesn't matter. Another time it'll be all right."

She was lying limp against him, her head on his breast. He could feel her heart beating. It seemed to flutter violently, as though she were taking some decision.

144

"I don't care," she said indistinctly, her face buried in his coat.

"Don't care about what?"

"The baby. I'll risk it. You can do what you like with me."

At these surrendering words a weak desire raised itself in him and died away at once. He knew why she had said it. It was not because, at this moment, she really wanted to be made love to. It was from a mere generous impulse to let him know that she loved him and would take a dreaded risk rather than disappoint him.

"Now?" he said.

"Yes, if you like."

He considered. He so wanted to be sure that she was his! But the cold night air flowed over them. Behind the hedges the long grass would be wet and chill. This was not the time or the place. Besides, that business of the eightpence had usurped his mind. He was not in the mood any longer.

"I can't," he said finally.

"You can't! But, Gordon! I thought——"

"I know. But it's all different now."

"You're still upset?"

"Yes. In a way."

"Why?"

He pushed her a little away from him. As well have the explanation now as later. Nevertheless he was so ashamed that he mumbled rather than said:

"I've got a beastly thing to say to you. It's been worrying me all the way along."

"What is it?"

"It's this. Can you lend me some money? I'm absolutely cleaned out. I had just enough for to-day, but that beastly hotel bill upset everything. I've only eightpence left."

Rosemary was amazed. She broke right out of his arms in her amazement.

"Only eightpence left! What *are* you talking about? What does it matter if you've only eightpence left?"

"Don't I tell you I shall have to borrow money off you in another minute? You'll have to pay for your own bus fares, and my bus fares, and your tea and Lord knows what. And I asked you to come out with me! You're supposed to be my guest. It's bloody."

"Your *guest!* Oh, Gordon! Is *that* what's been worrying you all this time?"

"Yes."

"Gordon, you *are* a baby! How can you let yourself be worried by a thing like that? As though I minded lending you money! Aren't I always telling you I want to pay my share when we go out together?"

"Yes, and you know how I hate your paying. We had that out the other night."

"Oh, how absurd, how absurd you are! Do you think there's anything to be ashamed of in having no money?"

"Of course there is! It's the only thing in the world there *is* to be ashamed of."

"But what's it got to do with you and me making love, anyway? I don't understand you. First you want to and then you don't want to. What's money got to do with it?"

"Everything."

He wound her arm in his and started down the road. She would never understand. Nevertheless he had got to explain.

"Don't you understand that one isn't a full human being—that one doesn't *feel* a human being—unless one's got money in one's pocket?"

"No. I think that's just silly."

"It isn't that I don't want to make love to you. I do. But I tell you I can't make love to you when I've only eightpence in my pocket. At least when you know I've only eightpence. I just can't do it. It's physically impossible."

"But why? Why?"

"You'll find it in Lemprière," he said obscurely.

That settled it. They talked no more about it. For the second time he had behaved grossly badly and yet had made her feel as if it were she who was in the wrong. They walked on. She did not understand him; on the other hand, she forgave him everything. Presently they reached Farnham Common, and, after a wait at the crossroad, got a bus to

146

Slough. In the darkness, as the bus loomed near, Rosemary found Gordon's hand and slipped half a crown into it, so that he might pay the fares and not be shamed in public by letting a woman pay for him.

For his own part Gordon would sooner have walked to Slough and saved the bus fares, but he knew Rosemary would refuse. In Slough, also, he was for taking the train straight back to London, but Rosemary said indignantly that she wasn't going to go without her tea, so they went to a large, dreary, draughty hotel near the station. Tea, with little wilting sandwiches and rock cakes like balls of putty, was two shillings a head. It was torment to Gordon to let her pay for his food. He sulked, ate nothing, and, after a whispered argument, insisted on contributing his eightpence towards the cost of the tea.

It was seven o'clock when they took the train back to London. The train was full of tired hikers in khaki shorts. Rosemary and Gordon did not talk much. They sat close together, Rosemary with her arm twined through his, playing with his hand, Gordon looking out of the window. People in the carriage eyed them, wondering what they had quarrelled about. Gordon watched the lamp-starred darkness streaming past. So the day to which he had looked forward was ended. And now back to Willowbed Road, with a penniless week ahead. For a whole week, unless some miracle happened, he wouldn't even be able to buy himself a cigarette. What a bloody fool he had been! Rosemary was not angry with him. By the pressure of her hand she tried to make it clear to him that she loved him. His pale discontented face, turned half away from her, his shabby coat and his unkempt mouse-coloured hair that wanted cutting more than ever, filled her with profound pity. She felt more tenderly towards him than she would have done if everything had gone well, because in her feminine way she grasped that he was unhappy and that life was difficult for him.

"See me home, will you?" she said as they got out at Paddington.

"If you don't mind walking. I haven't got the fare."

"But let *me* pay the fare. Oh, dear! I suppose you won't. But how are you going to get home yourself?"

"Oh, I'll walk. I know the way. It's not so very far."

"I hate to think of your walking all that way. You look so tired. Be a dear and let me pay your fare home. *Do!*"

"No. You've paid quite enough for me already."

"Oh, dear! You are so silly!"

They had halted at the entrance to the Underground. He took her hand. "I suppose we must say good-bye for the present," he said.

"Good-bye, Gordon dear. Thanks ever so much for taking me out. It was such fun this morning."

"Ah, this morning! It was different then." His mind went back to the morning hours, when they had been alone on the road together and there was still money in his pocket. Compunction seized him. On the whole he had behaved badly. He pressed her hand a little tighter. "You're not angry with me, are you?"

"No, silly, of course not."

"I didn't mean to be beastly to you. It was the money. It's always the money."

"Never mind, it'll be better next time. We'll go to some better place. We'll go down to Brighton for the week-end, or something."

"Perhaps, when I've got the money. You will write soon, won't you?"

"Yes."

"Your letters are the only things that keep me going. Tell me when you'll write, so that I can have your letter to look forward to."

"I'll write to-morrow night and post it on Tuesday. Then you'll get it last post on Tuesday night."

"Then good-bye, Rosemary dear."

"Good-bye, Gordon darling."

He left her at the booking-office. When he had gone twenty yards he felt a hand laid on his arm. He turned sharply. It was Rosemary. She thrust a packet of twenty Gold Flake, which she had bought at the tobacco kiosk, into his coat

148

pocket and ran back to the Underground before he could protest.

He trailed homeward through the wastes of Marylebone and Regent's Park. It was the fag-end of the day. The streets were dark and desolate, with that strange listless feeling of Sunday night when people are more tired after a day of idleness than after a day of work. It was vilely cold, too. The wind had risen when the night fell. *Sharply the menacing wind sweeps over.* Gordon was footsore, having walked a dozen or fifteen miles, and also hungry. He had had little food all day. In the morning he had hurried off without a proper breakfast, and the lunch at the Ravenscroft Hotel wasn't the kind of meal that did you much good; since then he had had no solid food. However, there was no hope of getting anything when he got home. He had told mother Wisbeach that he would be away all day.

When he reached the Hampstead Road he had to wait on the kerb to let a stream of cars go past. Even here everything seemed dark and gloomy, in spite of the glaring lamps and the cold glitter of the jewellers' windows. The raw wind pierced his thin clothes, making him shiver. *Sharply the menacing wind sweeps over The bending poplars, newly bare.* He had finished that poem, all except the last two lines. He thought again of those hours this morning—the empty misty roads, the feeling of freedom and adventure, of having the whole day and the whole country before you in which to wander at will. It was having money that did it, of course. Seven and elevenpence he had had in his pocket this morning. It had been a brief victory over the money-god; a morning's apostasy, a holiday in the groves of Ashtaroth. But such things never last. Your money goes and your freedom with it. Circumcise ye your foreskins, saith the Lord. And back we creep, duly snivelling.

Another shoal of cars swam past. One in particular caught his eye, a long slender thing, elegant as a swallow, all gleaming blue and silver; a thousand guineas it would have cost, he thought. A blue-clad chauffeur sat at the wheel, upright, immobile, like some scornful statue. At the back, in the pink-

149

lit interior, four elegant young people, two youths, and two girls, were smoking cigarettes and laughing. He had a glimpse of sleek bunny-faces; faces of ravishing pinkness and smoothness, lit by that peculiar inner glow that can never be counterfeited, the soft warm radiance of money.

He crossed the road. No food to-night. However, there was still oil in the lamp, thank God; he would have a secret cup of tea when he got back. At this moment he saw himself and his life without saving disguises. Every night the same—back to the cold lonely bedroom and the grimy, littered sheets of the poem that never got any further. It was a blind alley. He would never finish *London Pleasures,* he would never marry Rosemary, he would never set his life in order. He would only drift and sink, drift and sink, like the others of his family; but worse than them—down, down into some dreadful subworld that as yet he could only dimly imagine. It was what he had chosen when he declared war on money. Serve the money-god or go under; there is no other rule.

Something deep below made the stone street shiver. The tube-train, sliding through middle earth. He had a vision of London, of the western world; he saw a thousand million slaves toiling and grovelling about the throne of money. The earth is ploughed, ships sail, miners sweat in dripping tunnels underground, clerks hurry for the eight-fifteen with the fear of the boss eating at their vitals. And even in bed with their wives they tremble and obey. Obey whom? The money-priesthood, the pink-faced masters of the world. The Upper Crust. A welter of sleek young rabbits in thousand guinea motor cars, of golfing stockbrokers and cosmopolitan financiers, of Chancery lawyers and fashionable Nancy boys, of bankers, newspaper peers, novelists of all four sexes, American pugilists, lady aviators, film stars, bishops, titled poets and Chicago gorillas.

When he had gone another fifty yards the rhyme for the final stanza of his poem occurred to him. He walked homeward, repeating the poem to himself:

> *Sharply the menacing wind sweeps over*
> *The bending poplars, newly bare,*

And the dark ribbons of the chimneys
Veer downward; flicked by whips of air,

Torn posters flutter; coldly sound
The boom of trams and the rattle of hooves,
And the clerks who hurry to the station
Look, shuddering, over the eastern rooves,

Thinking, each one, "Here comes the winter!
"Please God I keep my job this year!"
And bleakly, as the cold strikes through
Their entrails like an icy spear,

They think of rent, rates, season tickets,
Insurance, coal, the skivvy's wages,
Boots, school-bills and the next instalment
Upon the two twin beds from Drage's.

For if in careless summer days
In groves of Ashtaroth we whored,
Repentant now, when winds blow cold,
We kneel before our rightful lord;

The lord of all, the money-god,
Who rules us blood and hand and brain,
Who gives the roof that stops the wind,
And, giving, takes away again;

Who spies with jealous, watchful care,
Our thoughts, our dreams, our secret ways,
Who picks our words and cuts our clothes,
And maps the pattern of our days;

Who chills our anger, curbs our hope,
And buys our lives and pays with toys,
Who claims as tribute broken faith,
Accepted insults, muted joys;

Who binds with chains the poet's wit,
The navvy's strength, the soldier's pride,
And lays the sleek, estranging shield
Between the lover and his bride.

Chapter Eight

As THE clock struck one Gordon slammed the shop door
to and hurried, almost ran, to the branch of the Westminster
Bank down the street.

With a half-conscious gesture of caution he was clutching
the lapel of his coat, holding it tight against him. In there,
stowed away in his right-hand inner pocket, was an object
whose very existence he partly doubted. It was a stout blue
envelope with an American stamp; in the envelope was a
cheque for fifty dollars; and the cheque was made out to
"Gordon Comstock"!

He could feel the square shape of the envelope outlined
against his body as clearly as though it had been red hot.
All the morning he had felt it there, whether he touched it
or whether he did not; he seemed to have developed a special
patch of sensitiveness in the skin below his right breast. As
often as once in ten minutes he had taken the cheque out of
its envelope and anxiously examined it. After all, cheques are
tricky things. It would be frightful if there turned out to be
some hitch about the date or the signature. Besides, he might
lose it—it might even vanish of its own accord like fairy gold.

The cheque had come from the *Californian Review*, that
American magazine to which, weeks or months ago, he had
despairingly sent a poem. He had almost forgotten about the
poem, it had been so long away, until this morning their
letter had come sailing out of the blue. And what a letter!
No English editor ever writes letters like that. They were
"very favorably impressed" by his poem. They would "en-

deavor" to include it in their next number. Would he "favor" them by showing them some more of his work? (Would he? Oh, boy—as Flaxman would say.) And the cheque had come with it. It seemed the most monstrous folly, in this year of blight 1934, that anyone should pay fifty dollars for a poem. However, there it was; and there was the cheque, which looked perfectly genuine however often he inspected it.

He would have no peace of mind till the cheque was cashed—for quite possibly the bank would refuse it—but already a stream of visions was flowing through his mind. Visions of girls' faces, visions of cobwebby claret bottles and quart pots of beer, visions of a new suit and his overcoat out of pawn, visions of a week-end at Brighton with Rosemary, visions of the crisp, crackling five pound note which he was going to give to Julia. Above all, of course, that fiver for Julia. It was almost the first thing he had thought of when the cheque came. Whatever else he did with the money, he must give Julia half of it. It was only the barest justice, considering how much he had "borrowed" from her in all these years. All the morning the thought of Julia and the money he owed her had been cropping up in his mind at odd moments. It was a vaguely distasteful thought, however. He would forget about it for half an hour at a time, would plan a dozen ways of spending his ten pounds to the uttermost farthing, and then suddenly he would remember about Julia. Good old Julia! Julia should have her share. A fiver at the very least. Even that was not a tenth of what he owed her. For the twentieth time, with a faint malaise, he registered the thought: five quid for Julia.

The bank made no trouble about the cheque. Gordon had no banking account, but they knew him well, for Mr. Mc-Kechnie banked there. They had cashed editors' cheques for Gordon before. There was only a minute's consultation, and then the cashier came back.

"Notes, Mr. Comstock?"

"One five pound and the rest pounds, please."

The flimsy luscious fiver and the five clean pound notes slid rustling under the brass rail. And after them the cashier pushed a little pile of half-crowns and pennies. In lordly style Gordon shot the coins into his pocket without even counting them. That was a bit of backsheesh. He had only expected ten pounds for fifty dollars. The dollar must be above par. The five pound note, however, he carefully folded up and stowed away in the American envelope. That was Julia's fiver. It was sacrosanct. He would post it to her presently.

He did not go home for dinner. Why chew leathery beef in the aspidistral dining-room when he had ten quid in pocket —five quid, rather? (He kept forgetting that half the money was already mortgaged to Julia.) For the moment he did not bother to post Julia's five pounds. This evening would be soon enough. Besides, he rather enjoyed the feeling of it in his pocket. It was queer how different you felt with all that money in your pocket. Not opulent, merely, but reassured, revivified, reborn. He felt a different person from what he had been yesterday. He *was* a different person. He was no longer the downtrodden wretch who made secret cups of tea over the oil stove at 31 Willowbed Road. He was Gordon Comstock, the poet, famous on both sides of the Atlantic. Publications: *Mice* (1932), *London Pleasures* (1935). He thought with perfect confidence of *London Pleasures* now. In three months it should see the light. Demy octavo, white buckram covers. There was nothing that he did not feel equal to now that his luck had turned.

He strolled into the Prince of Wales for a bite of food. A cut off the joint and two veg., one and twopence, a pint of pale ale ninepence, twenty Gold Flakes a shilling. Even after that extravagance he still had well over ten pounds in hand— or rather, well over five pounds. Beer-warmed, he sat and meditated on the things you can do with five pounds. A new suit, a week-end in the country, a day-trip to Paris, five rousing drunks, ten dinners in Soho restaurants. At this point it occurred to him that he and Rosemary and Ravelston must certainly have dinner together to-night. Just to celebrate his stroke of luck; after all, it isn't every day that ten pounds— five pounds—drops out of the sky into your lap. The thought of the three of them together, with good food and wine and money no object, took hold of him as something not to be resisted. He had just a tiny twinge of caution. Mustn't spend *all* his money, of course. Still, he could afford a quid—two quid. In a couple of minutes he had got Ravelston on the pub phone.

"Is that you, Ravelston? I say, Ravelston! Look here, you've got to have dinner with me to-night."

From the other end of the line Ravelston faintly demurred. "No, dash it! You have dinner with *me*." But Gordon overbore him. Nonsense! Ravelston had got to have dinner with *him* to-night. Unwillingly, Ravelston assented. All right, yes, thanks; he'd like it very much. There was a sort of apologetic misery in his voice. He guessed what had happened. Gordon had got hold of money from somewhere and was squandering it immediately; as usual, Ravelston felt he hadn't the right to interfere. Where should they go? Gordon was demanding. Ravelston began to speak in praise of those jolly little Soho restaurants where you get such a wonderful dinner for half a crown. But the Soho restaurants sounded beastly as soon as Ravelston mentioned them. Gordon wouldn't hear of it. Nonsense! They must go somewhere decent. Let's do it all regardless, was his private thought; might as well spend two quid—three quid, even. Where did Ravelston generally go? Modigliani's, admitted Ravelston. But Modigliani's was very —but no! not even over the phone could Ravelston frame that hateful word "expensive." How remind Gordon of his poverty? Gordon mightn't care for Modigliani's, he euphemistically said. But Gordon was satisfied. Modigliani's? Right you are—half-past eight. Good! After all, if he spent even three quid on the dinner he'd still have two quid to buy himself a new pair of shoes and a vest and a pair of pants.

He had fixed it up with Rosemary in another five minutes. The New Albion did not like their employees being rung up on the phone, but it did not matter once in a way. Since that disastrous Sunday journey, five days ago, he had heard from her once but had not seen her. She answered eagerly when she heard whose voice it was. Would she have dinner with him to-night? Of course! What fun! And so in ten minutes the whole thing was settled. He had always wanted Rosemary and Ravelston to meet, but somehow had never been able to contrive it. These things are so much easier when you've got a little money to spend.

The taxi bore him westward through the darkling streets. A three-mile journey—still, he could afford it. Why spoil the ship for a ha'porth of tar? He had dropped that notion of spending only two pounds to-night. He would spend three pounds, three pounds ten—four pounds if he felt like it. Slap up and regardless—that was the idea. And, oh! by the way! Julia's fiver. He hadn't sent it yet. No matter. Send it first thing in the morning. Good old Julia! She should have her fiver.

How voluptuous were the taxi cushions under his bum! He lolled this way and that. He had been drinking, of course —had had two quick ones, or possibly three, before coming away. The taxi-driver was a stout philosophic man with a weatherbeaten face and a knowing eye. He and Gordon understood one another. They had palled up in the bar where Gordon was having his quick ones. As they neared the West End the taximan drew up, unbidden, at a discreet pub on a corner. He knew what was in Gordon's mind. Gordon could do with a quick one. So could the taximan. But the drinks were on Gordon—that too was understood.

"You anticipate my thoughts," said Gordon, climbing out.

"Yes, sir."

"I could just about do with a quick one."

"Thought you might, sir."

"And could you manage one yourself, do you think?"

"Where there's a will there's a way," said the taximan.

"Come inside," said Gordon.

They leaned matily on the brass-edged bar, elbow to elbow, lighting two of the taximan's cigarettes. Gordon felt witty and expansive. He would have liked to tell the taximan the history of his life. The white-aproned barman hastened towards them.

"Yessir?" said the barman.

"Gin," said Gordon.

"Make it two," said the taximan.

More matily than ever, they clinked glasses.

"Many happy returns," said Gordon.

"Your birthday to-day, sir?"

"Only metaphorically. My re-birthday, so to speak."

"I never had much education," said the taximan.

"I was speaking in parables," said Gordon.

"English is good enough for me," said the taximan.

"It was the tongue of Shakespeare," said Gordon.

"Literary gentleman, are you, sir, by any chance?"

"Do I look as moth-eaten as all that?"

"Not moth-eaten, sir. Only intellectual-like."

"You're quite right. A poet."

"Poet! It takes all sorts to make a world, don't it now?" said the taximan.

"And a bloody good world it is," said Gordon.

His thoughts moved lyrically to-night. They had another gin and presently went back to the taxi all but arm in arm, after yet another gin. That made five gins Gordon had had this evening. There was an ethereal feeling in his veins; the gin seemed to be flowing there, mingled with his blood. He lay back in the corner of the seat, watching the great blazing sky-signs swim across the bluish dark. The evil red and blue of the Neon lights pleased him at this moment. How smoothly the taxi glided! More like a gondola than a car. It was having money that did that. Money greased the wheels. He thought of the evening ahead of him; good food, good wine, good talk —above all, no worrying about money. No damned niggling with sixpences and "We can't afford this" and "We can't afford that!" Rosemary and Ravelston would try to stop him being extravagant. But he would shut the... up. He'd spend every penny he had if he felt like it. Ten whole quid to bust! At least, five quid. The thought of Julia passed flickeringly through his mind and disappeared again.

He was quite sober when they got to Modigliani's. The monstrous commissionaire, like a great glittering waxwork with the minimum of joints, stepped stiffly forward to open the taxi door. His grim eye looked askance at Gordon's clothes.

Not that you were expected to "dress" at Modigliani's. They were tremendously Bohemian at Modigliani's, of course; but there are ways and ways of being Bohemian, and Gordon's way was the wrong way. Gordon did not care. He bade the taximan an affectionate farewell, and tipped him half a crown over his fare, whereat the commissionaire's eye looked a little less grim. At this moment Ravelston emerged from the doorway. The commissionaire knew Ravelston, of course. He lounged out on to the pavement, a tall distinguished figure, aristocratically shabby, his eye rather moody. He was worrying already about the money this dinner was going to cost Gordon.

"Ah, there you are, Gordon!"

"Hullo, Ravelston! Where's Rosemary?"

"Perhaps she's waiting inside. I don't know her by sight, you know. But I say, Gordon, look here! Before we go in, I wanted——"

"Ah, look, there she is!"

She was coming towards them, swift and debonair. She threaded her way through the crowd with the air of some neat little destroyer gliding between large clumsy cargo-boats. And she was nicely dressed, as usual. The sub-shovel hat was cocked at its most provocative angle. Gordon's heart stirred. There was a girl for you! He was proud that Ravelston should see her. She was very gay to-night. It was written all over her that she was not going to remind herself or Gordon of their last disastrous encounter. Perhaps she laughed and talked just a little too vivaciously as Gordon introduced them and they went inside. But Ravelston had taken a liking to her immediately. Indeed, everyone who met her did take a liking to Rosemary. The inside of the restaurant overawed Gordon for a moment. It was so horribly, artistically smart. Dark gate-leg tables, pewter candlesticks, pictures by modern French painters on the walls. One, a street scene, looked like a Utrillo. Gordon stiffened his shoulders. Damn it, what was there to be afraid of? The five pound note was tucked away in its envelope in his pocket. It was Julia's five pounds, of course; he wasn't going to spend it. Still, its presence gave him moral support. It was a kind of talisman. They were making for the corner

158

table—Ravelston's favourite table—at the far end. Ravelston took Gordon by the arm and drew him a little back, out of Rosemary's hearing.

"Gordon, look here!"

"What?"

"Look here, you're going to have dinner with *me* to-night."

"Bosh! This is on me."

"I do wish you would. I hate to see you spending all that money."

"We won't talk about money to-night," said Gordon.

"Fifty-fifty, then," pleaded Ravelston.

"It's on me," said Gordon firmly.

Ravelston subsided. The fat, white-haired Italian waiter was bowing and smiling beside the corner table. But it was at Ravelston, not at Gordon, that he smiled. Gordon sat down with the feeling that he must assert himself quickly. He waved away the menu which the waiter had produced.

"We must settle what we're going to drink first," he said.

"Beer for me," said Ravelston, with a sort of gloomy haste. "Beer's the only drink I care about."

"Me too," echoed Rosemary.

"Oh, rot! We've got to have some wine. What do you like, red or white? Give me the wine list," he said to the waiter.

"Then let's have a plain Bordeaux. Médoc or St. Julien or something," said Ravelston.

"I adore St. Julien," said Rosemary, who thought she remembered that St. Julien was always the cheapest wine on the list.

Inwardly, Gordon damned their eyes. There you are, you see! They were in league against him already. They were trying to prevent him from spending his money. There was going to be that deadly, hateful atmosphere of "You can't afford it" hanging over everything. It made him all the more anxious to be extravagant. A moment ago he would have compromised on Burgundy. Now he decided that they must have something really expensive—something fizzy, something with a kick in it. Champagne? No, they'd never let him have champagne. Ah!

159

"Have you got any Asti?" he said to the waiter.

The waiter suddenly beamed, thinking of his corkage. He had grasped now that Gordon and not Ravelston was the host. He answered in the peculiar mixture of French and English which he affected.

"Asti, sir? Yes, sir. Very nice Asti! Asti Spumanti. Très fin! Très vif!"

Ravelston's worried eye sought Gordon's across the table. You can't afford it! his eye pleaded.

"Is that one of those fizzy wines?" said Rosemary.

"Very fizzy, madame. Very lively wine. Très vif! Pop!" his fat hands made a gesture, picturing cascades of foam.

"Asti," said Gordon, before Rosemary could stop him.

Ravelston looked miserable. He knew that the Asti would cost Gordon ten or fifteen shillings a bottle. Gordon pretended not to notice. He began talking about Stendhal—association with Duchesse de Sanseverina and her "force vin d'Asti." Along came the Asti in a pail of ice—a mistake, that, as Ravelston could have told Gordon. Out came the cork. Pop! The wild wine foamed into the wide flat glasses. Mysteriously the atmosphere of the table changed. Something had happened to all three of them. Even before it was drunk the wine had worked its magic. Rosemary had lost her nervousness, Ravelston his worried preoccupation with the expense, Gordon his defiant resolve to be extravagant. They were eating anchovies and bread and butter, fried sole, roast pheasant with bread sauce and chipped potatoes; but principally they were drinking and talking. And how brilliantly they were talking—or so it seemed to them, anyway! They talked about the bloodiness of modern life and the bloodiness of modern books. What else is there to talk about nowadays? As usual (but, oh! how differently, now that there was money in his pocket and he didn't really believe what he was saying) Gordon descanted on the deadness, the dreadfulness of the age we live in. French letters and machine guns! The movies and the *Daily Mail*! It was a bone-deep truth when he walked the streets with a couple of coppers in his pocket; but it was a joke at this moment. It was great fun—it *is* fun when you have good food and good wine inside you—to demonstrate that we live in a dead and rotting world. He was being witty at the expense of modern literature; they were all being witty. With the fine scorn of the unpublished Gordon knocked down reputation after reputation. Shaw, Yeats, Eliot, Joyce, Huxley, Lewis, Hemingway—each with a careless phrase or two was shovelled into the dustbin. What fun it all was, if only it could last! And of course, at this particular moment, Gordon believed that it *could* last. Of the first bottle of Asti, Gordon drank three glasses, Ravelston two, Rosemary one. Gordon became aware that a girl at the table opposite was watching him. A tall elegant girl with a shell-pink skin and wonderful, almond-shaped eyes. Rich, obviously; one of the moneyed intelligentsia. She thought him interesting—was wondering who he was. Gordon found himself manufacturing special witticisms for her benefit. And he *was* being witty, there was no doubt about that. That too was money. Money greasing the wheels—wheels of thought as well as wheels of taxis.

But somehow the second bottle of Asti was not such a success as the first. To begin with there was uncomfortableness over its ordering. Gordon beckoned to the waiter.

"Have you got another bottle of this?"

The waiter beamed fatly. "Yes, sir! Mais certainement, monsieur!"

Rosemary frowned and tapped Gordon's foot under the table. "No, Gordon, *no!* You're not to."

"Not to what?"

"Order another bottle. We don't want it."

"Oh, bosh! Get us another bottle, waiter."

"Yes, sir."

Ravelston rubbed his nose. With eyes too guilty to meet Gordon's he looked at his wine glass. "Look here, Gordon. Let *me* stand this bottle. I'd like to."

"Bosh!" repeated Gordon.

"Get half a bottle, then," said Rosemary.

"A whole bottle, waiter," said Gordon.

After that nothing was the same. They still talked, laughed, argued, but things were not the same. The elegant girl at the table opposite had ceased watching Gordon. Somehow, Gordon wasn't being witty any longer. It is almost always a mistake to order a second bottle. It is like bathing for a second time on a summer day. However warm the day is, however much you have enjoyed your first bathe, you are always sorry for it if you go in a second time. The magic had departed from the wine. It seemed to foam and sparkle less, it was merely a clogging sourish liquid which you gulped down half in disgust and half in hopes of getting drunk the quicker. Gordon was now definitely though secretly drunk. One half of him was drunk and the other half sober. He was beginning to have that peculiar blurred feeling, as though your features had swollen and your fingers grown thicker, which you have in the second stage of drunkenness. But the sober half of him was still in command to outward appearance, anyway. The conversation grew more and more tedious. Gordon and Ravelston talked in the detached uncomfortable manner of people who have had a little scene and are not going to admit it. They talked about Shakespeare. The conversation tailed off into a long discussion about the meaning of Hamlet. It was very dull. Rosemary stifled a yawn. While Gordon's sober half talked, his drunken half stood aside and listened. Drunken half was very angry. They'd spoiled his evening, damn them! with their arguing about that second bottle. All he wanted now was to be properly drunk and have done with it. Of the six glasses in the second bottle he drank four—for Rosemary refused more wine. But you couldn't do much on this weak stuff. Drunken half clamoured for more drink, and more, and more. Beer by the quart and the bucket! A real good rousing drunk! And by God! he was going to have it later on. He thought of the five pound note stowed away in his inner pocket. He still had that to blue, anyway.

The musical clock that was concealed somewhere in Modigliani's interior struck ten.

"Shall we shove off?" said Gordon.

Ravelston's eyes looked pleadingly, guiltily across the table. Let me share the bill! his eyes said. Gordon ignored him.

"I vote we go to the Café Imperial," he said.

The bill failed to sober him. A little over two quid for the dinner, thirty bob for the wine. He did not let the others see the bill, of course, but they saw him paying. He threw four pound notes on to the waiter's salver and said casually, "Keep the change." That left him with about ten bob besides the fiver. Ravelston was helping Rosemary on with her coat; as she saw Gordon throw the notes to the waiter her lips parted in dismay. She had had no idea that the dinner was going to cost anything like four pounds. It horrified her to see him throwing money about like that. Ravelston looked gloomy and disapproving. Gordon damned their eyes again. Why did they have to keep on worrying? He could afford it, couldn't he? He still had that fiver. But by God, it wouldn't be his fault if he got home with a penny left!

But outwardly he was quite sober, and much more subdued than he had been half an hour ago. "We'd better have a taxi to the Café Imperial," he said.

"Oh, let's walk!" said Rosemary. "It's only a step."

"No, we'll have a taxi."

They got into the taxi and were driven away, Gordon sitting next to Rosemary. He had half a mind to put his arm round her, in spite of Ravelston's presence. But at that moment a swirl of cold night air came in at the window and blew against Gordon's forehead. It gave him a shock. It was like one of those moments in the night when suddenly from deep sleep you are broad awake and full of some dreadful realisation—as that you are doomed to die, for instance, or that your life is a failure. For perhaps a minute he was cold sober. He knew all about himself and the awful folly he was committing—knew that he had squandered five pounds on utter foolishness and was now going to squander the other five that belonged to Julia. He had a fleeting but terribly vivid vision of Julia, with her thin face and her greying hair, in the cold of her dismal bed-sitting room. Poor, good Julia! Julia who had been sacrificed to him all her life, from whom he had borrowed pound after pound after pound; and now he hadn't even the decency to keep her fiver intact! He recoiled from the thought; he fled back into his drunkenness as into a refuge.

163

Quick, quick, we're getting sober! Booze, more booze! Recapture that first fine careless rapture! Outside, the multi-coloured window of an Italian grocery, still open, swam towards them. He tapped sharply on the glass. The taxi drew up. Gordon began to climb out across Rosemary's knees.

"Where are you going, Gordon?"

"To recapture that first fine careless rapture," said Gordon, on the pavement.

"What?"

"It's time we laid in some more booze. The pubs'll be shutting in half an hour."

"No, Gordon, no! You're not to get anything more to drink. You've had quite enough already."

"Wait!"

He came out of the shop nursing a litre bottle of Chianti. The grocer had taken the cork out for him and put it in loosely again. The others had grasped now that he was drunk —that he must have been drinking before he met them. It made them both embarrassed. They went into the Café Imperial, but the chief thought in both their minds was to get Gordon away and to bed as quickly as possible. Rosemary whispered behind Gordon's back, *"Please* don't let him drink any more!" Ravelston nodded gloomily. Gordon was marching ahead of them to a vacant table, not in the least troubled by the stares everyone was casting at the wine-bottle which he carried on his arm. They sat down and ordered coffee, and with some difficulty Ravelston restrained Gordon from ordering brandy as well. All of them were ill at ease. It was horrible in the great garish café, stuffily hot and deafeningly noisy with the jabber of several hundred voices, the clatter of plates and glasses and the intermittent squalling of the band. All three of them wanted to get away. Ravelston was still worrying about the expense, Rosemary was worried because Gordon was drunk, Gordon was restless and thirsty. He had wanted to come here, but he was no sooner here than he wanted to escape. Drunken half was clamouring for a bit of fun. And drunken half wasn't going to be kept in check much longer. Beer, beer! cried drunken half. Gordon hated this stuffy place. He had visions of a pub taproom with great oozy barrels and quart pots topped with foam. He kept an eye on the clock. It was nearly half past ten and the pubs even in Westminster would shut at eleven. Mustn't miss his beer! The bottle of wine was for afterwards, when the pubs were shut. Rosemary was sitting opposite him, talking to Ravelston, uncomfortably but with a sufficient pretence that she was enjoying herself and there was nothing the matter. They were still talking in a rather futile way about Shakespeare. Gordon hated Shakespeare. As he watched Rosemary talking there came over him a violent, perverse desire for her. She was leaning forward, her elbows on the table; he could see her small breasts clearly through her dress. It came to him with a kind of shock, a catch of the breath, which once again almost sobered him, that he had seen her naked. She was his girl! He could have her whenever he wanted her! And by God, he was going to have her to-night! Why not? It was a fitting end to the evening. They would find a place easily enough; there are plenty of hotels round Shaftesbury Avenue where they don't ask questions if you can pay the bill. He still had his fiver. He felt for her foot under the table, meaning to imprint a delicate caress upon it, and only succeeded in treading on her toe. She drew her foot away from him.

"Let's get out of this," he said abruptly, and at once stood up.

"Oh, let's!" said Rosemary with relief.

They were in Regent Street again. Down on the left Piccadilly Circus blazed, a horrible pool of light. Rosemary's eyes turned towards the bus stop opposite.

"It's half past ten," she said doubtfully. "I've got to be back by eleven."

"Oh, rot! Let's look for a decent pub. I mustn't miss my beer."

"Oh, no, Gordon! No more pubs to-night. I couldn't drink any more. Nor ought you."

"It doesn't matter. Come this way."

He took her by the arm and began to lead her down towards the bottom of Regent Street, holding her rather tight

165

as though afraid she would escape. For the moment he had forgotten about Ravelston. Ravelston followed, wondering whether he ought to leave them to themselves or whether he ought to stay and keep an eye on Gordon. Rosemary hung back, not liking the way Gordon was pulling at her arm.

"Where are you taking me, Gordon?"

"Round the corner, where it's dark. I want to kiss you."

"I don't think I want to be kissed."

"Of course you do."

"No!"

"Yes!"

She let him take her. Ravelston waited on the corner by the Regent Palace, uncertain what to do. Gordon and Rosemary disappeared round the corner and were almost immediately in darker, narrower streets. The appalling faces of tarts, like skulls coated with pink powder, peered meaningly from several doorways. Rosemary shrank from them. Gordon was rather amused.

"They think you're one of them," he explained to her.

He stood his bottle on the pavement, carefully, against the wall, then suddenly seized her and twisted her backwards. He wanted her badly, and he did not want to waste time over preliminaries. He began to kiss her face all over, clumsily but very hard. She let him do it for a moment, but it frightened her; his face, so close to hers, looked pale, strange and distracted. He smelt very strongly of wine. She struggled, turning her face away so that he was only kissing her hair and neck.

"Gordon, you mustn't!"

"Why mustn't I?"

"What are you doing?"

"What do you suppose I'm doing?"

He shoved her back against the wall, and with the careful, preoccupied movements of a drunken man, tried to undo the front of her dress. It was of a kind that did not undo, as it happened. This time she was angry. She struggled violently, fending his hand aside.

"Gordon, stop that at once!"

166

"Why?"

"If you do it again I'll smack your face."

"Smack my face! Don't you come the Girl Guide with me."

"Let me go, will you!"

"Think of last Sunday," he said lewdly.

"Gordon, if you go on I'll hit you, honestly I will."

"Not you."

He thrust his hand right into the front of her dress. The movement was curiously brutal, as though she had been a stranger to him. She grasped that from the expression of his face. She was not Rosemary to him any longer, she was just a girl, a girl's body. That was the thing that upset her. She struggled and managed to free herself from him. He came after her again and clutched her arm. She smacked his face as hard as she could and dodged neatly out of his reach.

"What did you do that for?" he said, feeling his cheek but not hurt by the blow.

"I'm not going to stand that sort of thing. I'm going home. You'll be different to-morrow."

"Rot! You come along with me. You're going to bed with me."

"Good night!" she said, and fled up the dark side street.

For a moment he thought of following her, but found his legs too heavy. It did not seem worth while, anyway. He wandered back to where Ravelston was still waiting, looking moody and alone, partly because he was worried about Gordon and partly because he was trying not to notice two hopeful tarts who were on patrol just behind him. Gordon looked properly drunk, Ravelston thought. His hair was tumbling over his forehead, one side of his face was very pale and on the other there was a red smudge where Rosemary had slapped him. Ravelston thought this must be the flush of drunkenness.

"What have you done with Rosemary?" he said.

"She's gone," said Gordon, with a wave of his hand which was meant to explain everything. "But the night's still young."

"Look here, Gordon, it's time you were in bed."

"In bed, yes. But not alone."

He stood on the kerb gazing out into the hideous midnight-noon. For a moment he felt quite deathly. His face was burning. His whole body had a dreadful, swollen, fiery feeling. His head in particular seemed on the point of bursting. Somehow the baleful light was bound up with his sensations. He watched the sky-signs flicking on and off, glaring red and blue, arrowing up and down—the awful, sinister glitter of a doomed civilisation, like the still blazing lights of a sinking ship. He caught Ravelston's arm and made a gesture that comprehended the whole of Piccadilly Circus.

"The lights down in hell will look just like that."

"I shouldn't wonder."

Ravelston was looking out for a disengaged taxi. He must get Gordon home and to bed without further delay. Gordon wondered whether he was in joy or in agony. That burning, bursting feeling was dreadful. The sober half of him was not dead yet. Sober half still knew with ice-cold clarity what he had done and what he was doing. He had committed follies for which to-morrow he would feel like killing himself. He had squandered five pounds in senseless extravagance, he had robbed Julia, he had insulted Rosemary. And to-morrow— oh, to-morrow, we'll be sober! Go home, go home! cried sober half. —— to you! said drunken half contemptuously. Drunken half was still clamouring for a bit of fun. And drunken half was the stronger. A fiery clock somewhere opposite caught his eye. Twenty to eleven. Quick, before the pubs are shut! Haro! la gorge m'ard! Once again his thoughts moved lyrically. He felt a hard round shape under his arm, discovered that it was the Chianti bottle, and tweaked out the cork. Ravelston was waving to a taxi driver without managing to catch his eye. He heard a shocked squeal from the tarts behind. Turning, he saw with horror that Gordon had up-ended the bottle and was drinking from it.

"Hi! Gordon!"

He sprang towards him and forced his arm down. A gout of wine went down Gordon's collar.

"For God's sake be careful! You don't want the police to get hold of you, do you?"

"I want a drink," complained Gordon.

"But dash it! You can't start drinking here."

"Take me to a pub," said Gordon.

Ravelston rubbed his nose helplessly. "Oh, God! I suppose that's better than drinking on the pavement. Come on, we'll go to a pub. You shall have your drink there."

Gordon recorked his bottle carefully. Ravelston shepherded him across the circus, Gordon clinging to his arm, but not for support, for his legs were still quite steady. They halted on the island, then managed to find a gap in the traffic and went down the Haymarket.

In the pub the air seemed wet with beer. It was all a mist of beer shot through with the sickly tang of whisky. Along the bar a press of men seethed, downing with Faustlike eagerness their last drinks before eleven should sound its knell. Gordon slid easily through the crowd. He was not in a mood to worry about a few jostlings and elbowings. In a moment he had fetched up at the bar between a stout commercial traveller drinking Guinness and a tall, lean, decayed-major type of man with droopy moustaches, whose entire conversation seemed to consist of "What ho!" and "What, what!" Gordon threw half a crown on to the beer-wet bar.

"A quart of bitter, please!"

"No quart pots here!" cried the harassed barmaid, measuring pegs of whisky with one eye on the clock.

"Quart pots on the top shelf, Effie!" shouted the landlord over his shoulder, from the other side of the bar.

The barmaid hauled the beer-handle three times hurriedly. The monstrous glass pot was set before him. He lifted it. What a weight! A pint of pure water weighs a pound and a quarter. Down with it! Swish—gurgle! A long, long sup of beer flowed gratefully down his gullet. He paused for breath, and felt a little sickish. Come on, now for another. Swish—gurgle! It almost choked him this time. But stick it out, stick it out! Through the cascade of beer that poured down his throat and seemed to drown his ears he heard the landlord's shout: "Last orders, gentlemen, please!" For a moment he removed his face from the pot, gasped and got his breath back. Now for the last. Swish—gurgle! A-a-ah! Gordon set down the pot. Emptied in three gulps—not bad. He clattered it on the bar.

"Hi! Give me the other half of that—quick!"

"What ho!" said the major.

"Coming it a bit, aren't you?" said the commercial traveller.

Ravelston, further down the bar and hemmed in by several men, saw what Gordon was doing. He called to him, "Hi, Gordon!", frowned and shook his head, too shy to say in front of everybody, "Don't drink any more." Gordon settled himself on his legs. He was still steady, but consciously steady. His head seemed to have swollen to an immense size, his whole body had the same horrible, swollen, fiery feeling as before. Languidly he lifted the refilled beer-pot. He did not want it now. Its smell nauseated him. It was just a hateful, pale yellow, sickly-tasting liquid. Like urine, almost! That bucket-ful of stuff to be forced down into his bursting guts—horrible! But come on, no flinching! What else are we here for? Down with it! Here she is so near my nose, So tip her up and down she goes. Swish—gurgle!

In the same moment something dreadful happened. His gullet had shut up of its own accord, or the beer had missed his mouth. It was pouring all over him, a tidal wave of beer. He was drowning in beer like lay-brother Peter in the *Ingoldsby Legends*. Help! He tried to shout, choked, and let fall the beer-pot. There was a flurry all round him. People were leaping aside to avoid the jet of beer. Crash! went the pot. Gordon stood rocking. Men, bottles, mirrors were going round and round. He was falling, losing consciousness. But dimly visible before him was a black upright shape, sole point of stability in a reeling world—the beer-handle. He clutched it, swung, held tight. Ravelston started towards him.

The barmaid leaned indignantly over the bar. The round-about world slowed down and stopped. Gordon's brain was quite clear.

"Here! What are you hanging on to the beer-handle for?"

"All over my bloody trousers!" cried the commercial traveller.

"What am I hanging on to the beer-handle for?"

"*Yes!* What are you hanging on to the beer-handle for?"

Gordon swung himself sideways. The elongated face of the major peered down at him, with wet moustaches drooping.

"She says, 'What am I hanging on to the beer-handle for?' "

"What ho! What?"

Ravelston had forced his way between several men and reached him. He put a strong arm round Gordon's waist and hoisted him to his feet.

"Stand up, for God's sake! You're drunk."

"Drunk?" said Gordon.

Everyone was laughing at them. Ravelston's pale face flushed.

"Two and three those mugs cost," said the barmaid bitterly.

"And what about my bloody trousers?" said the commercial traveller.

"I'll pay for the mug," said Ravelston. He did so. "Now come on out of it. You're drunk."

He began to shepherd Gordon towards the door, one arm round his shoulder, the other holding the Chianti bottle, which he had taken from him earlier. Gordon freed himself. He could walk with perfect steadiness. He said in a dignified manner:

"Drunk did you say I was?"

Ravelston took his arm again. "Yes, I'm afraid you are. Decidedly."

"Swan swam across the sea, well swam swan," said Gordon.

"Gordon, you *are* drunk. The sooner you're in bed the better."

"First cast out the beam that is in thine own eye before thou castest out the mote that is in thy brother's," said Gordon.

Ravelston had got him out on to the pavement by this time. "We'd better get hold of a taxi," he said, looking up and down the street.

There seemed to be no taxis about, however. The people were streaming noisily out of the pub, which was on the point of closing. Gordon felt better in the open air. His brain had never been clearer. The red satanic gleam of a Neon light, somewhere in the distance, put a new and brilliant idea into his head. He plucked at Ravelston's arm.

"Ravelston! I say, Ravelston!"

"What?"

"Let's pick up a couple of tarts."

In spite of Gordon's drunken state, Ravelston was scandalised. "My dear old chap! You can't do that kind of thing."

"Don't be so damned upper-class. Why not?"

"But how could you, dash it! After you've just said good night to Rosemary—a really charming girl like that!"

"At night all cats are grey," said Gordon, with the feeling that he voiced a profound and cynical wisdom.

Ravelston decided to ignore this remark. "We'd better walk up to Piccadilly Circus," he said. "There'll be plenty of taxis there."

The theatres were emptying. Crowds of people and streams of cars flowed to and fro in the frightful corpse-light. Gordon's brain was marvellously clear. He knew what folly and evil he had committed and was about to commit. And yet after all it hardly seemed to matter. He saw as something far, far away, like something seen through the wrong end of the telescope, his thirty years, his wasted life, the blank future, Julia's five pounds, Rosemary. He said with a sort of philosophic interest:

"Look at the Neon lights! Look at those awful blue ones over the rubber shop. When I see those lights I know that I'm a damned soul."

"Quite," said Ravelston, who was not listening. "Ah, there's a taxi!" He signalled. "Damn! He didn't see me. Wait here a second."

He left Gordon by the tube station and hurried across the street. For a little while Gordon's mind receded into blankness. Then he was aware of two hard yet youthful faces, like the faces of young predatory animals, that had come close up to his own. They had blackened eyebrows and hats that were like vulgarer versions of Rosemary's. He was exchanging badinage with them. This seemed to him to have been going on for several minutes.

"Hullo, Dora! Hullo, Barbara! (He knew their names, it seemed.) And how are you? And how's old England's winding-sheet?"

"Oo—haven't you got a cheek, just!"

"And what are you up to at this time of night?"

"Oo—jes' strolling around."

"Like a lion, seeking whom he may devour?"

"Oo—you haven't half got a cheek! Hasn't he got a cheek, Barbara? You *have* got a cheek!"

Ravelston had caught the taxi and brought it round to where Gordon was standing. He stepped out, saw Gordon between the two girls, and stood aghast.

"Gordon! Oh, my God! What the devil have you been doing?"

"Let me introduce you. Dora and Barbara," said Gordon.

For a moment Ravelston looked almost angry. As a matter of fact, Ravelston was incapable of being properly angry. Upset, pained, embarrassed—yes; but not angry. He stepped forward with a miserable effort not to notice the two girls' existence. Once he noticed them the game was up. He took Gordon by the arm and would have bundled him into the taxi.

"Come on, Gordon, for God's sake! Here's the taxi. We'll go straight home and put you to bed."

Dora caught Gordon's other arm and hauled him out of reach as though he had been a stolen handbag.

"What bloody business is it of yours?" she cried ferociously.

"You don't want to insult these two ladies, I hope?" said Gordon.

Ravelston faltered, stepped back, rubbed his nose. It was a moment to be firm; but Ravelston had never in his life been firm. He looked from Dora to Gordon, from Gordon to Barbara. That was fatal. Once he had looked them in the face he was lost. Oh, God! What could he do? They were human beings—he couldn't insult them. The same instinct that sent his hand into his pocket at the very sight of a beggar made him helpless at this moment. The poor, wretched girls! He hadn't the heart to send them packing into the night. Suddenly he realised that he would have to go through with this abominable adventure into which Gordon had led him. For the first time in his life he was let in for going home with a tart.

"But dash it all!" he said feebly.

"Allons-y," said Gordon.

The taximan had taken his direction at a nod from Dora. Gordon slumped into the corner seat and seemed immediately to sink into some immense abyss from which he rose again more gradually and with only partial consciousness of what he had been doing. He was gliding smoothly through darkness starred with lights. Or were the lights moving and he stationary? It was like being on the ocean bottom, among the luminous, gliding fishes. The fancy returned to him that he was a damned soul in hell. The landscape in hell would be just like this. Ravines of cold evil-coloured fire, with darkness all above. But in hell there would be torment. Was this torment? He strove to classify his sensations. The momentary lapse into unconsciousness had left him weak, sick, shaken; his forehead seemed to be splitting. He put out a hand. It encountered a knee, a garter and a small soft hand which sought mechanically for his. He became aware that Ravelston, sitting opposite, was tapping his toe urgently and nervously.

"Gordon! Gordon! Wake up!"

"What?"

"Gordon! Oh, damn! Causons en français. Qu'est-ce que tu as fait? Crois-tu que je veux coucher avec une sale—oh, damnation!"

"Oo—parley-voo francey!" squealed the girls.

Gordon was mildly amused. Do Ravelston good, he thought. A parlour Socialist going home with a tart! The first genuinely proletarian action of his life. As though aware of this thought, Ravelston subsided into his corner in silent misery, sitting as far away from Barbara as possible. The taxi drew up at a hotel in a side-street; a dreadful, shoddy, low place it was. The "hotel" sign over the door looked skew-eyed. The windows were almost dark, but the sound of singing, boozy and dreary, trickled from within. Gordon staggered out of the taxi and felt for Dora's arm. Give us a hand, Dora. Mind the step. What ho!

A smallish, darkish, smelly hallway, lino-carpeted, mean, uncared-for and somehow impermanent. From a room somewhere on the left the singing swelled, mournful as a church organ. A cross-eyed, evil-looking chambermaid appeared from nowhere. She and Dora seemed to know one another. What a mug! No competition there. From the room on the left a single voice took up the song with would-be facetious emphasis:

> "The man that kisses a pretty girl
> And goes and tells his mother,
> Ought to have his lips cut off,
> Ought to——"

It tailed away, full of the ineffable, undisguisable sadness of debauchery. A very young voice it sounded. The voice of some poor boy who in his heart only wanted to be at home with his mother and sisters, playing hunt-the-slipper. There was a party of young fools in there, on the razzle with whisky and girls. The tune reminded Gordon. He turned to Ravelston as he came in, Barbara following.

"Where's my Chianti?" he said.

Ravelston gave him the bottle. His face looked pale, harassed, hunted, almost. With guilty restless movements he kept himself apart from Barbara. He could not touch her or even look at her, and yet to escape was beyond him. His eyes sought Gordon's. "For the love of God can't we get out of it somehow?" they signalled. Gordon frowned at him. Stick it out! No flinching! He took Dora's arm again. Come on, Dora! Now for those stairs. Ah! Wait a moment.

Her arm round his waist, supporting him, Dora drew him aside. Down the darkish, smelly stairs a young woman came mincingly, buttoning on a glove; after her a bald, middle-aged man in evening clothes, black overcoat and white silk muffler, his opera hat in his hand. He walked past them with small mean mouth tightened, pretending not to see them. A family man, by the guilty look in his eye. Gordon watched the gaslight gleam on the back of his bald head. His predecessor. In the same bed, probably. The mantle of Elisha. Now then,

Dora, up we go! Ah, these stairs! Difficilis ascensus Averni. That's right, here we are! "Mind the step," said Dora. They were on the landing. Black and white lino like a chessboard. White-painted doors. A smell of slops and a fainter smell of stale linen.

We this way, you that. At the other door Ravelston halted, his fingers on the handle. He could not—no, he *could* not do it. He could not enter that dreadful room. For the last time his eyes, like those of a dog about to be whipped, turned upon Gordon. "Must I, must I?" his eyes said. Gordon eyed him sternly. Stick it out, Regulus! March to your doom! Atqui sciebat quae sibi Barbara. It is a far, far more proletarian thing that you do. And then with startling suddenness Ravelston's face cleared. An expression of relief, almost of joy, stole over it. A wonderful thought had occurred to him. After all, you could always pay the girl without actually doing anything! Thank God! He set his shoulders, plucked up courage, went in. The door shut.

So here we are. A mean, dreadful room. Lino on the floor, gas-fire, huge double bed with sheets vaguely dingy. Over the bed, a framed coloured picture from *La Vie Parisienne*. A mistake, that. Sometimes the originals don't compare so well. And, by Jove! on the bamboo table by the window, positively an aspidistra! Hast thou found me, O mine enemy? But come here, Dora. Let's have a look at you.

He seemed to be lying on the bed. He could not see very well. Her youthful, rapacious face, with blackened eyebrows, leaned over him as he sprawled there.

"How about my present?" she demanded, half wheedling, half menacing.

Never mind that now. To work! Come here. Not a bad mouth. Come here. Come closer. Ah!

No. No use. Impossible. The will but not the way. The spirit is willing but the flesh is weak. Try again. No. The booze, it must be. See Macbeth. One last try. No, no use. Not this evening, I'm afraid.

All right, Dora, don't you worry. You'll get your two quid all right. We aren't paying by results.

176

He made a clumsy gesture. "Here, give us that bottle. That bottle off the dressing-table."

Dora brought it. Ah, that's better. That at least doesn't fail. With hands that had swollen to monstrous size he up-ended the Chianti bottle. The wine flowed down his throat, bitter and choking, and some of it went up his nose. It overwhelmed him. He was slipping, sliding, falling off the bed. His head met the floor. His legs were still on the bed. For a while he lay in this position. Is this the way to live? Down below the youthful voices were still mournfully singing:

> *"For to-night we'll merry be,*
> *For to-night we'll merry be,*
> *For to-night we'll merry be-e-e—*
> *To-morrow we'll be so-ober!"*

Chapter Nine

AND, BY Jove, to-morrow we *were* sober!

Gordon emerged from some long, sickly dream to the consciousness that the books in the lending library were the wrong way up. They were all lying on their sides. Moreover, for some reason their backs had turned white—white and shiny, like porcelain.

He opened his eyes a little wider and moved an arm. Small rivulets of pain, seemingly touched off by the movement, shot through his body at unexpected places—down the calves of his legs, for instance, and up both sides of his head. He perceived that he was lying on his side, with a hard smooth pillow under his cheek and a coarse blanket scratching his chin and pushing its hairs into his mouth. Apart from the minor pains that stabbed him every time he moved, there was a large, dull sort of pain which was not localised but which seemed to hover all over him.

Suddenly he flung off the blanket and sat up. He was in a police cell. At this moment a frightful spasm of nausea overcame him. Dimly perceiving a w.c. in the corner, he crept towards it and was violently sick, three or four times.

After that, for several minutes, he was in agonising pain. He could scarcely stand on his feet, his head throbbed as though it were going to burst, and the light seemed like some scalding white liquid pouring into his brain through the sockets of his eyes. He sat on the bed holding his head between his hands. Presently, when some of the throbbing had died down, he had another look about him. The cell measured about twelve feet long by six wide and was very high.

The walls were all of white porcelain bricks, horribly white and clean. He wondered dully how they cleaned as high up as the ceiling. Perhaps with a hose, he reflected. At one end there was a little barred window, very high up, and at the other end, over the door, an electric bulb let into the wall and protected by a stout grating. The thing he was sitting on was not actually a bed, but a shelf with one blanket and a canvas pillow. The door was of steel, painted green. In the door there was a little round hole with a flap on the outside.

Having seen this much he lay down and pulled the blanket over him again. He had no further curiosity about his surroundings. As to what had happened last night, he remembered everything—at least, he remembered everything up to the time when he had gone with Dora into the room with the aspidistra. God knew what had happened after that. There had been some kind of bust-up and he had landed in the clink. He had no notion of what he had done; it might be murder for all he knew. In any case he did not care. He turned his face to the wall and pulled the blanket over his head to shut out the light.

After a long time the spyhole in the door was pushed aside. Gordon managed to turn his head round. His neck-muscles seemed to creak. Through the spyhole he could see a blue eye and a semi-circle of pink chubby cheek.

" 'Ja do with a cup of tea?" a voice said.

Gordon sat up and instantly felt very sick again. He took his head between his hands and groaned. The thought of a cup of hot tea appealed to him, but he knew it would make him sick if it had sugar in it.

"Please," he said.

The police constable opened a partition in the top half of the door and passed in a thick white mug of tea. It had sugar in it. The constable was a solid rosy young man of about twenty-five, with a kind face, white eyelashes and a tremendous chest. It reminded Gordon of the chest of a carthorse. He spoke with a good accent but with vulgar turns of speech. For a minute or so he stood regarding Gordon.

"You weren't half bad last night," he said finally.

"I'm bad now."

"You was worse last night, though. What you go and hit the sergeant for?"

"Did I hit the sergeant?"

"Did you? Cool He wasn't half wild. He turns to me and he says—holding his ear he was, like this—he says, 'Now, if that man wasn't too drunk to stand, I'd knock his block off.' It's all gone down on your charge sheet. Drunk and disorderly. You'd only ha' bin drunk and incapable if you hadn't of hit the sergeant."

"Do you know what I shall get for this?"

"Five quid or fourteen days. You'll go up before Mr. Croom. Lucky for you it wasn't Mr. Walker. He'd give you a month without the option, Mr. Walker would. Very severe on the drunks he is. Teetotaller."

Gordon had drunk some of the tea. It was nauseatingly sweet but its warmth made him feel stronger. He gulped it down. At this moment a nasty, snarling sort of voice—the sergeant whom Gordon had hit, no doubt—yelped from somewhere outside:

"Take that man out and get him washed. Black Maria leaves at half past nine."

The constable hastened to open the cell door. As soon as Gordon stepped outside he felt worse than ever. This was partly because it was much colder in the passage than in the cell. He walked a step or two, and then suddenly his head was going round and round. "I'm going to be sick!" he cried. He was falling—he flung out a hand and stopped himself against the wall. The constable's strong arm went round him. Across the arm, as over a rail, Gordon sagged, doubled up and limp. A jet of vomit burst from him. It was the tea, of course. There was a gutter running along the stone floor. At the end of the passage the moustachio'd sergeant, in tunic without a belt, stood with his hand on his hip, looking on disgustedly.

"Dirty little tyke," he muttered, and turned away.

"Come on, old chap," said the constable. "You'll be better in half a mo'."

He half led, half dragged Gordon to a big stone sink at the

180

end of the passage and helped him to strip to the waist. His gentleness was astonishing. He handled Gordon almost like a nurse handling a child. Gordon had recovered enough strength to sluice himself with the ice-cold water and rinse his mouth out. The constable gave him a torn towel to dry himself with and then led him back to the cell.

"Now you sit quiet till the Black Maria comes. And take my tip—when you go up to the court, you plead guilty and say you won't do it again. Mr. Croom won't be hard on you."

"Where are my collar and tie?" said Gordon.

"We took 'em away last night. You'll get 'em back before you go up to court. We had a bloke hung himself with his tie, once."

Gordon sat down on the bed. For a little while he occupied himself by calculating the number of porcelain bricks in the walls, then sat with his elbows on his knees, his head between his hands. He was still aching all over; he felt weak, cold, jaded and, above all, bored. He wished that boring business of going up to the court could be avoided somehow. The thought of being put into some jolting vehicle and taken across London to hang about in chilly cells and passages, and of having to answer questions and be lectured by magistrates, bored him indescribably. All he wanted was to be left alone. But presently there was the sound of several voices further down the passage, and then of feet approaching. The partition in the door was opened.

"Couple of visitors for you," the constable said.

Gordon was bored by the very thought of visitors. Unwillingly he looked up, and saw Flaxman and Ravelston looking in upon him. How they had got there together was a mystery, but Gordon felt not the faintest curiosity about it. They bored him. He wished they would go away.

"Hullo, chappie!" said Flaxman.

"*You* here?" said Gordon with a sort of weary offensiveness.

Ravelston looked miserable. He had been up since the very early morning, looking for Gordon. This was the first time he had seen the interior of a police cell. His face shrank with disgust as he looked at the chilly white-tiled place with its shameless w.c. in the corner. But Flaxman was more accustomed to this kind of thing. He cocked a practised eye at Gordon.

"I've seen 'em worse," he said cheerfully. "Give him a prairie oyster and he'd buck up something wonderful. D'you know what your eyes look like, chappie?" he added to Gordon. "They look as if they'd been taken out and poached."

"I was drunk last night," said Gordon, his head between his hands.

"I gathered something of the kind, old chappie."

"Look here, Gordon," said Ravelston, "we came to bail you out, but it seems we're too late. They're taking you up to court in a few minutes' time. This is a bloody show. It's a pity you didn't give them a false name when they brought you here last night."

"Did I tell them my name?"

"You told them everything. I wish to God I hadn't let you out of my sight. You slipped out of that house somehow and into the street."

"Wandering up and down Shaftesbury Avenue, drinking out of a bottle," said Flaxman appreciatively. "But you oughn't to have hit the sergeant, old chappie! That was a bit of bloody foolishness. And I don't mind telling you Mother Wisbeach is on your track. When your pal here came round this morning and told her you'd been for a night on the tiles, she took on as if you'd done a bloody murder."

"And look here, Gordon," said Ravelston.

There was the familiar note of discomfort in his face. It was something about money, as usual. Gordon looked up. Ravelston was gazing into the distance.

"Look here."

"What?"

"About your fine. You'd better leave that to me. I'll pay it."

"No, you won't."

"My dear old chap! They'll send you to jail if I don't."

"Oh, hell! I don't care."

He did not care. At this moment he did not care if they sent him to prison for a year. Of course he couldn't pay his fine himself. He knew without even needing to look that he had no money left. He would have given it all to Dora, or more probably she would have pinched it. He lay down on the bed again and turned his back on the others. In the sulky, sluggish state that he was in, his sole desire was to get rid of them. They made a few more attempts to talk to him, but he would not answer, and presently they went away. Flaxman's voice boomed cheerfully down the passage. He was giving Ravelston minute instructions as to how to make a prairie oyster.

The rest of that day was very beastly. Beastly was the ride in the Black Maria, which, inside, was like nothing so much as a miniature public lavatory, with tiny cubicles down each side, into which you were locked and in which you had barely room to sit down. Beastlier yet was the long wait in one of the cells adjoining the magistrate's court. This cell was an exact replica of the cell at the police station, even to having precisely the same number of porcelain bricks. But it differed from the police station cell in being repulsively dirty. It was cold, but the air was so fetid as to be almost unbreathable. Prisoners were coming and going all the time. They would be thrust into the cell, taken out after an hour or two to go up to the court, and then perhaps brought back again to wait while the magistrate decided upon their sentence or fresh witnesses were sent for. There were always five or six men in the cell, and there was nothing to sit on except the plank bed. And the worst was that nearly all of them used the w.c.—there, publicly, in the tiny cell. They could not help it. There was nowhere else to go. And the plug of the beastly thing did not even pull properly.

Until the afternoon Gordon felt sick and weak. He had had no chance to shave, and his face was hatefully scrubby. At first he merely sat on the corner of the plank bed, at the end nearest the door, as far away from the w.c. as he could get, and took no notice of the other prisoners. They bored and disgusted him; later, as his headache wore off, he observed them with a faint interest. There was a professional burglar, a lean worried-looking man with grey hair, who was in a terrible stew about what would happen to his wife and kids if he were sent to jail. He had been arrested for "loitering with intent to enter"—a vague offence for which you generally get convicted if there are previous convictions against you. He kept walking up and down, flicking the fingers of his right hand with a curious nervous gesture, and exclaiming against the unfairness of it. There was also a deaf mute who stank like a ferret, and a small middle-aged Jew with a fur-collared overcoat, who had been buyer to a large firm of kosher butchers. He had bolted with twenty-seven pounds, gone to Aberdeen, of all places, and spent the money on tarts. He too had a grievance, for he said his case ought to have been tried in the rabbi's court instead of being turned over to the police. There was also a publican who had embezzled his Christmas club money. He was a big, hearty, prosperous-looking man of about thirty-five, with a loud red face and a loud blue overcoat—the sort of man who, if he were not a publican, would be a bookie. His relatives had paid back the embezzled money, all except twelve pounds, but the club members had decided to prosecute. There was something in this man's eyes that troubled Gordon. He carried everything off with a swagger, but all the while there was that blank, staring look in his eyes; he would fall into a kind of reverie at every gap in the conversation. It was somehow rather dreadful to see him. There he was, still in his smart clothes, with the splendour of a publican's life only a month or two behind him; and now he was ruined, probably for ever. Like all London publicans he was in the claw of the brewer, he would be sold up and his furniture and fittings seized, and when he came out of jail he would never have a pub or a job again.

The morning wore on with dismal slowness. You were allowed to smoke—matches were forbidden, but the constable on duty outside would give you a light through the trap in the door. Nobody had any cigarettes except the publican, who had his pockets full of them and distributed them freely. Prisoners came and went. A ragged dirty man who claimed to be a coster "up" for obstruction was put into the cell for half an hour. He talked a great deal, but the others were deeply suspicious of him; when he was taken out again they all de-

184

clared he was a "split." The police, it was said, often put a "split" into the cells, disguised as a prisoner, to pick up information. Once there was great excitement when the constable whispered through the trap that a murderer, or would-be murderer, was being put into the cell next door. He was a youth of eighteen who had stabbed his "tart" in the belly, and she was not expected to live. Once the trap opened and the tired, pale face of a clergyman looked in. He saw the burglar, said wearily, "*You* here again, Jones?" and went away again. Dinner, so-called, was served out at about twelve o'clock. All you got was a cup of tea and two slices of bread-and-marg. You could have food sent in, though, if you could pay for it. The publican had a good dinner sent in in covered dishes; but he had no appetite for it, and gave most of it away. Ravelston was still hanging about the court, waiting for Gordon's case to come on, but he did not know the ropes well enough to have food sent in to Gordon. Presently the burglar and the publican were taken away, sentenced, and brought back to wait till the Black Maria should take them off to jail. They each got nine months. The publican questioned the burglar about what prison was like. There was a conversation of unspeakable obscenity about the lack of women there.

Gordon's case came on at half past two, and it was over so quickly that it seemed preposterous to have waited all that time for it. Afterwards he could remember nothing about the court except the coat-of-arms over the magistrate's chair. The magistrate was dealing with the drunks at the rate of two a minute. To the tune of "John-Smith-drunk-and-incapable-drunk?-yes-six-shillings-move-on-*next!*" they filed past the railings of the dock, precisely like a crowd taking tickets at a booking-office. Gordon's case, however, took two minutes instead of thirty seconds, because he had been disorderly and the sergeant had to testify that Gordon had struck him on the ear and called him a —— bastard. There was also a mild sensation in the court because Gordon, when questioned at the police station, had described himself as a poet. He must have been very drunk to say a thing like that. The magistrate looked at him suspiciously.

"I see you call yourself a *poet. Are* you a poet?"

"I write poetry," said Gordon sulkily.

"Hm! Well, it doesn't seem to teach you to behave yourself, does it? You will pay five pounds or go to prison for fourteen days. *Next!*"

And that was all. Nevertheless, somewhere at the back of the court a bored reporter had pricked up his ears.

On the other side of the court there was a room where a police sergeant sat with a large ledger, entering up the drunks' fines and taking payment. Those who could not pay were taken back to the cells. Gordon had expected this to happen to himself. He was quite resigned to going to prison. But when he emerged from the court it was to find that Ravelston was waiting there and had already paid his fine for him. Gordon did not protest. He allowed Ravelston to pack him into a taxi and take him back to the flat in Regent's Park. As soon as they got there Gordon had a hot bath; he needed one, after the beastly contaminating grime of the last twelve hours. Ravelston lent him a razor, lent him a clean shirt and pyjamas and socks and underclothes, even went out of doors and bought him a toothbrush. He was strangely solicitous about Gordon. He could not rid himself of a guilty feeling that what had happened last night was mainly his own fault; he ought to have put his foot down and taken Gordon home as soon as he showed signs of being drunk. Gordon scarcely noticed what was being done for him. Even the fact that Ravelston had paid his fine failed to trouble him. For the rest of that afternoon he lay in one of the armchairs in front of the fire, reading a detective story. About the future he refused to think. He grew sleepy very early. At eight o'clock he went to bed in the spare bedroom and slept like a log for nine hours.

It was not till next morning that he began to think seriously about his situation. He woke in the wide caressing bed, softer and warmer than any bed he had ever slept in, and began to grope about for his matches. Then he remembered that in places like this you didn't need matches to get a light, and felt for the electric switch that hung on a cord at the bedhead. Soft light flooded the room. There was a syphon of soda water on the bed-table. Gordon discovered that even after thirty-six hours there was still a vile taste in his mouth. He had a drink and looked about him.

It was a queer feeling, lying there in somebody else's pyjamas in somebody else's bed. He felt that he had no business here—that this wasn't the sort of place where he belonged. There was a sense of guilt in lying here in luxury when he was ruined and hadn't a penny in the world. For he was ruined right enough, there was no doubt about that. He seemed to know with perfect certainty that his job was lost. God knew what was going to happen next. The memory of that stupid dull debauch rolled back upon him with beastly vividness. He could recall everything, from his first pink gin before he started out to Dora's peach-coloured garters. He squirmed when he thought of Dora. *Why* does one do these things? Money again, always money! The rich don't behave like that. The rich are graceful even in their vices. But if you have no money you don't even know how to spend it when you get it. You just splurge it frantically away, like a sailor in a bawdy-house his first night ashore.

He had been in the clink twelve hours. He thought of the cold fæcal stench of that cell at the police court. A foretaste of future days. And everyone would know that he had been in the clink. With luck it might be kept from Aunt Angela and Uncle Walter, but Julia and Rosemary probably knew already. With Rosemary it didn't matter so much, but Julia would be ashamed and miserable. He thought of Julia. Her long thin back as she bent over the tea-caddy; her good, goose-like, defeated face. She had never lived. From childhood she had been sacrificed to him—to Gordon, to "the boy." It might be a hundred quid he had "borrowed" from her in all these years; and then even five quid he couldn't spare her. Five quid he had set aside for her, and then spent it on a tart!

He turned out the light and lay on his back, wide awake. At this moment he saw himself with frightful clarity. He took a sort of inventory of himself and his possessions. Gordon Comstock, last of the Comstocks, thirty years old, with twenty-six teeth left; with no money and no job; in borrowed pyjamas in a borrowed bed; with nothing before him except cadging and destitution, and nothing behind him except squalid fooleries. His total wealth a puny body and two cardboard suitcases full of worn-out clothes.

At seven Ravelston was awakened by a tap on his door. He rolled over and said sleepily, "Hullo?" Gordon came in, a dishevelled figure almost lost in the borrowed silk pyjamas. Ravelston roused himself, yawning. Theoretically he got up at the proletarian hour of seven. Actually he seldom stirred until Mrs. Beaver, the charwoman, arrived at eight. Gordon pushed the hair out of his eyes and sat down on the foot of Ravelston's bed.

"I say, Ravelston, this is bloody. I've been thinking things over. There's going to be hell to pay."

"What?"

"I shall lose my job. McKechnie can't keep me on after I've been in the clink. Besides, I ought to have been at work yesterday. Probably the shop wasn't opened all day."

Ravelston yawned. "It'll be all right, I think. That fat chap—what's his name? Flaxman—rang McKechnie up and told him you were down with 'flu. He made it pretty convincing. He said your temperature was a hundred and three. Of course your landlady knows. But I don't suppose she'd tell McKechnie."

"But suppose it's got into the papers!"

"Oh, lord! I suppose that might happen. The char brings the papers up at eight. But do they report drunk cases? Surely not?"

Mrs. Beaver brought the *Telegraph* and the *Herald*. Ravelston sent her out for the *Mail* and the *Express*. They searched hurriedly through the police-court news. Thank God! it hadn't "got into the papers" after all. There was no reason why it should, as a matter of fact. It was not as if Gordon had been a racing motorist or a professional footballer. Feeling better, Gordon managed to eat some breakfast, and after breakfast Ravelston went out. It was agreed that he should go up to the shop, see Mr. McKechnie, give him further details of Gordon's illness and find out how the land lay. It seemed quite natural to Ravelston to waste several days in getting Gordon out of his scrape. All the morning Gordon hung about the flat, restless and out of sorts, smoking cigarettes in an endless chain. Now that he was alone, hope had deserted him. He knew by profound instinct that Mr. McKechnie would have heard about his arrest. It wasn't the kind of thing you could keep dark. He had lost his job, and that was all about it.

He lounged across to the window and looked out. A desolate day; the whitey-grey sky looked as if it could never be blue again; the naked trees wept slowly into the gutters. Down a neighbouring street the cry of the coal-man echoed mournfully. Only a fortnight to Christmas now. Jolly to be out of work at this time of year! But the thought, instead of frightening him, merely bored him. The peculiar lethargic feeling, the stuffy heaviness behind the eyes, that one has after a fit of drunkenness, seemed to have settled upon him permanently. The prospect of searching for another job bored him even more than the prospect of poverty. Besides, he would never find another job. There are no jobs to be had nowadays. He was going down, down into the sub-world of the unemployed —down, down into God knew what workhouse depths of dirt and hunger and futility. And chiefly he was anxious to get it over with as little fuss and effort as possible.

Ravelston came back at about one o'clock. He pulled his gloves off and threw them into a chair. He looked tired and depressed. Gordon saw at a glance that the game was up.

"He's heard, of course?" he said.

"Everything, I'm afraid."

"How? I suppose that cow of a Wisbeach woman went and sneaked to him?"

"No. It was in the paper after all. The local paper. He got it out of that."

"Oh, hell! I'd forgotten that."

Ravelston produced from his coat pocket a folded copy of a bi-weekly paper. It was one that they took in at the shop because Mr. McKechnie advertised in it—Gordon had forgotten that. He opened it. Gosh! What a splash! It was all over the middle page.

"BOOKSELLER'S ASSISTANT FINED.
MAGISTRATE'S SEVERE STRICTURE.
'DISGRACEFUL FRACAS.' "

There were nearly two columns of it. Gordon had never been so famous before and never would be again. They must have been very hard up for a bit of news. But these local papers have a curious notion of patriotism. They are so avid for local news that a bicycle-accident in the Harrow Road will occupy more space than a European crisis, and such items of news as "Hampstead Man on Murder Charge" or "Dismembered Baby in Cellar in Camberwell" are displayed with positive pride.

Ravelston described his interview with Mr. McKechnie. Mr. McKechnie, it seemed, was torn between his rage against Gordon and his desire not to offend such a good customer as Ravelston. But of course, after a thing like that, you could hardly expect him to take Gordon back. These scandals were bad for trade, and besides, he was justly angry at the lies Flaxman had told him over the phone. But he was angriest of all at the thought of *his* assistant being drunk and disorderly. Ravelston said that the drunkenness seemed to anger him in a way that was peculiar. He gave the impression that he would almost have preferred Gordon to pinch money out of the till. Of course, he was a teetotaller himself. Gordon had sometimes wondered whether he wasn't also a secret drinker, in the traditional Scottish style. His nose was certainly very red. But perhaps it was snuff that did it. Anyway, that was that. Gordon was in the soup, full fathom five.

"I suppose the Wisbeach will stick to my clothes and things," he said. "I'm not going round there to fetch them. Besides, I owe her a week's rent."

"Oh, don't you worry about that. I'll see to your rent and everything."

"My dear chap, I can't let you pay my rent!"

"Oh, dash it!" Ravelston's face grew faintly pink. He looked miserably into the distance, and then said what he had to say all in a sudden burst: "Look here, Gordon, we must get this settled. You've just got to stay here till this business has blown over. I'll see you through about money and all that. You needn't think you're being a nuisance, because you're not. And anyway, it's only till you get another job."

Gordon moved moodily away from him, his hands in his pockets. He had foreseen all this, of course. He knew that he ought to refuse, he *wanted* to refuse, and yet he had not quite the courage.

"I'm not going to sponge on you like that," he said sulkily.

"Don't use such expressions, for God's sake! Besides, where could you go if you didn't stay here?"

"I don't know—into the gutter, I suppose. It's where I belong. The sooner I get there the better."

"Rot! You're going to stay here till you've found another job."

"But there isn't a job in the world. It might be a year before I found a job. I don't *want* a job."

"You mustn't talk like that. You'll find a job right enough. Something's bound to turn up. And for God's sake don't talk about *sponging* on me. It's only an arrangement between friends. If you really want to, you can pay it all back when you've got the money."

"Yes—*when!*"

But in the end he let himself be persuaded. He had known that he would let himself be persuaded. He stayed on at the flat, and allowed Ravelston to go round to Willowbed Road and pay his rent and recover his two cardboard suitcases; he even allowed Ravelston to "lend" him a further two pounds for current expenses. His heart sickened while he did it. He was living on Ravelston—sponging on Ravelston. How could there ever be real friendship between them again? Besides, in his heart he didn't want to be helped. He only wanted to be left alone. He was headed for the gutter; better to reach the gutter quickly and get it over. Yet for the time being he stayed, simply because he lacked the courage to do otherwise.

But as for this business of getting a job, it was hopeless from the start. Even Ravelston, though rich, could not manufacture jobs out of nothing. Gordon knew beforehand that there were no jobs going begging in the book trade. During the next three days he wore his shoes out traipsing from book-seller to bookseller. At shop after shop he set his teeth, marched in, demanded to see the manager, and three minutes later marched out again with his nose in the air. The answer was always the same—no jobs vacant. A few booksellers were taking on an extra man for the Christmas rush, but Gordon was not the type they were looking for. He was neither smart nor servile; he wore shabby clothes and spoke with the accent of a gentleman. Besides, a few questions always brought it out that he had been sacked from his last job for drunken-ness. After only three days he gave it up. He knew it was no use. It was only to please Ravelston that he had even been pretending to look for work.

In the evening he trailed back to the flat, footsore and with his nerves on edge from a series of snubs. He was making all his journeys on foot, to economise Ravelston's two pounds. When he got back Ravelston had just come up from the office and was sitting in one of the armchairs in front of the fire, with some long galley-proofs over his knee. He looked up as Gordon came in.

"Any luck?" he said as usual.

Gordon did not answer. If he had answered it would have been with a stream of obscenities. Without even looking at Ravelston he went straight into his bedroom, kicked off his shoes and flung himself on the bed. He hated himself at this moment. Why had he come back? What right had he to come back and sponge on Ravelston when he hadn't even the in-tention of looking for a job any longer? He ought to have stayed out in the streets, slept in Trafalgar Square, begged—anything. But he hadn't the guts to face the streets as yet. The prospect of warmth and shelter had tugged him back. He lay with his hands beneath his head, in a mixture of apathy and self-hatred. After about half an hour he heard the door-bell ring and Ravelston get up to answer it. It was that bitch Hermione Slater, presumably. Ravelston had in-troduced Gordon to Hermione a couple of days ago, and she had treated him like dirt. But a moment later there was a knock at the bedroom door.

192

"What is it?" said Gordon.

"Somebody's come to see you," said Ravelston.

"To see *me?*"

"Yes. Come on into the other room."

Gordon swore and rolled sluggishly off the bed. When he got to the other room he found that the visitor was Rosemary. He had been half expecting her, of course, but it wearied him to see her. He knew why she had come; to sympathise with him, to pity him, to reproach him—it was all the same. In his despondent, bored mood he did not want to make the effort of talking to her. All he wanted was to be left alone. But Ravelston was glad to see her. He had taken a liking to her in their single meeting and thought she might cheer Gordon up. He made a transparent pretext to go downstairs to the office, leaving the two of them together.

They were alone, but Gordon made no move to embrace her. He was standing in front of the fire, round-shouldered, his hands in his coat pockets, his feet thrust into a pair of Ravelston's slippers which were much too big for him. She came rather hesitantly towards him, not yet taking off her hat or her coat with the lamb-skin collar. It hurt her to see him. In less than a week his appearance had deteriorated strangely. Already he had that unmistakable, seedy, lounging look of a man who is out of work. His face seemed to have grown thinner, and there were rings round his eyes. Also it was obvious that he had not shaved that day.

She laid her hand on his arm, rather awkwardly, as a woman does when it is she who has to make the first embrace.

"Gordon——"

"Well?"

He said it almost sulkily. The next moment she was in his arms. But it was she who had made the first movement, not he. Her head was on his breast, and behold! she was struggling with all her might against the tears that almost overwhelmed her. It bored Gordon dreadfully. He seemed so often to reduce her to tears! And he didn't want to be cried over; he only wanted to be left alone—alone to sulk and despair. As he held her there, one hand mechanically caressing her shoulder, his main feeling was boredom. She had made things more difficult for him by coming here. Ahead of him were dirt, cold, hunger, the streets, the workhouse and the jail. It was against *that* that he had got to steel himself. And he could steel himself, if only she would leave him alone and not come plaguing him with these irrelevant emotions.

He pushed her a little way from him. She had recovered herself quickly, as she always did.

"Gordon, my dear one! Oh, I'm so sorry, so sorry!"

"Sorry about what?"

"You losing your job and everything. You look so unhappy."

"I'm not unhappy. Don't pity me, for God's sake."

He disengaged himself from her arms. She pulled her hat off and threw it into a chair. She had come here with something definite to say. It was something she had refrained from saying all these years—something that it had seemed to her a point of chivalry not to say. But now it had got to be said, and she would come straight out with it. It was not in her nature to beat about the bush.

"Gordon, will you do something to please me?"

"What?"

"Will you go back to the New Albion?"

So that was it! Of course he had foreseen it. She was going to start nagging at him like all the others. She was going to add herself to the band of people who worried him and badgered him to "get on." But what else could you expect? It was what any woman would say. The marvel was that she had never said it before. Go back to the New Albion! It had been the sole significant action of his life, leaving the New Albion. It was his religion, you might say, to keep out of that filthy money-world. Yet at this moment he could not remember with any clarity the motives for which he had left the New Albion. All he knew was that he would never go back, not if the skies fell, and that the argument he foresaw bored him in advance.

He shrugged his shoulders and looked away. "The New Albion wouldn't take me back," he said shortly.

"Yes, they would. You remember what Mr. Erskine said.

194

It's not so long ago—only two years. And they're always on the look-out for good copywriters. Everyone at the office says so. I'm sure they'd give you a job if you went and asked them. And they'd pay you at least four pounds a week."

"Four pounds a week! Splendid! I could afford to keep an aspidistra on that, couldn't I?"

"No, Gordon, don't joke about it now."

"I'm not joking. I'm serious."

"You mean you won't go back to them—not even if they offered you a job?"

"Not in a thousand years. Not if they paid me fifty pounds a week."

"But why? Why?"

"I've told you why," he said wearily.

She looked at him helplessly. After all, it was no use. There was this money-business standing in the way—these meaningless scruples which she had never understood but which she had accepted merely because they were his. She felt all the impotence, the resentment of a woman who sees an abstract idea triumphing over common sense. How maddening it was, that he should let himself be pushed into the gutter by a thing like that! She said almost angrily:

"I don't understand you, Gordon, I really don't. Here you are out of work, you may be starving in a little while for all you know; and yet when there's a good job which you can have almost for the asking, you won't take it."

"No, you're quite right. I won't."

"But you must have *some* kind of job, mustn't you?"

"A job, but not a *good* job. I've explained that God knows how often. I dare say I'll get a job of sorts sooner or later. The same kind of job as I had before."

"But I don't believe you're even *trying* to get a job, are you?"

"Yes, I am. I've been out all to-day seeing booksellers."

"And you didn't even shave this morning!" she said, changing her ground with feminine swiftness.

He felt his chin. "I don't believe I did, as a matter of fact."

195

"And then you expect people to give you a job! Oh, Gordon!"

"Oh, well, what does it matter? It's too much fag to shave every day."

"You're letting yourself go to pieces," she said bitterly. "You don't seem to *want* to make any effort. You want to sink—just *sink!*"

"I don't know—perhaps. I'd sooner sink than rise."

There were further arguments. It was the first time she had ever spoken to him like this. Once again the tears came into her eyes, and once again she fought them back. She had come here swearing to herself that she would not cry. The dreadful thing was that her tears, instead of distressing him, merely bored him. It was as though he *could* not care, and yet at his very centre there was an inner heart that cared because he could not care. If only she would leave him alone! Alone, alone! Free from the nagging consciousness of his failure; free to sink, as she had said, down, down into quiet worlds where money and effort and moral obligation did not exist. Finally he got away from her and went back to the spare bedroom. It was definitely a quarrel—the first really deadly quarrel they had ever had. Whether it was to be final he did not know. Nor did he care, at this moment. He locked the door behind him and lay on the bed smoking a cigarette. He must get out of this place, and quickly! To-morrow morning he would clear out. No more sponging on Ravelston! No more blackmail to the gods of decency! Down, down, into the mud —down to the streets, the workhouse and the jail. It was only there that he could be at peace.

Ravelston came upstairs to find Rosemary alone and on the point of departure. She said good-bye and then suddenly turned to him and laid her hand on his arm. She felt that she knew him well enough now to take him into her confidence.

"Mr. Ravelston, please—*will* you try and persuade Gordon to get a job?"

"I'll do what I can. Of course it's always difficult. But I expect we'll find him a job of sorts before long."

"It's so dreadful to see him like this! He goes absolutely to pieces. And all the time, you see, there's a job he could quite easily get if he wanted it—a really *good* job. It's not that he can't, it's simply that he won't."

She explained about the New Albion. Ravelston rubbed his nose.

"Yes. As a matter of fact I've heard all about that. We talked it over when he left the New Albion."

"But you don't think he was right to leave them?" she said, promptly divining that Ravelston *did* think Gordon right.

"Well—I grant you it wasn't very wise. But there's a certain amount of truth in what he says. Capitalism's corrupt and we ought to keep outside it—that's his idea. It's not practicable, but in a way it's sound."

"Oh, I dare say it's all right as a theory! But when he's out of work and when he could get this job if he chose to ask for it—*surely* you don't think he's right to refuse?"

"Not from a common-sense point of view. But in principle —well, yes."

"Oh, in principle! We can't afford principles, people like us. *That's* what Gordon doesn't seem to understand."

Gordon did not leave the flat next morning. One resolves to do these things, one *wants* to do them; but when the time comes, in the cold morning light, they somehow don't get done. He would stay just one day more, he told himself; and then again it was "just one day more," until five whole days had passed since Rosemary's visit, and he was still lurking there, living on Ravelston, with not even a flicker of a job in sight. He still made some pretence of searching for work, but he only did it to save his face. He would go out and loaf for hours in public libraries, and then come home to lie on the bed in the spare bedroom, dressed except for his shoes, smoking endless cigarettes. And for all that inertia and the fear of the streets still held him there, those five days were awful, damnable, unspeakable. There is nothing more dreadful in the world than to live in somebody else's house, eating his bread and doing nothing in return for it. And perhaps it is worst of all when your benefactor won't for a moment admit that he is your benefactor. Nothing could have exceeded Ravelston's delicacy. He would have perished rather than admit that Gordon was sponging on him. He had paid Gordon's fine, he had paid his arrears of rent, he had kept him for a week and he had "lent" him two pounds on top of that; but it was nothing, it was a mere arrangement between friends, Gordon would do the same for him another time. From time to time Gordon made feeble efforts to escape, which always ended in the same way.

"Look here, Ravelston, I can't stay here any longer. You've kept me long enough. I'm going to clear out to-morrow morning."

"But my dear old chap! Do be sensible. You haven't—" But no! Not even now, when Gordon was openly on the rocks, could Ravelston say, "You haven't got any money." One can't say things like that. He compromised: "Where are you going to live, anyway?"

"God knows—I don't care. There are common lodging-houses and places. I've got a few bob left."

"Don't be such an ass. You'd much better stay here till you've found a job."

"But it might be months, I tell you. I can't live on you like this."

"Rot, my dear chap! I like having you here."

But of course, in his inmost heart, he didn't really like having Gordon there. How should he? It was an impossible situation. There was a tension between them all the time. It is always so when one person is living on another. However delicately it is disguised, charity is still horrible; there is a malaise, almost a secret hatred, between the giver and the receiver. Gordon knew that his friendship with Ravelston would never be the same again. Whatever happened afterwards, the memory of this evil time would be between them. The feeling of his dependent position, of being in the way, unwanted, a nuisance, was with him night and day. At meals he would scarcely eat, he would not smoke Ravelston's cigarettes, but bought himself cigarettes out of his few remaining shillings. He would not even light the gas-fire in his bedroom.

198

He would have made himself invisible if he could. Every day, of course, people were coming and going at the flat and at the office. All of them saw Gordon and grasped his status. Another of Ravelston's pet scroungers, they all said. He even detected a gleam of professional jealousy in one or two of the hangers-on of *Antichrist*. Three times during that week Hermione Slater came. After his first encounter with her he fled from the flat as soon as she appeared; on one occasion, when she came at night, he had to stay out of doors till after midnight. Mrs. Beaver, the charwoman, had also "seen through" Gordon. She knew his type. He was another of those good-for-nothing young "writing gentlemen" who sponged on poor Mr. Ravelston. So in none too subtle ways she made things uncomfortable for Gordon. Her favourite trick was to rout him out with broom and pan—"Now, Mr. Comstock, I've got to do this room out, *if* you please"—from whichever room he had settled down in.

But in the end, unexpectedly and through no effort of his own, Gordon did get a job. One morning a letter came for Ravelston from Mr. McKechnie. Mr. McKechnie had relented —not to the extent of taking Gordon back, of course, but to the extent of helping him to find another job. He said that a Mr. Cheeseman, a bookseller in Lambeth, was looking for an assistant. From what he said it was evident that Gordon could get the job if he applied for it; it was equally evident that there was some snag about the job. Gordon had vaguely heard of Mr. Cheeseman—in the book trade everybody knows everybody else. In his heart the news bored him. He didn't really want this job. He didn't want ever to work again; all he wanted was to sink, sink, effortless, down into the mud. But he couldn't disappoint Ravelston after all Ravelston had done for him. So the same morning he went down to Lambeth to enquire about the job.

The shop was in the desolate stretch of road south of Waterloo Bridge. It was a poky, mean-looking shop, and the name over it, in faded gilt, was not Cheeseman but Eldridge. In the window, however, there were some valuable calf folios, and some sixteenth-century maps which Gordon thought must be worth money. Evidently Mr. Cheeseman specialised in "rare" books. Gordon plucked up his courage and went in.

As the door-bell ping'd, a tiny, evil-looking creature, with a sharp nose and heavy black eyebrows, emerged from the office behind the shop. He looked up at Gordon with a kind of nosy malice. When he spoke it was in an extraordinary clipped manner, as though he were biting each word in half before it escaped from him. "Ot c'n I do f'yer!"—that approximately was what it sounded like. Gordon explained why he had come. Mr. Cheeseman shot a meaning glance at him and answered in the same clipped manner as before:

"Oh, eh? Comstock, eh? Come 'is way. Got mi office back here. Bin 'specting you."

Gordon followed him. Mr. Cheeseman was a rather sinister little man, almost small enough to be called a dwarf, with very black hair, and slightly deformed. As a rule a dwarf, when malformed, has a full-sized torso and practically no legs. With Mr. Cheeseman it was the other way about. His legs were of normal length, but the top half of his body was so short that his buttocks seemed to sprout almost immediately below his shoulder blades. This gave him, in walking, a resemblance to a pair of scissors. He had the powerful bony shoulders of the dwarf, the large ugly hands, and the sharp nosing movements of the head. His clothes had that peculiar hardened, shiny texture of clothes that are very old and very dirty. They were just going into the office when the door-bell ping'd again, and a customer came in, holding out a book from the sixpenny box outside and half a crown. Mr. Cheeseman did not take the change out of the till—apparently there was no till—but produced a very greasy wash-leather purse from some secret place under his waistcoat. He handled the purse, which was almost lost in his big hands, in a peculiarly secretive way, as though trying to hide it from sight.

"I like keep mi money i' mi pocket," he explained, with an upward glance, as they went into the office.

It was apparent that Mr. Cheeseman clipped his words from a notion that words cost money and ought not to be wasted. In the office they had a talk, and Mr. Cheeseman extorted from Gordon the confession that he had been sacked for drunkenness. As a matter of fact he knew all about this already. He had heard about Gordon from Mr. McKechnie, whom he had met at an auction a few days earlier. He had pricked up his ears when he heard the story, for he was on the look-out for an assistant, and clearly an assistant who had been sacked for drunkenness would come at reduced wages. Gordon saw that his drunkenness was going to be used as a weapon against him. Yet Mr. Cheeseman did not seem absolutely unfriendly. He seemed to be the kind of person who will cheat you if he can, and bully you if you give him the chance, but who will also regard you with a contemptuous good-humour. He took Gordon into his confidence, talked of conditions in the trade and boasted with much chuckling of his own astuteness. He had a peculiar chuckle, his mouth curving upwards at the corners and his large nose seeming about to disappear into it.

Recently, he told Gordon, he had had an idea for a profitable side-line. He was going to start a twopenny library; but it would have to be quite separate from the shop, because anything so low-class would frighten away the book-lovers who came to the shop in search of "rare" books. He had taken premises a little distance away, and in the lunch-hour he took Gordon to see them. They were further down the dreary street, between a fly-blown ham-and-beef shop and a smartish undertaker. The ads in the undertaker's window caught Gordon's eye. It seems you can get underground for as little as two pounds ten nowadays. You can even get buried on the hire-purchase. There was also an ad for cremations—"Reverent, Sanitary and Inexpensive."

The premises consisted of a single narrow room—a mere pipe of a room with a window as wide as itself, furnished with a cheap desk, one chair and a card index. The new-painted shelves were ready and empty. This was not, Gordon saw at a glance, going to be the kind of library that he had presided over at McKechnie's. McKechnie's library had been comparatively highbrow. It had dredged no deeper than Dell, and it had even had books by Lawrence and Huxley. But this was

201

one of those cheap and evil little libraries ("mushroom libraries," they are called) which are springing up all over London and are deliberately aimed at the uneducated. In libraries like these there is not a single book that is ever mentioned in the reviews or that any civilised person has ever heard of. The books are published by special low-class firms and turned out by wretched hacks at the rate of four a year, as mechanically as sausages and with much less skill. In effect they are merely fourpenny novelettes disguised as novels, and they only cost the library-proprietor one and eightpence a volume. Mr. Cheeseman explained that he had not ordered the books yet. He spoke of "ordering the books" as one might speak of ordering a ton of coals. He was going to start with five hundred assorted titles, he said. The shelves were already marked off into sections—"Sex," "Crime," "Wild West," and so forth.

He offered Gordon the job. It was very simple. All you had to do was to remain there ten hours a day, hand out the book, take the money and choke off the more obvious book-pinchers. The pay, he added with a measuring, sidelong glance, was thirty shillings a week.

Gordon accepted promptly. Mr. Cheeseman was perhaps faintly disappointed. He had expected an argument, and would have enjoyed crushing Gordon by reminding him that beggars can't be choosers. But Gordon was satisfied. The job would do. There was no *trouble* about a job like this; no room for ambition, no effort, no hope. Ten bob less—ten bob nearer the mud. It was what he wanted.

He "borrowed" another two pounds from Ravelston and took a furnished bed-sitting-room, eight bob a week, in a filthy alley parallel to Lambeth Cut. Mr. Cheeseman ordered the five hundred assorted titles, and Gordon started work on the twentieth of December. This, as it happened, was his thirtieth birthday.

Chapter Ten

Under ground, under ground! Down in the safe soft womb of earth, where there is no getting of jobs or losing of jobs, no relatives or friends to plague you, no hope, fear, ambition, honour, duty—no *duns* of any kind. That was where he wished to be.

Yet it was not death, actual physical death, that he wished for. It was a queer feeling that he had. It had been with him ever since that morning when he had woken up in the police cell. The evil, mutinous mood that comes after drunkenness seemed to have set into a habit. That drunken night had marked a period in his life. It had dragged him downward with strange suddenness. Before, he had fought against the money-code, and yet he had clung to his wretched remnant of decency. But now it was precisely from decency that he wanted to escape. He wanted to go down, deep down, into some world where decency no longer mattered; to cut the strings of his self-respect, to submerge himself—to *sink*, as Rosemary had said. It was all bound up in his mind with the thought of being *under ground*. He liked to think about the lost people, the under ground people, tramps, beggars, criminals, prostitutes. It is a good world that they inhabit, down there in their frowzy kips and spikes. He liked to think that beneath the world of money there is that great sluttish underworld where failure and success have no meaning; a sort of kingdom of ghosts where all are equal. That was where he wished to be, down in the ghost-kingdom, *below* ambition. It comforted him somehow to think of the smoke-dim slums of South London sprawling on and on, a huge graceless wilderness where you could lose yourself for ever.

And in a way this job was what he wanted; at any rate, it was something near what he wanted. Down there in Lambeth, in winter, in the murky streets where the sepia-shadowed faces of tea-drunkards drifted through the mist, you had a *submerged* feeling. Down here you had no contact with money or with culture. No highbrow customers to whom you had to act the highbrow; no one who was capable of asking you, in that prying way that prosperous people have, "What are you, with your brains and education, doing in a job like this?" You were just part of the slum, and, like all slum-dwellers, taken for granted. The youths and girls and draggled middle-aged women who came to the library scarcely even spotted the fact that Gordon was an educated man. He was just "the bloke at the library," and practically one of themselves.

The job itself, of course, was of inconceivable futility. You just sat there, ten hours a day, six hours on Thursdays, handing out books, registering them and receiving twopences. Between whiles there was nothing to do except read. There was nothing worth watching in the desolate street outside. The principal event of the day was when the hearse drove up to the undertaker's establishment next door. This had a faint interest for Gordon, because the dye was wearing off one of the horses and it was assuming by degrees a curious purplish-brown shade. Much of the time, when no customers came, he spent reading the yellow-jacketed trash that the library contained. Books of that type you could read at the rate of one an hour. And they were the kind of books that suited him nowadays. It is real "escape literature," that stuff in the twopenny libraries. Nothing has ever been devised that puts less strain on the intelligence; even a film, by comparison, demands a certain effort. And so when a customer demanded a book of this category or that, whether it was "Sex" or "Crime" or "Wild West" or "Romance" (always with the accent on the *o*), Gordon was ready with expert advice.

Mr. Cheeseman was not a bad person to work for, so long as you understood that if you worked till the Day of Judgment you would never get a rise of wages. Needless to say, he suspected Gordon of pinching the till-money. After a week or two he devised a new system of booking, by which he could tell how many books had been taken out and check this with the day's takings. But it was still (he reflected) in Gordon's power to issue books and make no record of them; and so the possibility that Gordon might be cheating him of sixpence or even a shilling a day continued to trouble him, like the pea under the princess's mattress. Yet he was not absolutely unlikeable, in his sinister dwarfish way. In the evenings, after he had shut the shop, when he came along to the library to collect the day's takings, he would stay talking to Gordon for a while and recounting with nosy chuckles any particularly astute swindles that he had worked lately. From these conversations Gordon pieced together Mr. Cheeseman's history. He had been brought up in the old-clothes trade, which was his spiritual vocation, so to speak, and had inherited the bookshop from an uncle three years ago. At that time it was one of those dreadful bookshops in which there are not even any shelves, in which the books lie about in monstrous dusty piles with no attempt at classification. It was frequented to some extent by book-collectors, because there was occasionally a valuable book among the piles of rubbish, but mainly it kept going by selling second-hand paper-covered thrillers at twopence each. Over this dustheap Mr. Cheeseman had presided, at first, with intense disgust. He loathed books and had not yet grasped that there was money to be made out of them. He was still keeping his old-clothes shop going by means of a deputy, and intended to return to it as soon as he could get a good offer for the bookshop. But presently it was borne in upon him that books, properly handled, are worth money. As soon as he had made this discovery he developed an astonishing flair for book-dealing. Within two years he had worked his shop up till it was one of the best "rare" bookshops of its size in London. To him a book was as purely an article of merchandise as a pair of second-hand trousers. He had never in his life *read* a book himself, nor could he conceive why anyone should want to do so. His attitude towards the collectors who pored so lovingly over his rare editions was that of a sexually cold prostitute towards her clientèle. Yet he seemed to know by the mere feel of a book whether it was valuable or not. His head was a perfect mine of auction-records and first-edition dates, and he had a marvellous nose for a bargain. His favourite way of acquiring stock was to buy up the libraries of people who had just died, especially clergy-men. Whenever a clergyman died Mr. Cheeseman was on the spot with the promptness of a vulture. Clergymen, he explained to Gordon, so often have good libraries and ignorant widows. He lived over the shop, was unmarried, of course, and had no amusements and seemingly no friends. Gordon used sometimes to wonder what Mr. Cheeseman did with himself in the evenings, when he was not out snooping after bargains. He had a mental picture of Mr. Cheeseman sitting in a double-locked room with the shutters over the windows, count-ing piles of half-crowns and bundles of pound notes which he stowed carefully away in cigarette-tins.

Mr. Cheeseman bullied Gordon and was on the look-out for an excuse to dock his wages; yet he did not bear him any particular ill-will. Sometimes in the evening when he came to the library he would produce a greasy packet of Smith's Potato Crisps from his pocket, and, holding it out, say in his clipped style:

"Hassome chips?"

The packet was always grasped so firmly in his large hand that it was impossible to extract more than two or three chips. But he meant it as a friendly gesture.

As for the place where Gordon lived, in Brewer's Yard, parallel to Lambeth Cut on the south side, it was a filthy kip. His bed-sitting-room was eight shillings a week and was just under the roof. With its sloping ceiling—it was a room shaped like a wedge of cheese—and its skylight window, it was the nearest thing to the proverbial poet's garret that he had ever lived in. There was a large, low, broken-backed bed with a ragged patchwork quilt and sheets that were changed once fortnightly; a deal table ringed by dynasties of teapots; a rickety kitchen chair; a tin basin for washing in; a gas-ring in the fender. The bare floorboards had never been stained but were dark with dirt. In the cracks in the pink wallpaper dwelt multitudes of bugs; however, this was winter and they were torpid unless you over-warmed the room. You were expected to make your own bed. Mrs. Meakin, the landlady, theoretically "did out" the rooms daily, but four days out of five she found the stairs too much for her. Nearly all the lodgers cooked their own squalid meals in their bedrooms. There was no gas-stove, of course; just the gas-ring in the fender, and, down two flights of stairs, a large evil-smelling sink which was common to the whole house.

In the garret adjoining Gordon's there lived a tall handsome old woman who was not quite right in the head and whose face was often as black as a Negro's from dirt. Gordon could never make out where the dirt came from. It looked like coal dust. The children of the neighbourhood used to shout "Blackie!" after her as she stalked along the pavement like a tragedy queen, talking to herself. On the floor below there was a woman with a baby which cried, cried everlastingly; also a young couple who used to have frightful quarrels and frightful reconciliations which you could hear all over the house. On the ground floor a house-painter, his wife and five children existed on the dole and an occasional odd job. Mrs. Meakin, the landlady, inhabited some burrow or other in the basement. Gordon liked this house. It was all so different from Mrs. Wisbeach's. There was no mingy lower-middle class decency here, no feeling of being spied upon and disapproved of. So long as you paid your rent you could do almost exactly as you liked; come home drunk and crawl up the stairs, bring women in at all hours, lie in bed all day if you wanted to. Mother Meakin was not the type to interfere. She was a dishevelled, jelly-soft old creature with a figure like a cottage loaf. People said that in her youth she had been no better than she ought, and probably it was true. She had a loving manner towards anything in trousers. Yet it seemed that traces of respectability lingered in her breast. On the day when Gordon installed himself he heard her puffing and struggling up the stairs, evidently bearing some burden. She knocked softly on the door with her knee, or the place where her knee ought to have been, and he let her in.

" 'Ere y'are, then," she wheezed kindly as she came in with her arms full. "I knew as 'ow you'd like this. I likes all my lodgers to feel comfortable-like. Lemme put it on the table for you. There! That makes the room like a bit more 'ome-like, don't it now?"

It was an aspidistra. It gave him a bit of a twinge to see it. Even here, in this final refuge! Hast thou found me, O mine enemy? But it was a poor weedy specimen—indeed, it was obviously dying.

In this place he could have been happy if only people would let him alone. It was a place where you *could* be happy, in a sluttish way. To spend your days in meaningless mechanical work, work that could be slovened through in a sort of coma; to come home and light the fire when you had any coal (there were sixpenny bags at the grocer's) and get the stuffy little attic warm; to sit over a squalid meal of bacon, bread-and-marg and tea, cooked over the gas-ring; to lie on the frowzy bed, reading a thriller or doing the Brain Brighteners in *Tit Bits* until the small hours; it was the kind of life he wanted. All his habits had deteriorated rapidly. He never shaved more than three times a week nowadays, and only washed the parts that showed. There were good public baths near by, but he hardly went to them as often as once in a month. He never made his bed properly, but just turned back the sheets, and never washed his few crocks till all of them had been used twice over. There was a film of dust on everything. In the fender there was always a greasy frying-pan and a couple of plates coated with the remnants of fried eggs. One night the bugs came out of one of the cracks and marched across the ceiling two by two. He lay on his bed, his hands under his head, watching them with interest. Without regret, almost intentionally, he was letting himself go to pieces. At the bottom of all his feelings there was a sulkiness, a je m'en fous in the face of the world. Life had beaten him; but you can still beat life by turning your face away. Better to sink than rise. Down, down into the ghost-kingdom, the shadowy world where shame, effort, decency do not exist!

To sink! How easy it ought to be, since there are so few competitors! But the strange thing is that often it is harder to sink than to rise. There is always something that drags one upwards. After all, one is never quite alone; there are always friends, lovers, relatives. Everyone Gordon knew seemed to be writing him letters, pitying him or bullying him. Aunt Angela had written, Uncle Walter had written, Rosemary had written over and over again, Ravelston had written, Julia had written. Even Flaxman had sent a line to wish him luck. Flaxman's wife had forgiven him, and he was back at Peckham, in aspidistral bliss. Gordon hated getting letters nowadays. They were a link with that other world from which he was trying to escape.

Even Ravelston had turned against him. That was after he had been to see Gordon in his new lodgings. Until this visit he had not realised what kind of neighbourhood Gordon was living in. As his taxi drew up at the corner, in the Waterloo Road, a horde of ragged shock-haired boys came swooping from nowhere, to fight round the taxi door like fish at a bait. Three of them clung to the handle and hauled the door open simultaneously. Their servile, dirty little faces, wild with hope, made him feel sick. He flung some pennies among them and fled up the alley without looking at them again. The narrow pavements were smeared with a quantity of dogs' excrement that was surprising, seeing that there were no dogs in sight. Down in the basement Mother Meakin was boiling a haddock, and you could smell it half way up the stairs. In the attic Ravelston sat on the rickety chair, with the ceiling sloping down just behind his head. The fire was out and there was no light in the room except four candles guttering in a saucer beside the aspidistra. Gordon lay on the ragged bed, fully dressed but with no shoes on. He had scarcely stirred when Ravelston came in. He just lay there, flat on his back, sometimes smiling a little, as though there were some private joke between himself and the ceiling. The room had already the stuffy sweetish smell of rooms that have been lived in a long time and never cleaned. There were dirty crocks lying about in the fender.

"Would you like a cup of tea?" Gordon said, without stirring.

"No, thanks awfully—no," said Ravelston, a little too hastily.

He had seen the brown-stained cups in the fender and the repulsive common sink downstairs. Gordon knew quite well why Ravelston refused the tea. The whole atmosphere of this place had given Ravelston a kind of shock. That awful mixed smell of slops and haddock on the stairs! He looked at Gordon, supine on the ragged bed. And, dash it, Gordon was a gentleman! At another time he would have repudiated that thought; but in this atmosphere pious humbug was impossible. All the class-instincts which he believed himself not to possess rose in revolt. It was dreadful to think of anyone with brains and refinement living in a place like this. He wanted to tell Gordon to get out of it, pull himself together, earn a decent income and live like a gentleman. But of course he didn't say so. You can't say things like that. Gordon was aware of what was going on inside Ravelston's head. It amused him, rather. He felt no gratitude towards Ravelston for coming here and seeing him; on the other hand, he was not ashamed of his surroundings as he would once have been. There was a faint, amused malice in the way he spoke.

"You think I'm a B.F., of course," he remarked to the ceiling.

"No, I don't. Why should I?"

"Yes, you do. You think I'm a B.F. to stay in this filthy place instead of getting a proper job. You think I ought to try for that job at the New Albion."

"No, dash it! I never thought that. I see your point absolutely. I told you that before. I think you're perfectly right in principle."

"And you think principles are all right so long as one doesn't go and put them into practice."

"No. But the question always is, when *is* one putting them into practice?"

"It's quite simple. I've made war on money. This is where it's led me."

Ravelston rubbed his nose, then shifted uneasily on his chair.

"The mistake you make, don't you see, is in thinking one can live in a corrupt society without being corrupt oneself. After all, what do you achieve by refusing to make money? You're trying to behave as though one could stand right outside our economic system. But one can't. One's got to change the system, or one changes nothing. One can't put things right in a hole-and-corner way, if you take my meaning."

Gordon waved a foot at the buggy ceiling.

"Of course this *is* a hole-and-corner, I admit."

"I didn't mean that," said Ravelston, pained.

"But let's face facts. You think I ought to be looking about for a *good* job, don't you?"

"It depends on the job. I think you're quite right not to sell yourself to that advertising agency. But it does seem rather a pity that you should stay in that wretched job you're in at present. After all, you *have* got talents. You ought to be using them somehow."

"There are my poems," said Gordon, smiling at his private joke.

Ravelston looked abashed. This remark silenced him. Of course, there *were* Gordon's poems. There was *London Pleasures,* for instance. Ravelston knew, and Gordon knew, and each knew that the other knew, that *London Pleasures* would never be finished. Never again, probably, would Gordon write a line of poetry; never, at least, while he remained in this vile place, this blind-alley job and this defeated mood. He had finished with all that. But this could not be said, as yet. The pretence was still kept up that Gordon was a struggling poet —the conventional poet-in-garret.

It was not long before Ravelston rose to go. This smelly place oppressed him, and it was increasingly obvious that Gordon did not want him here. He moved hesitantly towards the door, pulling on his gloves, then came back again, pulling off his left glove and flicking it against his leg.

"Look here, Gordon, you won't mind my saying it—this is a filthy place, you know. This house, this street—everything."

"I know. It's a pigsty. It suits me."

"But do you *have* to live in a place like this?"

"My dear chap, you know what my wages are. Thirty bob a week."

"Yes, but——! Surely there *are* better places? What rent are you paying?"

"Eight bob."

"Eight bob? You could get a fairly decent unfurnished room for that. Something a bit better than this, anyway. Look here, why don't you take an unfurnished place and let me lend you ten quid for furniture?"

"'Lend' me ten quid! After all you've 'lent' me already? *Give* me ten quid, you mean."

Ravelston gazed unhappily at the wall. Dash it, what a thing to say! He said flatly:

"All right, if you like to put it like that. *Give* you ten quid."

"But as it happens, you see, I don't want it."

"But dash it all! You might as well have a decent place to live in."

"But I don't want a decent place. I want an indecent place. This one, for instance."

"But why? Why?"

"It's suited to my station," said Gordon, turning his face to the wall.

A few days later Ravelston wrote him a long, diffident sort of letter. It reiterated most of what he had said in their conversation. Its general effect was that Ravelston saw Gordon's point entirely, that there was a lot of truth in what Gordon said, that Gordon was absolutely right in principle, but——! It was the obvious, the inevitable "but." Gordon did not answer. It was several months before he saw Ravelston again. Ravelston made various attempts to get in touch with him. It was a curious fact—rather a shameful fact from a Socialist's point of view—that the thought of Gordon, who had brains and was of gentle birth, lurking in that vile place and that almost menial job, worried him more than the thought of ten thousand unemployed in Middlesbrough. Several times, in hope of cheering Gordon up, he wrote asking him to send contributions to *Antichrist*. Gordon never answered. Their friendship was at an end, it seemed to him. The evil time when he had lived on Ravelston had spoiled everything. Charity kills friendship.

And then there were Julia and Rosemary. They differed from Ravelston in this, that they had no shyness about speaking their minds. They did not say euphemistically that Gordon was "right in principle"; they knew that to refuse a "good" job can never be right. Over and over again they besought him to go back to the New Albion. The worst was that he had both of them in pursuit of him together. Before this business they had never met, but now Rosemary had got to know Julia somehow. They were in feminine league against him. They used to get together and talk about the "maddening" way in which Gordon was behaving. It was the only thing they had in common, their feminine rage against his "maddening" behaviour. Simultaneously and one after the other, by letter and by word of mouth, they harried him. It was unbearable.

Thank God, neither of them had seen his room at Mother Meakin's yet. Rosemary might have endured it, but the sight of that filthy attic would have been almost the death of Julia. They had been round to see him at the library, Rosemary a number of times, Julia once, when she could make a pretext to get away from the teashop. Even that was bad enough. It dismayed them to see what a mean, dreary little place the library was. The job at McKechnie's, though wretchedly paid, had not been the kind of job that you need actually be ashamed of. It brought Gordon into touch with cultivated people; seeing that he was a "writer" himself, it might conceivably "lead to something." But here, in a street that was almost a slum, serving out yellow-jacketed trash at thirty bob a week—what hope was there in a job like that? It was just a derelict's job, a blind-alley job. Evening after evening, walking up and down the dreary misty street after the library was shut, Gordon and Rosemary argued about it and about. She kept on and on

213

at him. *Would* he go back to the New Albion? *Why* wouldn't he go back to the New Albion? He always told her that the New Albion wouldn't take him back. After all, he hadn't applied for the job and there was no knowing whether he could get it; he preferred to keep it uncertain. There was something about him now that dismayed and frightened her. He seemed to have changed and deteriorated so suddenly. She divined, though he did not speak to her about it, that desire of his to escape from all effort and all decency, to sink down, down into the ultimate mud. It was not only from money but from life itself that he was turning away. They did not argue now as they had argued in the old days before Gordon had lost his job. In those days she had not paid much attention to his preposterous theories. His tirades against the money-morality had been a kind of joke between them. And it had hardly seemed to matter that time was passing and that Gordon's chance of earning a decent living was infinitely remote. She had still thought of herself as a young girl and of the future as limitless. She had watched him fling away two years of his life—two years of *her* life, for that matter; and she would have felt it ungenerous to protest.

But now she was growing frightened. Time's wingèd chariot was hurrying near. When Gordon lost his job she had suddenly realised, with the sense of making a startling discovery, that after all she was no longer very young. Gordon's thirtieth birthday was past; her own was not far distant. And what lay ahead of them? Gordon was sinking effortless into grey, deadly failure. He seemed to *want* to sink. What hope was there that they could ever get married now? Gordon knew that she was right. The situation was impossible. And so the thought, unspoken as yet, grew gradually in both their minds that they would have to part—for good.

One night they were to meet under the railway arches. It was a horrible January night; no mist, for once, only a vile wind that screeched round corners and flung dust and torn paper into your face. He waited for her, a small slouching figure, shabby almost to raggedness, his hair blown about

214

by the wind. She was punctual, as usual. She ran towards him, pulled his face down and kissed his cold cheek.

"Gordon, dear, how cold you are! Why did you come out without an overcoat?"

"My overcoat's up the spout. I thought you knew."

"Oh, dear! Yes."

She looked up at him, a small frown between her black brows. He looked so haggard, so despondent, there in the ill-lit archway, his face full of shadows. She wound her arm through his and pulled him out into the light.

"Let's keep walking. It's too cold to stand about. I've got something serious I want to say to you."

"What?"

"I expect you'll be very angry with me."

"What is it?"

"This afternoon I went and saw Mr. Erskine. I asked leave to speak to him for a few minutes."

He knew what was coming. He tried to free his arm from hers, but she held on to it.

"Well?" he said sulkily.

"I spoke to him about you. I asked him if he'd take you back. Of course he said trade was bad and they couldn't afford to take on new staff and all that. But I reminded him of what he'd said to you, and he said, Yes, he'd always thought you were very promising. And in the end he said he'd be quite ready to find a job for you if you'd come back. So you see I *was* right. They *will* give you the job."

He did not answer. She squeezed his arm. "So *now* what do you think about it?" she said.

"You know what I think," he said coldly.

Secretly he was alarmed and angry. This was what he had been fearing. He had known all along that she would do it sooner or later. It made the issue more definite and his own blame clearer. He slouched on, his hands still in his coat pockets, letting her cling to his arm but not looking towards her.

"You're angry with me?" she said.

"No, I'm not. But I don't see why you had to do it—behind my back."

That wounded her. She had had to plead very hard before she had managed to extort that promise from Mr. Erskine. And it had needed all her courage to beard the managing director in his den. She had been in deadly fear that she might be sacked for doing it. But she wasn't going to tell Gordon anything of that.

"I don't think you ought to say *behind your back*. After all, I was only trying to help you."

"How does it help me to get the offer of a job I wouldn't touch with a stick?"

"You mean you won't go back, even now?"

"Never."

"Why?"

"*Must* we go into it again?" he said wearily.

She squeezed his arm with all her strength and pulled him round, making him face her. There was a kind of desperation in the way she clung to him. She had made her last effort and it had failed. It was as though she could feel him receding, fading away from her like a ghost.

"You'll break my heart if you go on like this," she said.

"I wish you wouldn't trouble about me. It would be so much simpler if you didn't."

"But why do you have to throw your life away?"

"I tell you I can't help it. I've got to stick to my guns."

"You know what this will mean?"

With a chill at his heart, and yet with a feeling of resignation, even of relief, he said: "You mean we shall have to part—not see each other again?"

They had walked on, and now they emerged into the Westminster Bridge Road. The wind met them with a scream, whirling at them a cloud of dust that made both of them duck their heads. They halted again. Her small face was full of lines, and the cold wind and the cold lamplight did not improve it.

"You want to get rid of me," he said.

"No. No. It's not exactly that."

216

"But you feel we ought to part."

"How can we go on like this?" she said desolately.

"It's difficult, I admit."

"It's all so miserable, so hopeless! Wh t can it ever lead to?"

"So you don't love me after all?" he said.

"I do, I do! You know I do."

"In a way, perhaps. But not enough to go on loving me when it's certain I'll never have the money to keep you. You'll have me as a husband, but not as a lover. It's still a question of money, you see."

"It is *not* money, Gordon! It's *not* that."

"Yes, it's just money. There's been money between us from the start. Money, always money!"

The scene continued, but not for very much longer. Both of them were shivering with cold. There is no emotion that matters greatly when one is standing at a street corner in a biting wind. When finally they parted it was with no irrevo cable farewell. She simply said, "I must get back," kissed him and ran across the road to the tram-stop. Mainly with relief he watched her go. He could not stop now to ask himself whether he loved her. Simply he wanted to get away—away from the windy street, away from scenes and emotional demands, back in the frowzy solitude of his attic. If there were tears in his eyes it was only from the cold of the wind.

With Julia it was almost worse. She asked him to go and see her one evening. This was after she had heard, from Rosemary, of Mr. Erskine's offer of a job. The dreadful thing with Julia was that she understood nothing, absolutely nothing, of his motives. All she understood was that a "good" job had been offered him and that he had refused it. She implored him almost on her knees not to throw this chance away. And when he told her that his mind was made up, she wept, actually wept. That was dreadful. The poor goose-like girl, with streaks of grey in her hair, weeping without grace or dignity in her little Drage-furnished bed-sitting-room! This was the death of all her hopes. She had watched the family go down and down, moneyless and childless, into grey obscurity. Gordon alone had had it in him to succeed; and he, from mad perverseness, would not. He knew what she was thinking; he had to induce in himself a kind of brutality to stand firm. It was only because of Rosemary and Julia that he cared. Ravelston did not matter, because Ravelston understood. Aunt Angela and Uncle Walter, of course, were bleating weakly at him in long, fatuous letters. But them he disregarded.

In desperation Julia asked him, what did he mean to *do* now that he had flung away his last chance of succeeding in life. He answered simply, "My poems." He had said the same to Rosemary and to Ravelston. With Ravelston the answer had sufficed. Rosemary had no longer any belief in his poems, but she would not say so. As for Julia, his poems had never at any time meant anything to her. "I don't see much sense in writing if you can't make money out of it," was what she had always said. And he himself did not believe in his poems any longer. But he still struggled to "write," at least at times. Soon after he changed his lodgings he had copied out on to clean sheets the completed portions of *London Pleasures*—not quite four hundred lines, he discovered. Even the labour of copying it out was a deadly bore. Yet he still worked on it occasionally; cutting out a line here, altering another there, not making or even expecting to make any progress. Before long the pages were as they had been before, a scrawled, grimy labyrinth of words. He used to carry the wad of grimy manuscript about with him in his pocket. The feeling of it there upheld him a little; after all it was a kind of achievement, demonstrable to himself though to nobody else. There it was, sole product of two years—of a thousand hours' work, it might be. He had no feeling for it any longer as a poem. The whole concept of poetry was meaningless to him now. It was only that if *London Pleasures* were ever finished it would be something snatched from fate, a thing created *outside* the money-world. But he knew, far more clearly than before, that it never would be finished. How was it possible that any creative impulse should remain to him, in the life he was living now? As time went on, even the desire to finish *London Pleasures* vanished. He still carried the manuscript about in his pocket; but it was only a gesture, a symbol of his private war.

He had finished for ever with that futile dream of being a "writer." After all, was not that too a species of ambition? He wanted to get away from all that, *below* all that. Down, down! Into the ghost kingdom, out of the reach of hope, out of the reach of fear! Under ground, under ground! That was where he wished to be.

Yet in a way it was not so easy. One night about nine he was lying on his bed, with the ragged counterpane over his feet, his hands under his head to keep them warm. The fire was out. The dust was thick on everything. The aspidistra had died a week ago and was withering upright in its pot. He slid a shoeless foot from under the counterpane, held it up and looked at it. His sock was full of holes—there were more holes than sock. So here he lay, Gordon Comstock, in a slum attic on a ragged bed, with his feet sticking out of his socks, with one and fourpence in the world, with three decades behind him and nothing, nothing accomplished! Surely *now* he was past redemption? Surely, try as they would, they couldn't prise him out of a hole like this? He had wanted to reach the mud—well, this was the mud, wasn't it?

Yet he knew that it was not so. That other world, the world of money and success, is always so strangely near. You don't escape it merely by taking refuge in dirt and misery. He had been frightened as well as angry when Rosemary told him about Mr. Erskine's offer. It brought the danger so close to him. A letter, a telephone message, and from this squalor he could step straight back into the money-world—back to four quid a week, back to effort and decency and slavery. Going to the devil isn't so easy as it sounds. Sometimes your salvation haunts you down like the Hound of Heaven.

For a while he lay in an almost mindless state, gazing at the ceiling. The utter futility of just lying there, dirty and cold, comforted him a little. But presently he was roused by a light tap at the door. He did not stir. It was Mother Meakin, presumably, though it did not sound like her knock.

"Come in," he said.

The door opened. It was Rosemary.

She stepped in, and then stopped as the dusty sweetish smell of the room caught her. Even in the bad light of the lamp she could see the state of filth the room was in—the litter of food and papers on the table, the grate full of cold ashes, the foul crocks in the fender, the dead aspidistra. As she came slowly towards the bed she pulled her hat off and threw it on to the chair.

"*What* a place for you to live in!" she said.

"So you've come back?" he said.

"Yes."

He turned a little away from her, his arm over his face. "Come back to lecture me some more, I suppose?"

"No."

"Then why?"

"Because——"

She had knelt down beside the bed. She pulled his arm away, put her face forward to kiss him, then drew back, surprised, and began to stroke the hair over his temple with the tips of her fingers.

"Oh, Gordon!"

"What?"

"You've got grey in your hair!"

"Have I? Where?"

"Here—over the temple. There's quite a little patch of it. It must have happened all of a sudden."

" 'My golden locks time hath to silver turned,' " he said indifferently.

"So we're both going grey," she said.

She bent her head to show him the three white hairs on her crown. Then she wriggled herself on to the bed beside him, put an arm under him, pulled him towards her, covered his face with kisses. He let her do it. He did not want this to happen—it was the very thing that he least wanted. But she had wriggled herself beneath him; they were breast to breast. Her body seemed to melt into his. By the expression of her face he knew what had brought her here. After all, she was virgin. She did not know what she was doing. It was magnanimity, pure magnanimity, that moved her. His wretchedness had drawn her back to him. Simply because he was penniless and a failure she had got to yield to him, even if it was only once.

"I had to come back," she said.

"Why?"

"I couldn't bear to think of you here alone. It seemed so awful, leaving you like that."

"You did quite right to leave me. You'd much better not have come back. You know we can't ever get married."

"I don't care. That isn't how one behaves to people one loves. I don't care whether you marry me or not. I love you."

"This isn't wise," he said.

"I don't care. I wish I'd done it years ago."

"We'd much better not."

"Yes."

"No."

"Yes!"

After all, she was too much for him. He had wanted her so long, and he could not stop to weigh the consequences. So it was done at last, without much pleasure, on Mother Meakin's dingy bed. Presently Rosemary got up and rearranged her clothes. The room, though stuffy, was dreadfully cold. They were both shivering a little. She pulled the coverlet further over Gordon. He lay without stirring, his back turned to her, his face hidden against his arm. She knelt down beside the bed, took his other hand and laid it for a moment against her cheek. He scarcely noticed her. Then she shut the door quietly behind her and tiptoed down the bare, evil-smelling stairs. She felt dismayed, disappointed and very cold.

Chapter Eleven

SPRING, spring! Bytuene Mershe ant Averil, when spray biginneth to spring! When shaws be sheene and swards full fayre, and leaves both large and longe! When the hounds of spring are on winter's traces, in the spring time, the only pretty ring time, when the birds do sing, hey-ding-a-ding ding, cuckoo, jug-jug, pu-wee, ta-witta-woo! And so on and so on and so on. See almost any poet between the Bronze Age and 1850.

But how absurd that even now, in the era of central heating and tinned peaches, a thousand so-called poets are still writing in the same strain! For what difference does spring or winter or any other time of year make to the average civilised person nowadays? In a town like London the most striking seasonal change, apart from the mere change of temperature, is in the things you see lying about on the pavement. In late winter it is mainly cabbage leaves. In July you tread on cherry stones, in November on burnt-out fireworks. Towards Christmas the orange peel grows thicker. It was a different matter in the Middle Ages. There was some sense in writing poems about spring when spring meant fresh meat and green vegetables after months of frowsting in some windowless hut on a diet of salt fish and mouldy bread.

If it was spring Gordon failed to notice it. March in Lambeth did not remind you of Persephone. The days grew longer, there were vile dusty winds and sometimes in the sky patches of harsh blue appeared. Probably there were a few sooty buds on the trees if you cared to look for them. The aspidistra, it

222

turned out, had not died after all; the withered leaves had dropped off it, but it was putting forth a couple of dull green shoots near its base.

Gordon had been three months at the library now. The stupid slovenly routine did not irk him. The library had swelled to a thousand "assorted titles" and was bringing Mr. Cheeseman a pound a week clear profit, so Mr. Cheeseman was happy after his fashion. He was, nevertheless, nurturing a secret grudge against Gordon. Gordon had been sold to him, so to speak, as a drunkard. He had expected Gordon to get drunk and miss a day's work at least once, thus giving a sufficient pretext for docking his wages; but Gordon had failed to get drunk. Queerly enough, he had no impulse to drink nowadays. He would have gone without beer even if he could have afforded it. Tea seemed a better poison. All his desires and discontents had dwindled. He was better off on thirty bob a week than he had been previously on two pounds. The thirty bob covered, without too much stretching, his rent, cigarettes, a washing bill of about a shilling a week, a little fuel, and his meals, which consisted almost entirely of bacon, bread-and-marg and tea, and cost about two bob a day, gas included. Sometimes he even had sixpence over for a seat at a cheap but lousy picture-house near the Westminster Bridge Road. He still carried the grimy manuscript of *London Pleasures* to and fro in his pocket, but it was from mere force of habit; he had dropped even the pretence of working. All his evenings were spent in the same way. There in the remote frowzy attic, by the fire if there was any coal left, in bed if there wasn't, with teapot and cigarettes handy, reading, always reading. He read nothing nowadays except twopenny weekly papers. *Tit Bits, Answers, Peg's Paper, The Gem, The Magnet, Home Notes, The Girl's Own Paper*—they were all the same. He used to get them a dozen at a time from the shop. Mr. Cheeseman had great dusty stacks of them, left over from his uncle's day and used for wrapping paper. Some of them were as much as twenty years old.

He had not seen Rosemary for weeks past. She had written a number of times and then, for some reason, abruptly stopped

223

writing. Ravelston had written once, asking him to contribute an article on twopenny libraries to *Antichrist*. Julia had sent a desolate little letter, giving family news. Aunt Angela had had bad colds all the winter, and Uncle Walter was complaining of bladder trouble. Gordon did not answer any of their letters. He would have forgotten their existence if he could. They and their affection were only an encumbrance. He would not be free, free to sink down into the ultimate mud, till he had cut his links with all of them, even with Rosemary.

One afternoon he was choosing a book for a tow-headed factory girl, when someone he only saw out of the corner of his eye came into the library and hesitated just inside the door.

"What kind of book did you want?" he asked the factory girl.

"Oo—jest a kind of a *romance*, please."

Gordon selected a *romance*. As he turned, his heart bounded violently. The person who had just come in was Rosemary. She did not make any sign, but stood waiting, pale and worried-looking, with something ominous in her appearance.

He sat down to enter the book on the girl's ticket, but his hands had begun trembling so that he could hardly do it. He pressed the rubber stamp in the wrong place. The girl trailed out, peeping into the book as she went. Rosemary was watching Gordon's face. It was a long time since she had seen him by daylight, and she was struck by the change in him. He was shabby to the point of raggedness, his face had grown much thinner and had the dingy, greyish pallor of people who live on bread and margarine. He looked much older—thirty-five at the least. But Rosemary herself did not look quite as usual. She had lost her gay trim bearing, and her clothes had the appearance of having been thrown on in a hurry. It was obvious that there was something wrong.

He shut the door after the factory girl. "I wasn't expecting you," he began.

"I had to come. I got away from the studio at lunch time. I told them I was ill."

"You don't look well. Here, you'd better sit down."

There was only one chair in the library. He brought it out

from behind the desk and was moving towards her, rather vaguely, to offer some kind of caress. Rosemary did not sit down, but laid her small hand, from which she had removed the glove, on the top rung of the chair-back. By the pressure of her fingers he could see how agitated she was.

"Gordon, I've a most awful thing to tell you. It's happened after all."

"What's happened?"

"I'm going to have a baby."

"A baby? Oh, Christ!"

He stopped short. For a moment he felt as though someone had struck him a violent blow under the ribs. He asked the usual fatuous question:

"Are you sure?"

"Absolutely. It's been weeks now. If you knew the time I've had! I kept hoping and hoping—I took some pills—oh, it was too beastly!"

"A baby! Oh, God, what fools we were! As though we couldn't have foreseen it!"

"I know. I suppose it was my fault. I——"

"Damn! Here comes somebody."

The door-bell ping'd. A fat, freckled woman with an ugly under-lip came in at a rolling gait and demanded "Something with a murder in it." Rosemary had sat down and was twisting her glove round and round her fingers. The fat woman was exacting. Each book that Gordon offered her she refused on the ground that she had "had it already" or that it "looked dry." The deadly news that Rosemary had brought had unnerved Gordon. His heart pounding, his entrails constricted, he had to pull out book after book and assure the fat woman that this was the very book she was looking for. At last, after nearly ten minutes, he managed to fob her off with something which she said grudgingly she "didn't think she'd had before."

He turned back to Rosemary. "Well, what the devil are we going to do about it?" he said as soon as the door had shut.

"I don't see what I can do. If I have this baby I'll lose my job, of course. But it isn't only that I'm worrying about. It's

225

my people finding out. My mother—oh, dear! It simply doesn't bear thinking of."

"Ah, your people! I hadn't thought of them. One's people! What a cursed incubus they are!"

"*My* people are all right. They've always been good to me. But it's different with a thing like this."

He took a pace or two up and down. Though the news had scared him he had not really grasped it as yet. The thought of a baby, his baby, growing in her womb had awoken in him no emotion except dismay. He did not think of the baby as a living creature; it was a disaster pure and simple. And already he saw where it was going to lead.

"We shall have to get married, I suppose," he said flatly.

"Well, shall we? That's what I came here to ask you."

"But I suppose you want me to marry you, don't you?"

"Not unless *you* want to. I'm not going to tie you down. I know it's against your ideas to marry. You must decide for yourself."

"But we've no alternative—if you're really going to have this baby."

"Not necessarily. That's what you've got to decide. Because after all there *is* another way."

"What way?"

"Oh, *you* know. A girl at the studio gave me an address. A friend of hers had it done for only five pounds."

That pulled him up. For the first time he grasped, with the only kind of knowledge that matters, what they were really talking about. The words "a baby" took on a new significance. They did not mean any longer a mere abstract disaster, they meant a bud of flesh, a bit of himself, down there in her belly, alive and growing. His eyes met hers. They had a strange moment of sympathy such as they had never had before. For a moment he did feel that in some mysterious way they were one flesh. Though they were feet apart he felt as though they were joined together—as though some invisible living cord stretched from her entrails to his. He knew then that it was a dreadful thing they were contemplating—a blasphemy, if that word had any meaning. Yet if it had been put otherwise he might not have recoiled from it. It was the squalid detail of the five pounds that brought it home.

"No fear!" he said. "Whatever happens we're not going to do *that*. It's disgusting."

"I know it is. But I can't have the baby without being married."

"No! If that's the alternative I'll marry you. I'd sooner cut my right hand off than do a thing like that."

Ping! went the door-bell. Two ugly louts in cheap bright blue suits, and a girl with a fit of the giggles, came in. One of the youths asked with a sort of sheepish boldness for "something with a kick in it—something smutty." Silently, Gordon indicated the shelves where the "sex" books were kept. There were hundreds of them in the library. They had titles like *Secrets of Paris* and *The Man She Trusted;* on their tattered yellow jackets were pictures of half-naked girls lying on divans with men in dinner-jackets standing over them. The stories inside, however, were painfully harmless. The two youths and the girl ranged among them, sniggering over the pictures on their covers, the girl letting out little squeals and pretending to be shocked. They disgusted Gordon so much that he turned his back on them till they had chosen their books.

When they had gone he came back to Rosemary's chair. He stood behind her, took hold of her small firm shoulders, then slid a hand inside her coat and felt the warmth of her breast. He liked the strong springy feeling of her body; he liked to think that down there, a guarded seed, his baby was growing. She put a hand up and caressed the hand that was on her breast, but did not speak. She was waiting for him to decide.

"If I marry you I shall have to turn respectable," he said musingly.

"Could you?" she said with a touch of her old manner.

"I mean I shall have to get a proper job—go back to the New Albion. I suppose they'd take me back."

He felt her grow very still and knew that she had been waiting for this. Yet she was determined to play fair. She was not going to bully him or cajole him.

"I never said I wanted you to do that. I want you to marry

me—yes, because of the baby. But it doesn't follow you've got to keep me."

"There's no sense in marrying if I can't keep you. Suppose I married you when I was like I am at present—no money and no proper job? What would you do then?"

"I don't know. I'd go on working as long as I could. And afterwards, when the baby got too obvious—well, I suppose I'd have to go home to father and mother."

"That would be jolly for you, wouldn't it? But you were so anxious for me to go back to the New Albion before. You haven't changed your mind?"

"I've thought things over. I know you'd hate to be tied to a regular job. I don't blame you. You've got your own life to live."

He thought it over a little while longer. "It comes down to this. Either I marry you and go back to the New Albion, or you go to one of those filthy doctors and get yourself messed about for five pounds."

At that she twisted herself out of his grasp and stood up facing him. His blunt words had upset her. They had made the issue clearer and uglier than before.

"Oh, why did you say that?"

"Well, those *are* the alternatives."

"I'd never thought of it like that. I came here meaning to be fair. And now it sounds as if I was trying to bully you into it—trying to play on your feelings by threatening to get rid of the baby. A sort of beastly blackmail."

"I didn't mean that. I was only stating facts."

Her face was full of lines, the black brows drawn together. But she had sworn to herself that she would not make a scene. He could guess what this meant to her. He had never met her people, but he could imagine them. He had some notion of what it might mean to go back to a country town with an illegitimate baby; or, what was almost as bad, with a husband who couldn't keep you. But she was going to play fair. No blackmail! She drew a sharp inward breath, taking a decision.

"All right, then, I'm not going to hold *that* over your head.

228

It's too mean. Marry me or don't marry me, just as you like. But I'll have the baby, anyway."

"You'd do that? Really?"

"Yes, I think so."

He took her in his arms. Her coat had come open, her body was warm against him. He thought he would be a thousand kinds of fool if he let her go. Yet the alternative was impossible, and he did not see it any less clearly because he held her in his arms.

"Of course, you'd like me to go back to the New Albion," he said.

"No, I wouldn't. Not if you don't want to."

"Yes, you would. After all, it's natural. You want to see me earning a decent income again. In a *good* job, with four pounds a week and an aspidistra in the window. Wouldn't you, now? Own up."

"All right, then—yes, I would. But it's only something I'd *like* to see happening; I'm not going to *make* you do it. I'd just hate you to do it if you didn't really want to. I want you to feel free."

"Really and truly free?"

"Yes."

"You know what that means? Supposing I decided to leave you and the baby in the lurch?"

"Well—if you really wanted to. You're free—quite free."

After a little while she went away. Later in the evening or to-morrow he would let her know what he decided. Of course it was not absolutely certain that the New Albion would give him a job even if he asked them; but presumably they would, considering what Mr. Erskine had said. Gordon tried to think and could not. There seemed to be more customers than usual this afternoon. It maddened him to have to bounce out of his chair every time he had sat down and deal with some fresh influx of fools demanding crime-stories and sex-stories and romances. Suddenly, about six o'clock, he turned out the lights, locked up the library and went out. He had got to be alone. The library was not due to shut for two hours yet. God knew what Mr. Cheeseman would say when he found out. He might even give Gordon the sack. Gordon did not care.

He turned westward, up Lambeth Cut. It was a dull sort of evening, not cold. There was muck underfoot, white lights, and hawkers screaming. He had got to think this thing out, and he could think better walking. But it was so hard, so hard! Back to the New Albion, or leave Rosemary in the lurch; there was no other alternative. It was no use thinking, for instance, that he might find some "good" job which would offend his sense of decency a bit less. There aren't so many "good" jobs waiting for moth-eaten people of thirty. The New Albion was the only chance he had or ever would have.

At the corner, on the Westminster Bridge Road, he paused a moment. There were some posters opposite, livid in the lamplight. A monstrous one, ten feet high at least, advertised Bovex. The Bovex people had dropped Corner Table and got on to a new tack. They were running a series of four-line poems—Bovex Ballads, they were called. There was a picture of a horribly eupeptic family, with grinning ham-pink faces, sitting at breakfast; underneath, in blatant lettering:

> *"Why should you be thin and white?*
> *And have that washed-out feeling?*
> *Just take hot Bovex every night—*
> *Invigorating—healing!"*

Gordon gazed at the thing. He drank in its puling silliness. God, what trash! "Invigorating—healing!" The weak incompetence of it! It hadn't even the vigorous badness of the slogans that really stick. Just soppy, lifeless drivel. It would have been almost pathetic in its feebleness if one hadn't reflected that all over London and all over every town in England that poster was plastered, rotting the minds of men. He looked up and down the graceless street. Yes, war is coming soon. You can't doubt it when you see the Bovex ads. The electric drills in our streets presage the rattle of the machine guns. Only a little while before the aeroplanes come. Zoom—bang! A few tons of T.N.T. to send our civilisation back to hell where it belongs.

He crossed the road and walked on, southward. A curious

230

thought had struck him. He did not any longer want that war to happen. It was the first time in months—years, perhaps—that he had thought of it and not wanted it.

If he went back to the New Albion, in a month's time he might be writing Bovex Ballads himself. To go back to *that!* Any "good" job was bad enough; but to be mixed up in *that!* Christ! Of course he oughtn't to go back. It was just a question of having the guts to stand firm. But what about Rosemary? He thought of the kind of life she would live at home, in her parents' house, with a baby and no money; and of the news running through that monstrous family that Rosemary had married some awful rotter who couldn't even keep her. She would have the whole lot of them nagging at her together. Besides, there was the baby to think about. The money-god is so cunning. If he only baited his traps with yachts and race-horses, tarts and champagne, how easy it would be to dodge him. It is when he gets at you through your sense of decency that he finds you helpless.

The Bovex Ballad jingled in Gordon's head. He ought to stand firm. He had made war on money—he ought to stick it out. After all, hitherto he *had* stuck it out, after a fashion. He looked back over his life. No use deceiving himself. It had been a dreadful life—lonely, squalid, futile. He had lived thirty years and achieved nothing except misery. But that was what he had chosen. It was what he *wanted,* even now. He wanted to sink down, down into the muck where money does not rule. But this baby-business had upset everything. It was a pretty banal predicament, after all. Private vices, public virtues—the dilemma is as old as the world.

He looked up and saw that he was passing a public library. A thought struck him. That baby. What did it mean, anyway, having a baby? What was it that was actually happening to Rosemary at this moment? He had only vague and general ideas of what pregnancy meant. No doubt they would have books in there that would tell him about it. He went in. The lending library was on the left. It was there that you had to ask for works of reference.

The woman at the desk was a university graduate, young,

colourless, spectacled and intensely disagreeable. She had a fixed suspicion that no one—at least, no male person—ever consulted works of reference except in search of pornography. As soon as you approached she pierced you through and through with a flash of her pince-nez and let you know that your dirty secret was no secret from *her*. After all, all works of reference are pornographical, except perhaps Whitaker's *Almanac*. You can put even the Oxford Dictionary to evil purposes by looking up words like —— and ——.

Gordon knew her type at a glance, but he was too preoccupied to care.

"Have you any books on gynæcology?" he said.

"Any *what?*" demanded the young woman with a pince-nez flash of unmistakable triumph. As usual! Another male in search of dirt!

"Well, any books on midwifery? About babies being born, and so forth."

"We don't issue books of that description to the general public," said the young woman frostily.

"I'm sorry—there's a point I particularly want to look up."

"Are you a medical student?"

"No."

"Then I don't *quite* see what you want with books on midwifery."

Curse the woman! Gordon thought. At another time he would have been afraid of her; at present, however, she merely bored him.

"If you want to know, my wife's going to have a baby. We neither of us know much about it. I want to see whether I can find out anything useful."

The young woman did not believe him. He looked too shabby and worn, she decided, to be a newly-married man. However, it was her job to lend out books, and she seldom actually refused them, except to children. You always got your book in the end, after you had been made to feel yourself a dirty swine. With an aseptic air she led Gordon to a small table in the middle of the library and presented him with two fat books in brown covers. Thereafter she left him alone, but kept

232

an eye on him from whatever part of the library she happened to be in. He could feel her pince-nez probing the back of his neck at long range, trying to decide from his demeanour whether he was really searching for information or merely picking out the dirty bits.

He opened one of the books and searched inexpertly through it. There were acres of close-printed text full of Latin words. That was no use. He wanted something simple—pictures, for choice. How long had this thing been going on? Six weeks—nine weeks, perhaps. Ah! This must be it.

He came on a print of a nine weeks' fœtus. It gave him a shock to see it, for he had not expected it to look in the least like that. It was a deformed, gnomelike thing, a sort of clumsy caricature of a human being, with a huge domed head as big as the rest of its body. In the middle of the great blank expanse of head there was a tiny button of an ear. The thing was in profile; its boneless arm was bent, and one hand, crude as a seal's flipper, covered its face—fortunately, perhaps. Below were little skinny legs, twisted like a monkey's, with the toes turned in. It was a monstrous thing, and yet strangely human. It surprised him that they should begin looking human so soon. He had pictured something much more rudimentary; a mere blob with a nucleus, like a bubble of frog-spawn. But it must be very tiny, of course. He looked at the dimensions marked below. Length 30 millimetres. About the size of a large gooseberry.

But perhaps it had not been going on quite so long as that. He turned back a page or two and found a print of a six weeks' fœtus. A really dreadful thing this time—a thing he could hardly even bear to look at. Strange that our beginnings and endings are so ugly—the unborn as ugly as the dead. This thing looked as if it were dead already. Its huge head, as though too heavy to hold upright, was bent over at right angles at the place where its neck ought to have been. There was nothing you could call a face, only a wrinkle representing the eye—or was it the mouth? It had no human semblance this time; it was more like a dead puppy-dog. Its short thick arms were very doglike, the hands being mere stumpy paws. 15.5 millimetres long—no bigger than a hazel nut.

He pored for a long time over the two pictures. Their ugliness made them more credible and therefore more moving. His baby had seemed real to him from the moment when Rosemary spoke of abortion; but it had been a reality without visual shape—something that happened in the dark and was only important after it had happened. But here was the actual process taking place. Here was the poor ugly thing, no bigger than a gooseberry, that he had created by his heedless act. Its future, its continued existence perhaps, depended on him. Besides, it was a bit of himself—it *was* himself. Dare one dodge such a responsibility as that?

But what about the alternative? He got up, handed over his books to the disagreeable young woman, and went out; then, on an impulse, turned back and went into the other part of the library, where the periodicals were kept. The usual crowd of mangy-looking people were dozing over the papers. There was one table set apart for women's papers. He picked up one of them at random and bore it off to another table.

It was an American paper of the more domestic kind, mainly adverts with a few stories lurking apologetically among them. And *what* adverts! Quickly he flicked over the shiny pages. Lingerie, jewellery, cosmetics, fur coats, silk stockings flicked up and down like the figures in a child's peepshow. Page after page, advert after advert. Lipsticks, undies, tinned food, patent medicines, slimming cures, face-creams. A sort of cross-section of the money-world. A panorama of ignorance, greed, vulgarity, snobbishness, whoredom and disease.

And *that* was the world they wanted him to re-enter! *That* was the business in which he had a chance of Making Good. He flicked over the pages more slowly. Flick, flick. Adorable—until she smiles. The food that is shot out of a gun. Do you let foot-fag affect your personality? Get back that peach-bloom on a Beautyrest Mattress. Only a *penetrating* face-cream will reach that under-surface dirt. Pink toothbrush is *her* trouble. How to alkalise your stomach almost instantly. Roughage for husky kids. Are you one of the four out of five? The world-famed Culturequick Scrapbook. Only a drummer and yet he quoted Dante.

Christ, what muck!

But of course it was an American paper. The Americans always go one better on any kind of beastliness, whether it is ice-cream soda, racketeering or theosophy. He went over to the women's table and picked up another paper. An English one this time. Perhaps the ads in an English paper wouldn't be quite so bad—a little less brutally offensive?

He opened the paper. Flick, flick. Britons never shall be slaves!

Flick, flick. Get that waist-line back to normal! She *said* "Thanks awfully for the lift," but she *thought*, "Poor boy, why doesn't somebody tell him?" How a woman of thirty-two stole her young man from a girl of twenty. Prompt relief for feeble kidneys. Silkyseam—the smooth-sliding bathroom tissue. Asthma was choking her! Are *you* ashamed of your undies? Kiddies clamour for their Breakfast Crisps. Now I'm school-girl complexion all over. Hike all day on a slab of Vitamalt!

To be mixed up in *that!* To be in it and of it—part and parcel of it! God, God, God!

Presently he went out. The dreadful thing was that he knew already what he was going to do. His mind was made up—had been made up for a long time past. When this problem appeared it had brought its solution with it; all his hesitation had been a kind of make-believe. He felt as though some force outside himself were pushing him. There was a telephone booth near by. Rosemary's hostel was on the phone —she ought to be at home by now. He went into the booth, feeling in his pocket. Yes, exactly two pennies. He dropped them into the slot, swung the dial.

A refaned, adenoidal feminine voice answered him: "Who's thyah, please?"

He pressed Button A. So the die was cast.

"Is Miss Waterlow in?"

"Who's *thyah*, please?"

"Say it's Mr. Comstock. She'll know. Is she at home?"

"Ay'll see. Hold the lane, please."

235

A pause.

"Hullo! Is that you, Gordon?"

"Hullo! Hullo! Is that you, Rosemary? I just wanted to tell you. I've thought it over—I've made up my mind."

"Oh!" There was another pause. With difficulty mastering her voice, she added: "Well, what did you decide?"

"It's all right. I'll take the job—if they'll give it me, that is."

"Oh, Gordon, I'm so glad! You're not angry with me? You don't feel I've sort of bullied you into it?"

"No, it's all right. It's the only thing I can do. I've thought everything out. I'll go up to the office and see them to-morrow."

"I *am* so glad!"

"Of course, I'm assuming they'll give me the job. But I suppose they will, after what old Erskine said."

"I'm sure they will. But, Gordon, there's just one thing. You will go there nicely dressed, won't you? It might make a lot of difference."

"I know. I'll have to get my best suit out of pawn. Ravelston will lend me the money."

"Never mind about Ravelston. I'll lend you the money. I've got four pounds put away. I'll run out and wire it you before the post-office shuts. I expect you'll want some new shoes and a new tie as well. And, oh, Gordon!"

"What?"

"Wear a hat when you go up to the office, won't you? It looks better, wearing a hat."

"A hat! God! I haven't worn a hat for two years. Must I?"

"Well—it does look more business-like, doesn't it?"

"Oh, all right. A bowler hat, even, if you think I ought."

"I think a soft hat would do. But get your hair cut, won't you, there's a dear?"

"Yes, don't you worry. I'll be a smart young business man. Well groomed, and all that."

"Thanks ever so, Gordon dear. I must run out and wire that money. Good night and good luck."

"Good night."

He came out of the booth. So that was that. He had torn it now, right enough.

He walked rapidly away. What had he done? Chucked up the sponge! Broken all his oaths! His long and lonely war had ended in ignominious defeat. Circumcise ye your foreskins, saith the Lord. He was coming back to the fold, repentant. He seemed to be walking faster than usual. There was a peculiar sensation, an actual physical sensation, in his heart, in his limbs, all over him. What was it? Shame, misery, despair? Rage at being back in the clutch of money? Boredom when he thought of the deadly future? He dragged the sensation forth, faced it, examined it. It was relief.

Yes, that was the truth of it. Now that the thing was done he felt nothing but relief; relief that now at last he had finished with dirt, cold, hunger and loneliness and could get back to decent, fully human life. His resolutions, now that he had broken them, seemed nothing but a frightful weight that he had cast off. Moreover, he was aware that he was only fulfilling his destiny. In some corner of his mind he had always known that this would happen. He thought of the day when he had given them notice at the New Albion; and Mr. Erskine's kind, red, beefish face, gently counselling him not to chuck up a "good" job for nothing. How bitterly he had sworn, then, that he was done with "good" jobs for ever! Yet it was foredoomed that he should come back, and he had known it even then. And it was not merely because of Rosemary and the baby that he had done it. That was the obvious cause, the precipitating cause, but even without it the end would have been the same; if there had been no baby to think about, something else would have forced his hand. For it was what, in his secret heart, he had desired.

After all he did not lack vitality, and that moneyless existence to which he had condemned himself had thrust him ruthlessly out of the stream of life. He looked back over the last two frightful years. He had blasphemed against money, rebelled against money, tried to live like an anchorite outside the money-world; and it had brought him not only misery, but also a frightful emptiness, an inescapable sense of futility. To abjure money is to abjure life. Be not righteous over much; why shouldst thou die before thy time? Now he was

237

back in the money-world, or soon would be. To-morrow he would go up to the New Albion, in his best suit and overcoat (he must remember to get his overcoat out of pawn at the same time as his suit), in homburg hat of the correct gutter-crawling pattern, neatly shaved and with his hair cut short. He would be as though born anew. The sluttish poet of to-day would be hardly recognisable in the natty young business man of to-morrow. They would take him back, right enough; he had the talent they needed. He would buckle to work, sell his soul and hold down his job.

And what about the future? Perhaps it would turn out that these last two years had not left much mark upon him. They were merely a gap, a small setback in his career. Quite quickly, now that he had taken the first step, he would develop the cynical, blinkered business mentality. He would forget his fine disgusts, cease to rage against the tyranny of money—cease to be aware of it, even—cease to squirm at the ads for Bovex and Breakfast Crisps. He would sell his soul so utterly that he would forget it had ever been his. He would get married, settle down, prosper moderately, push a pram, have a villa and a radio and an aspidistra. He would be a law-abiding little cit like any other law-abiding little cit—a soldier in the strap-hanging army. Probably it was better so.

He slowed his pace a little. He was thirty and there was grey in his hair, yet he had a queer feeling that he had only just grown up. It occurred to him that he was merely repeating the destiny of every human being. Everyone rebels against the money-code, and everyone sooner or later surrenders. He had kept up his rebellion a little longer than most, that was all. And he had made such a wretched failure of it! He wondered whether every anchorite in his dismal cell pines secretly to be back in the world of men. Perhaps there were a few who did not. Somebody or other had said that the modern world is only habitable by saints and scoundrels. He, Gordon, wasn't a saint. Better, then, to be an unpretending scoundrel along with the others. It was what he had secretly pined for; now that he had acknowledged his desire and surrendered to it, he was at peace.

He was making roughly in the direction of home. He looked up at the houses he was passing. It was a street he did not know. Oldish houses, mean-looking and rather dark, let off in flatlets and single rooms for the most part. Railed areas, smoke-grimed bricks, whited steps, dingy lace curtains. "Apartments" cards in half the windows, aspidistras in nearly all. A typical lower-middle-class street. But not, on the whole, the kind of street that he wanted to see blown to hell by bombs.

He wondered about the people in houses like those. They would be, for example, small clerks, shop-assistants, commercial travellers, insurance touts, tram conductors. Did *they* know that they were only puppets dancing when money pulled the strings? You bet they didn't. And if they did, what would they care? They were too busy being born, being married, begetting, working, dying. It mightn't be a bad thing, if you could manage it, to feel yourself one of them, one of the ruck of men. Our civilisation is founded on greed and fear, but in the lives of common men the greed and fear are mysteriously transmuted into something nobler. The lower-middle-class people in there, behind their lace curtains, with their children and their scraps of furniture and their aspidistras—they lived by the money-code, sure enough, and yet they contrived to keep their decency. The money-code as they interpreted it was not merely cynical and hoggish. They had their standards, their inviolable points of honour. They "kept themselves respectable"—kept the aspidistra flying. Besides, they were *alive*. They were bound up in the bundle of life. They begot children, which is what the saints and the soul-savers never by any chance do.

The aspidistra is the tree of life, he thought suddenly.

He was aware of a lumpish weight in his inner pocket. It was the manuscript of *London Pleasures*. He took it out and had a look at it under a street lamp. A great wad of paper, soiled and tattered, with that peculiar, nasty, grimed-at-the-edges look of papers which have been a long time in one's pocket. About four hundred lines in all. The sole fruit of his exile, a two years' fœtus which would never be born. Well, he had finished with all that. Poetry! *Poetry*, indeed! In 1935.

What should he do with the manuscript? Best thing, shove it down the w.c. But he was a long way from home and had not the necessary penny. He halted by the iron grating of a drain. In the window of the nearest house an aspidistra, a striped one, peeped between the yellow lace curtains.

He unrolled a page of *London Pleasures*. In the middle of the labyrinthine scrawlings a line caught his eye. Momentary regret stabbed him. After all, parts of it weren't half bad! If only it could ever be finished! It seemed such a shame to shy it away after all the work he had done on it. Save it, perhaps? Keep it by him and finish it secretly in his spare time? Even now it might come to something.

No, no! Keep your parole. Either surrender or don't surrender.

He doubled up the manuscript and stuffed it between the bars of the drain. It fell with a plop into the water below.

Vicisti, O aspidistra!

Chapter Twelve

Ravelston wanted to say good-bye outside the registry office, but they would not hear of it, and insisted on dragging him off to have lunch with them. Not at Modigliani's, however. They went to one of those jolly little Soho restaurants where you get such a wonderful four-course lunch for half a crown. They had garlic sausage with bread and butter, fried plaice, entrecôte aux pommes frites and a rather watery caramel pudding; also a bottle of Médoc Supérieur, three and sixpence the bottle.

Only Ravelston was at the wedding. The other witness was a poor meek creature with no teeth, a professional witness whom they picked up outside the registry office and tipped half a crown. Julia hadn't been able to get away from the teashop, and Gordon and Rosemary had only got the day off from the office by pretexts carefully manœuvred a long time ahead. Nobody knew they were getting married, except Ravelston and Julia. Rosemary was going to go on working at the studio for another month or two. She had preferred to keep her marriage a secret until it was over, chiefly for the sake of her innumerable brothers and sisters, none of whom could afford wedding presents. Gordon, left to himself, would have done it in a more regular manner. He had even wanted to be married in church. But Rosemary had put her foot down on that idea.

Gordon had been back at the office two months now. Four ten a week he was getting. It would be a tight pinch when Rosemary stopped working, but there was hope of a rise next

241

year. They would have to get some money out of Rosemary's parents, of course, when the baby was due to arrive. Mr. Clew had left the New Albion a year ago, and his place had been taken by a Mr. Warner, a Canadian who had been five years with a New York publicity firm. Mr. Warner was a live wire but quite a likeable person. He and Gordon had a big job on hand at the moment. The Queen of Sheba Toilet Requisites Co. were sweeping the country with a monster campaign for their deodorant, April Dew. They had decided that B.O. and halitosis were worked out, or nearly, and had been racking their brains for a long time past to think of some new way of scaring the public. Then some bright spark had suggested, What about smelling feet? That field had never been exploited and had immense possibilities. The Queen of Sheba had turned the idea over to the New Albion. What they asked for was a really telling slogan; something in the class of "Nightstarvation"—something that would rankle in the public consciousness like a poisoned arrow. Mr. Warner had thought it over for three days and then emerged with the unforgettable phrase. "P.P." "P.P." stood for Pedic Perspiration. It was a real flash of genius, that. It was so simple and so arresting. Once you knew what they stood for, you couldn't possibly see those letters "P.P." without a guilty tremor. Gordon had searched for the word "pedic" in the Oxford Dictionary and found that it did not exist. But Mr. Warner had said, Hell! what did it matter, anyway? It would put the wind up them just the same. The Queen of Sheba had jumped at the idea, of course.

They were putting every penny they could spare into the campaign. On every hoarding in the British Isles huge accusing posters were hammering "P.P." into the public mind. All the posters were identically the same. They wasted no words, but just demanded with sinister simplicity:

"P.P."
What about
YOU?

242

Just that—no pictures, no explanations. There was no longer any need to say what "P.P." stood for; everyone in England knew it by this time. Mr. Warner, with Gordon to help him, was designing the smaller ads for the newspapers and magazines. It was Mr. Warner who supplied the bold sweeping ideas, sketched the general lay-out of the ads and decided what pictures would be needed; but it was Gordon who wrote most of the letterpress—wrote the harrowing little stories, each a realistic novel in a hundred words, about despairing virgins of thirty, and lonely bachelors whose girls had unaccountably thrown them over, and overworked wives who could only afford to change their stockings once a week and who saw their husbands subsiding into the clutches of "the other woman." He did it very well; he did it far better than he had ever done anything else in his life. Mr. Warner gave golden reports of him. There was no doubt about Gordon's literary ability. He could use words with the economy that is only learned by years of effort. So perhaps his long agonising struggles to be a "writer" had not been wasted after all.

They said good-bye to Ravelston outside the restaurant. The taxi bore them away. Ravelston had insisted on paying for the taxi from the registry office, so they felt they could afford another taxi. Warmed with wine, they lolled together, in the dusty May sunshine that filtered through the taxi window. Rosemary's head on Gordon's shoulder, their hands together in her lap. He played with the very slender wedding ring on Rosemary's ring finger. Rolled gold, five and sixpence. It looked all right, however.

"I must remember to take it off before I go to the studio to-morrow," said Rosemary reflectively.

"To think we're really married! Till death do us part. We've done it now, right enough."

"Terrifying, isn't it?"

"I expect we'll settle down all right, though. With a house of our own and a pram and an aspidistra."

He lifted her face up to kiss her. She had a touch of make-up on to-day, the first he had ever seen on her, and not too skilfully applied. Neither of their faces stood the spring sunshine very well. There were fine lines on Rosemary's, deep seams on Gordon's. Rosemary looked twenty-eight, perhaps; Gordon looked at least thirty-five. But Rosemary had pulled the three white hairs out of her crown yesterday.

"Do you love me?" he said.

"Adore you, silly."

"I believe you do. It's queer. I'm thirty and moth-eaten."

"I don't care."

They began to kiss, then drew hurriedly apart as they saw two scrawny upper-middle-class women, in a car that was moving parallel to their own, observing them with catty interest.

The flat off the Edgware Road wasn't too bad. It was a dull quarter and rather a slummy street, but it was convenient for the centre of London; also it was quiet, being a blind alley. From the back window (it was a top floor) you could see the roof of Paddington Station. Twenty-one and six a week, unfurnished. One bed, one reception, kitchenette, bath (with geyser) and w.c. They had got their furniture already, most of it on the never-never. Ravelston had given them a complete set of crockery for a wedding present—a very kindly thought, that. Julia had given them a rather dreadful "occasional" table, veneered walnut with a scalloped edge. Gordon had begged and implored her not to give them anything. Poor Julia! Christmas had left her utterly broke, as usual, and Aunt Angela's birthday had been in March. But it would have seemed to Julia a kind of crime against nature to let a wedding go by without giving a present. God knew what sacrifices she had made to scrape together thirty bob for that "occasional" table. They were still very short of linen and cutlery. Things would have to be bought piecemeal, when they had a few bob to spare.

They ran up the last flight of stairs in their excitement to get to the flat. It was all ready to inhabit. They had spent their evenings for weeks past getting the stuff in. It seemed to them a tremendous adventure to have this place of their own. Neither of them had ever owned furniture before; they had been living in furnished rooms ever since their childhood. As soon as they got inside they made a careful tour of the flat, checking, examining and admiring everything as though they did not know by heart already every item that was there. They fell into absurd raptures over each separate stick of furniture. The double bed with the clean sheet ready turned down over the pink eiderdown! The linen and towels stowed away in the chest of drawers! The gateleg table, the four hard chairs, the two armchairs, the divan, the bookcase, the red Indian rug, the copper coal-scuttle which they had picked up cheap in the Caledonian market! And it was all their own, every bit of it was their own—at least, so long as they didn't get behind with the instalments! They went into the kitchenette. Everything was ready, down to the minutest detail. Gas stove, meat safe, enamel-topped table, plate rack, saucepans, kettle, sink basket, mops, dish-cloths—even a tin of Panshine, a packet of soapflakes and a pound of washing soda in a jamjar. It was all ready for use, ready for life. You could have cooked a meal in it here and now. They stood hand in hand by the enamel-topped table, admiring the view of Paddington Station.

"Oh, Gordon, what fun it all is! To have a place that's really our own and no landladies interfering!"

"What I like best of all is to think of having breakfast together. You opposite me on the other side of the table, pouring out coffee. How queer it is! We've known each other all these years and we've never once had breakfast together."

"Let's cook something now. I'm dying to use those saucepans."

She made some coffee and brought it into the front room on the red lacquered tray which they had bought in Selfridge's Bargain Basement. Gordon wandered over to the "occasional" table by the window. Far below the mean street was drowned in a haze of sunlight, as though a glassy yellow sea had flooded it fathoms deep. He laid his coffee cup down on the "occasional" table.

245

"This is where we'll put the aspidistra," he said.

"Put the *what?*"

"The aspidistra."

She laughed. He saw that she thought he was joking, and added: "We must remember to go out and order it before all the florists are shut."

"Gordon! You don't mean that? You aren't *really* thinking of having an aspidistra?"

"Yes, I am. We won't let ours get dusty, either. They say an old toothbrush is the best thing to clean them with."

She had come over to his side, and she pinched his arm.

"You aren't serious, by any chance, are you?"

"Why shouldn't I be?"

"An aspidistra! To think of having one of those awful depressing things in here! Besides, where could we put it? I'm not going to have it in this room, and in the bedroom it would be worse. Fancy having an aspidistra in one's bedroom!"

"We don't want one in the bedroom. This is the place for an aspidistra. In the front window, where the people opposite can see it."

"Gordon, you *are* joking—you must be joking!"

"No, I'm not. I tell you we've got to have an aspidistra."

"But why?"

"It's the proper thing to have. It's the first thing one buys after one's married. In fact, it's practically part of the wedding ceremony."

"Don't be so absurd! I simply couldn't bear to have one of those things in here. You shall have a geranium if you really must. But not an aspidistra."

"A geranium's no good. It's an aspidistra we want."

"Well, we're not going to have one, that's flat."

"Yes, we are. Didn't you promise to obey me just now?"

"No, I did not. We weren't married in church."

"Oh, well, it's implied in the marriage service. 'Love, honour and obey' and all that."

"No, it isn't. Anyway we aren't going to have that aspidistra."

"Yes, we are."

"We are *not*, Gordon!"

"Yes."

"No!"

"Yes!"

"*No!*"

She did not understand him. She thought he was merely being perverse. They grew heated, and, according to their habit, quarrelled violently. It was their first quarrel as man and wife. Half an hour later they went out to the florist's to order the aspidistra.

But when they were half-way down the first flight of stairs Rosemary stopped short and clutched the banister. Her lips parted; she looked very queer for a moment. She pressed a hand against her middle.

"Oh, Gordon!"

"What?"

"I felt it move!"

"Felt what move?"

"The baby. I felt it move inside me."

"You did?"

A strange, almost terrible feeling, a sort of warm convulsion, stirred in his entrails. For a moment he felt as though he were sexually joined to her, but joined in some subtle way that he had never imagined. He had paused a step or two below her. He fell on his knees, pressed his ear to her belly and listened.

"I can't hear anything," he said at last.

"Of course not, silly! Not for months yet."

"But I shall be able to hear it later on, shan't I?"

"I think so. *You* can hear it at seven months, *I* can feel it at four. I think that's how it is."

"But it did really move? You're sure? You really felt it move?"

"Oh, yes. It moved."

For a long time he remained kneeling there, his head pressed against the softness of her belly. She clasped her hands behind his head and pulled it closer. He could hear nothing, only the blood drumming in his own ear. But she could not have been mistaken. Somewhere in there, in the safe, warm, cushioned darkness, it was alive and stirring.

Well, once again things were happening in the Comstock family.

Books by George Orwell
available from Harcourt Brace & Company
in Harvest paperback editions

BURMESE DAYS

A CLERGYMAN'S DAUGHTER

A COLLECTION OF ESSAYS

COMING UP FOR AIR

DICKENS, DALI & OTHERS

DOWN AND OUT IN PARIS AND LONDON

HOMAGE TO CATALONIA

IN FRONT OF YOUR NOSE: THE COLLECTED ESSAYS,
JOURNALISM AND LETTERS OF GEORGE ORWELL, 1945–1950

KEEP THE ASPIDISTRA FLYING

THE ORWELL READER: FICTION, ESSAYS AND REPORTAGE

THE ROAD TO WIGAN PIER